CW01506717

Roade Local History Society is grateful
to the following for their generous
financial support for this book

Mr Christopher Denton, Roade

·

Roade Parish Council

·

**MILTON KEYNES
HERITAGE ASSOCIATION**

ABOUT THE AUTHOR

Chris Hillyard is a lifelong resident of Roade whose family have resided in the village since the late 15th century. With the coming of the railways many of his forebears left the land to work in that industry, subsequent generations were to follow, railways were 'in the blood'.

He attended both the local Primary and Comprehensive Schools, and upon leaving school joined the British Rail Engineering Limited Training School at Wolverton Works where he commenced a four year electrical apprenticeship.

Appointed to the Royal Train staff in 1977, the attachment lasted for the following thirty-three years, fifteen of which were as Royal Train Foreman. During his service he accompanied Her Majesty the Queen, members of the Royal Family and visiting Heads of State on 792 Royal Trains, travelling 488,631 miles. He was awarded the Golden Jubilee Medal in 2002 and the Royal Victorian Medal, (Silver), in 2003 for services to the Royal Household.

ROADE LOCAL HISTORY SOCIETY

RLHS was formed in 2005 and its mission is to collect, record, protect and share documents, images and physical ephemera of local historical significance for the benefit of residents, the local community and future generations.

Sir Frank Brangwyn
(*victorianweb.com*)

First published in 2021 by 'Roade Local History Society'

ISBN No: 9780956349620

© Roade Local History Society, unless otherwise indicated

RLHS, Scratter Edge, 26 Fox Covert Drive, Roade NN7 2LL

www.roaderemembered.org.uk
www.roadehistorysociety.org.uk

Other Publications: Roade Roll of Honour
Roade Through the Camera, ISBN No: 9780956349606
Roade Village Scrapbook 1953, ISBN: 9780956349613

Cover design – Alan Atkinson

Printed and bound by –
Cambrian Printers, Pontllanfraith, NP12 2YA

CONTENTS

FOREWORD

By: Stuart Wilkinson
Chairman of the Council
National Transport Trust

Patron: HRH Anne, the Princess Royal.
President: Judy, Lady McAlpine

The National Transport Trust is very privileged to have added a small element to the very colourful history of Roade and it's Cutting through the mounting of a commemorative plaque on Overbridge 208, and I am delighted to be invited to contribute this foreword. The plaque is the 103rd to have been erected by the Trust (out of 147 at time of writing), and was the first to be requested from outside the Trust rather than nominated from within.

Each of these plaques commemorates a site of transport heritage significance, whether that be related to transport by road, rail, water or air, and they are to be found from the north of Scotland to Lands End and while the information presented on each plaque is limited by space considerations, the information on the website behind the plaques suffers no such constraint.

Like the cutting itself, this work is of considerable breadth and depth, and it charts the effect the cutting has had on the development of Roade and its people over a period approaching 200 years. Our nation's transport history has shaped it, and nowhere is this more evident than at Roade; the Roade Local History Society and in particular Christopher Hillyard are to be congratulated on this work which appeals equally to the technically minded and the social enquirer.

Stuart Wilkinson
October 2021

NOTES FOR THE READER

The railway lines and their directions within this publication are described as Up and Down, with Up being towards the line's principle destination, London. Multiple tracks are further defined by destination or permissible line speeds.

TERM	MEANING
UP	Destination London.
DOWN	Destination away from London.
FAST	Mainly Inter-City express usage.
SLOW	Mainly freight, commuter and local passenger train services

Railway Companies

L&BR	London & Birmingham Railway
L&NWR	London & North Western Railway
LM&SR	London Midland & Scottish Railway
BR	British Railways
TR&OJR	Towcester Roade & Olney Junction Railway
ENMTR&OJR	Easton Neston Mineral, Towcester, Roade & Olney Junction Railway
ST&MJR	Stratford-upon-Avon, Towcester & Midland Junction Railway
MR	Midland Railway
S&MJR	Stratford-upon-Avon & Midland Junction Railway
NR	Network Rail

Since 1994 all railway lines, supporting infrastructure and route maintenance has been undertaken by the Department for Transport, initially as Railtrack until 2002, and Network Rail thereafter. Multiple operating franchises have access to the national railway network.

Bridge Numbering (See Map page 17)

ST&MJR	As built 1890
West Coast Main Line	Numbering as adopted by L&NWR c1881

Weights, Measures & Currency

Imperial System pre 15th February 1971
Metric System post decimalisation

PREAMBLE

Of the numerous challenges which Robert Stephenson faced during the construction of the London & Birmingham railway, Roade's railway Cutting remains one of the most visibly awe-inspiring engineering achievements of the nation's railway infrastructure. It is the timeless legacy which Stephenson and his engineers left to our village and the nation.

Designation as a 'Site of Special Scientific Interest' in 1986 ensured its protection as an asset of National Geological Significance. In 2018 its engineering excellence was recognised with the award of a prestigious 'Red Wheel' from the National Transport Trust, designating it as a 'Transport Heritage Site'.

The inspiration for this publication was sparked by Mr Alvin Barby, a Roade resident with a lifelong interest in the history and development of the railways, and especially, its impact on the Northamptonshire village of Roade. In 2010 Alvin compiled and produced a booklet entitled 'Railways around Roade', the content therein derived from his research, official documents, press cuttings and images collected over many years.

As a former career railwayman, also possessing more than a passing interest in the subject matter, I was honoured to be asked to write the foreword for Alvin's compilation. However, for me, the narrative therein instilled a desire to seek a much greater understanding of the profound social and economic impacts which the railways had upon our once rustic and rural community. In addition, I felt compelled to draw back the veil of time in order to gain an insight into the lives of our forebears i.e. families and individuals who lived with or were part of the railway's intrusion into the community, welcome or otherwise.

What was not anticipated was the sheer volume and diversity of the media material and information on this somewhat obscure subject matter, which exists if you dig deep enough! 'Remarkable' was one comment received, which provided the title 'Cutting Remarks'. Much of the content herein derives from newspaper reports and contemporary publications of the time. These have been purposely reproduced, in the main, 'as written'; giving a further insight into the changing social structure and conventions over the last 183 years.

Christopher Hillyard, RVM
Roade Local History Society
17 September 2021

CHAPTER 1

The London & Birmingham Railway
'In the Beginning'

The entrepreneurs of the industrial revolution were quick to realise the commercial rewards available from investment in *rail-way* transportation, enabling the rapid supply and distribution of bulk quantities of goods and materials. This leap forward, fuelled by public interest and the 'railway mania' which followed the opening of the 25-mile Stockton and Darlington Railway in 1825 and the 31-mile Liverpool and Manchester Railway five years later, was to be irreversible. The development of the steam locomotive and the provision of carriages for increased public conveyance further demonstrated the boundless potential of this mode of transport.

Even now, some two hundred years later, the ambition of the London and Birmingham Railway Company to build a line between these two giant industrial conurbations seems a monumental risk. The sheer magnitude of the required works, the primitive mechanical aids available to the engineers and the enormous amount of private finance required would, even in this day and age, be considered incredible.

However, the desire was unstoppable and the objective was achieved. The completion of the Cutting enabled the world's first long-distance Inter-City railway to be opened to the public on the 17th September 1839, and the rest, as they say, is history.

The stories recorded herein cover the 200-year evolution of a mere three or so miles of the 112½ mile line, depicting the trials, tribulations and community impacts resultant of such a project upon a rural South Northamptonshire village. There is much to be told. –

Roade Cutting is a notable 'landmark' on the British railway system. Throughout the planning of the London to Birmingham Railway route, it was referred to as 'The Blisworth Cutting' – it being the civil engineering work required to progress the line northward through the geological landform known as the Blisworth Ridge, and from there to Rugby and beyond. Its recognised name changed to Roade Cutting when Roade Station was sited at the start of the excavation. It was considered to be one of, if not the most, formidable engineering challenges to be overcome during the construction of the line. It is one and a half miles in length, and the second longest open excavation on the entire route. Originally it was 57 feet in depth and subsequently, after widening in the late 1870s and early 1880s, it became the deepest excavation on the line, at an average depth of 65 feet, a major part of which consisted of a very hard rock – Great Oolite Limestone.

CUTTING REMARKS

Proposals for the railway were first published in 1822, and there followed lengthy debate and legal proceedings. These were compounded by political pressures and financial constraints over many years in the acquisition of the required land and permissions. In 1830 Sir William Wake, 9th Baronet, presided at a meeting held at the White Bear, Towcester, of landowners and gentry opposed to the plans. Reflecting on this process, the *London & Birmingham Railway Pocket Book* later described the opposition as selfish, anti-social, anti-national and vexatious.

Initially, two routes between the capital and the midland city were considered. One was via Bletchley, Rugby and Coventry, proposed by Francis Giles, the other, proposed by Sir John Rennie, being via Banbury and Oxford. It is recorded that in the summer of 1830 Robert Stephenson (son of railway pioneer George) personally surveyed both, walking each of the proposed routes on over 20 occasions, in order to determine the least challenging lie-of-the-land over which the rails would be laid.

Surveying the Route
(www.havershamvillage.co.uk)

Contained within the 1822 document was a detailed description of both of the proposed routes, the land ownership of each portion, and a list of buildings which would need to be removed. Locally these demolitions were: at Ashton, four houses, a hovel, a yard and two cottages with gardens; at Roade, a yard and hovel; and at Blisworth, a plantation. All these were situated on land owned by the Duke of Grafton who had sole ownership of the land throughout both Ashton and Blisworth Parish. The land at Courteenhall was owned exclusively by Sir William Wake, 9th Baronet.

In respect of the proposed route through Roade Parish, the majority of the arable and pasture land ownership was split between the Duke and Sir William, in addition to a further 20 individual land owners and interested parties. These included the Revd John Risley the Revd William Butlin and the Revd Miles Walker. One area of Arable land to the north of the Parish was owned by the Provost and Fellows of

The London & Birmingham Railway
'In the Beginning'

Worcester College, Oxford, and farmed by William Burgess. The remaining interested parties being Messrs. Baggins, Beckett, Blunt, Boyes, Burgess, Cave, Goodridge, Hands, Longstaff, Markham, Pagett, Pittam, Tite, Wilcox, Winter and Wood.

In 1831, prior to the coming of the railway, the population of Roade was 553, residing in 113 houses. The prime sources of employment were farming and related local industry. The London and Birmingham Railway Act was finally passed by Parliament on 6th May 1833, by which time the Bletchley, Rugby and Coventry route had been favoured. A further year was to elapse for the construction contracts to be awarded. Robert Stephenson was appointed Chief Engineer in March 1834, and the excavation of the Cutting commenced.

London & Birmingham Railway
Chief Engineer
Robert Stephenson (1803-1859)
(*The Practical Mechanics Journal*)

London & Birmingham Railway
Armorial device
(*Wikimedia.org*)

CHAPTER 2

Making the Cut – The Navvy Invasion

The excavation would require a considerable workforce and offered an alternative source of employment to many local men and boys for the duration of its construction. However, the local labour supply was wholly inadequate to support such a task, and the local population was to be considerably increased by native journeymen and Scottish and Irish 'navvies' who came to the area in search of employment. The name navvies originates from 'navigator' or 'navigational engineer', although they were known as *'Banditti'* by the Assistant Engineer, Lieutenant Peter Lecount, RN, a civil engineer and railway enthusiast, now ashore on half-pay.

The Revd Daniel William Barrett was from Northamptonshire, and although a humble, devout and pious ecclesiastical personage, he had this to say about the navvies –

> *The term 'navvy' is simply an abridgement of the longer poetical word navigator, which savours too much of the sound of alligator to be pleasant. And in fact some people have a rough idea that the navvy is a sort of human alligator who feeds on helpless women and timid men, and frightens children into fits.*

The navvy
(*www.lookandlearn.com*)

The impact of such vast numbers descending upon the area and its economy was soon to be felt, including clogging up the highways with carts and wagons containing all the needful items and impediments to support a somewhat nomadic lifestyle.

CUTTING REMARKS

Roade and the neighbouring settlements were inadequately provisioned or prepared to give lodgings to all the men to be employed.

The Revd Maze W. Gregory, Vicar of Roade (1853-1866) and a noted local historian, said that "The number of houses in the village quickly increased from 100 to 150, besides which, a row of huts called "The Sixty" was erected in a field hard by the works, in which lived from 800 to 1,000 navvies. From what I hear there was a very scanty supply of furniture in these places, little else indeed than beds of straw, which the day gangs turned into when the night gangs turned out, and *vice versa*. The village was filled with the higher class of workmen and overlookers, and the houses made to hold a far greater number than they ought".

At the northern end of the excavation a temporary village was built, close to one of the excavation's over-bridges, Accommodation Bridge. This area was near to Woodleys Farmhouse, the former New Inn public house, and consisted of several houses built from limestone which had been excavated from the Cutting. Those who were not fortunate enough to be lodged locally, lived in turf shantytowns, built by either themselves, or the contractor. Some were accompanied by their wives, or 'female companions'. Others found comfort with the local womenfolk, "The females were corrupted, many of them", said a contractor of the mid-Northamptonshire villages in the 1830s, "and went away with the men, and lived amongst them in habits that civilised language will scarcely allow a description of". Mary Anne Warren of Ashton was one such young lady who had absconded with one of the navvies, a Scot called Alexander Bethune, after her father had forbidden their marriage. Bethune was killed whilst working on the railway at Kilsby not long after the couple had eloped and married. Mary Anne returned to the village and subsequently married a former sweetheart and raised 12 children.

The modern perception of the rough & ready navvy is somewhat of a misconception. Numerous literary sources describe their attire as instantly recognisable. Generally consisting of moleskin trousers, double-canvas shirts, velveteen square-tailed coats over a distinctive rainbow waistcoat, hobnail boots, gaudy handkerchiefs and felt hats with upturned brims.

Clothing for the navvies
(Illustrated London News)

Making the Cut – The Navvy Invasion

This increase in the local population, whilst large enough in itself, accounts for only one third of the number of men engaged on the various works throughout the surrounding area. Overall, around 3,000 men were employed within a few miles to the north and south of the excavation (between Kilsby Tunnel and the Wolverton Viaduct). The navvies' impact on a rustic and traditionally rural population both enlivened and challenged the social framework, as it was an enormous drain on resources and upset and aggravated the local gentry.

Another consequence of the considerable population increase, and the building of rudimentary accommodation with little or no sanitation, was a serious outbreak of typhus and smallpox in the lodgings and shanties. This quickly spread to the village where there were over 100 funerals in 12 months, against about six normally.

The navvies were paid once a month, sometimes less frequently. Payment was made in a local ale house (The New Inn probably), which resulted in them drinking their wage over the following days, selling their shovels for more beer, fighting and rioting. One contemporary account described them as –

> … possessed of all the daring recklessness of the smuggler without having any of his redeeming qualities, their ferocious behaviour can only be equalled by the brutality of their language. From being long known to each other they in general act in concert and put at defiance any local constabulary force.

Navvies pay parade
(By Betty Harrington)

However, not all the navvies were without morals and principles, as some originating from Bletchley brought with them the Wesleyan Methodist faith to Roade. For a short period they were allowed to worship in the Baptist Church, but their enthusiastic form of worship was frowned upon and they were forced to move to a rented room attached to a row of 6 cottages in the High Street built for railway workers. It later became a cottage and is now 35 High Street. They were again forced to relocate after the congregation suffered mocking and ridicule from people outside the building during services, moving to a rented cottage in Barn Lane close to The Green and owned by Thomas Clarke, a Baptist!

CUTTING REMARKS

Mr Frank Foster, a close friend of Stephenson, was given responsibility for supervising the excavation of the Cutting, along with the tunnel at Kilsby, a few miles further north. Under Foster's authority, the contract for the excavation at Roade was let to Mr William Hughes. Hughes was an experienced contractor who had successfully undertaken canal construction in both the United Kingdom and Northern Europe. Hughes was faced with a formidable task as the excavation cut through three distinct strata – a mixed layer of clays over 20 feet deep on average and overlying limestone, under which lay yet more clay and waterlogged shale, although this mix varied along the length of the excavation.

Under Hughes' charge was a chief engineer with a number of sub-assistants, these in turn were supported by a team of inspectors, responsible for building, mining, excavating and construction of the permanent way. The sub-assistants and any sub-contractors engaged were then responsible for employing navvies to undertake the tasks. The navvies themselves were sub-divided into three groups, excavators, trenchers and runners, each group overseen by a ganger. In addition, the Company appointed 'Over-lookers' to monitor progress.

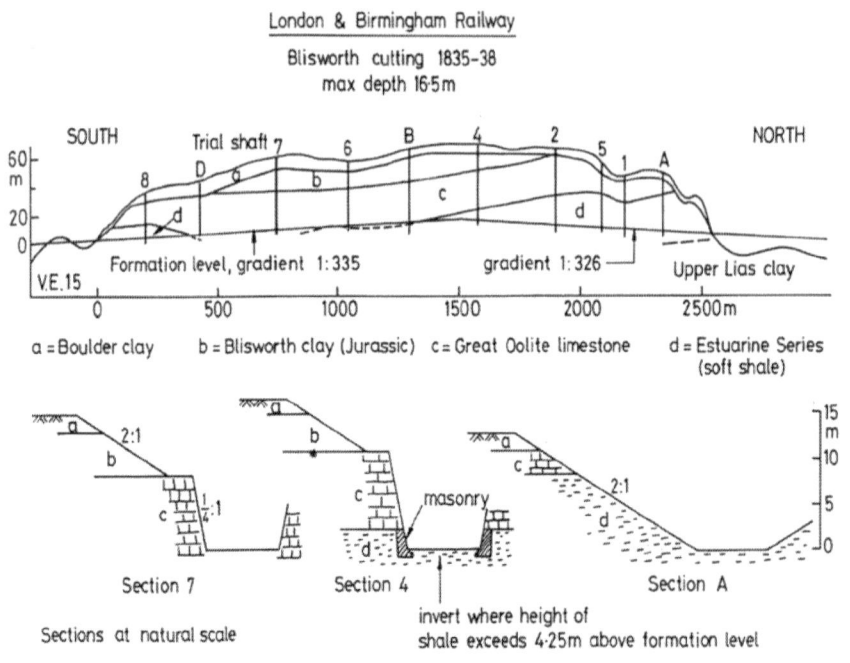

Section and detail drawing
(Prof. A.W. Skepton)

The difficulties that the engineers encountered in cutting through the mixed layers of clay, shale and hard rock, were observed by geologists with great interest as its depth increased. One observer recorded –

> *The different beds of rock in this excavation abound with fossil shells, in a good state of preservation: they consist of nautilus, terebratula, oysters, etc. There were also two or three fossils of very considerable magnitude discovered; they were of the Saurian or Lizard tribe, and were found embedded in a stratum immediately on the top of the rock, which is a type*

Making the Cut – The Navvy Invasion

of half-formed stone of considerable hardness when dry, but becoming soon softened when exposed to the air and damp.

The building of the railway dates from the days when railway engineers had little experience of the effect of gradients on locomotives. In fact, railways were aligned much as the canals had been, following the land with the easier gradients, and only using tunnels and embankments where absolutely necessary. This is not surprising as most of the contractors and labourers had been previously employed on canal construction. With this in mind, the ruling gradient of the line was to be predominantly 1 in 330, hence the requirement for the huge Cutting at Roade. The following extracts are from the specification and other correspondence, and give an insight into the scale of works required –

> *The whole of the Walls and Buttresses to be of masonry; the stones to be procured from the excavations. The courses to run as thick as the material obtained from the excavation will afford when properly quarried. The facing stones to be at least 18 inches; the beds to be square with the face of the buttress, or wall. The stones to be hammer dressed, and brought to a rough bed, but perfectly true; special care being taken to prevent too full a bearing in the centre of them, the object of this arrangement being to secure a sound support to the rock and to effect by the dove-tailed stones a connexion with the rock, to prevent the top of the wall being pushed out.*

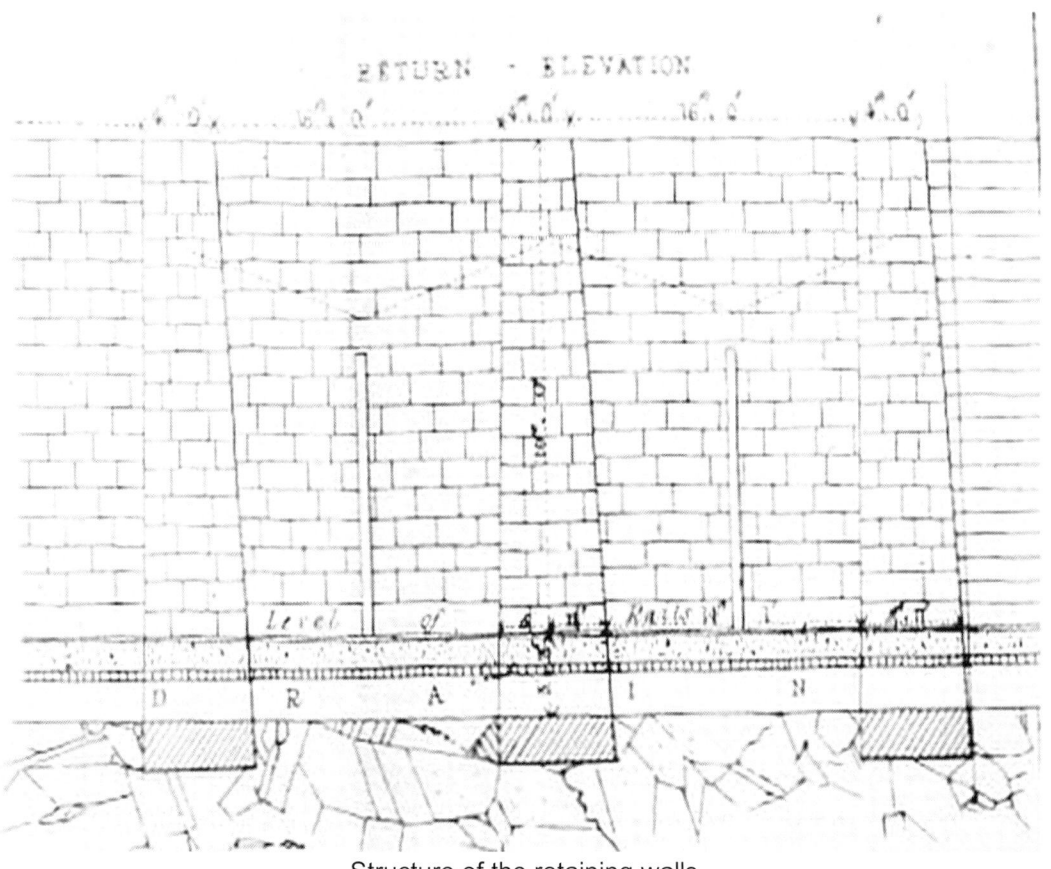

Structure of the retaining walls
(Gail Ling)

CUTTING REMARKS

To prevent any injury to the Slopes by the springs of water issuing from the rock and other strata in this excavation, the strictest attention will be required on the part of the Contractor, and the modes of drainage adapted to the varying thickness of the shale and other strata .The central Drain to be made according to the dimensions in the plan. Where it crosses the inverts, they will form its bottom; and between the inverts, the bottom to be laid to a uniform inclination. At a depth, never falling short of 1 foot below any wet stratum that may occur, two courses of the recess wall and buttresses to be projected beyond the back of the wall; the lower course to project beyond the upper, so as to receive a stone, to rise 1 foot above the upper course, forming a Drain 12 inches deep and 6 inches wide; to be surrounded at the bottom and back with a casing of sound Puddle, and filled in at the top with Rubble stone, to allow the top water to have access to the drain .This drain is to have a regular fall from the centre of each buttress. The water, when thus collected, shall be carried through the recess wall, and down the sunken channel in its face . . . .

Cutting section
(Encyclopaedia Britannica 9th Edition 1902)

In the southern and central sections of the Cutting the slopes were at two gradients:1:4 in the limestone (the lower shale in the central section being contained by retaining walls) at the top of which a nine feet wide 'bench' separated a shallower slope of 2:1 in the upper levels of clay –

The object of the bench is to catch any loose portions of clay which might be detached from above; they have also been found very useful as affording foundations for walls of pebble-stone, which it has been found necessary to erect in many places, to retain the numerous slips of clay above.

At the bottom of the central section a rubble wall, averaging 20 feet in height, was built on each side underneath the limestone layer. This was strengthened by buttresses at intervals of 20 feet, resting on inverted arches carried underneath the line. To reduce the risks of both slip and flooding by the strata of clay and water-bearing shale, Stephenson paid the strictest attention to drainage. A puddle-dam was to be formed to prevent water from reaching the back of the wall, with a small drain through the wall to let off the water from behind. A drain was also formed beneath the track along the central section of the Cutting.

Making the Cut – The Navvy Invasion

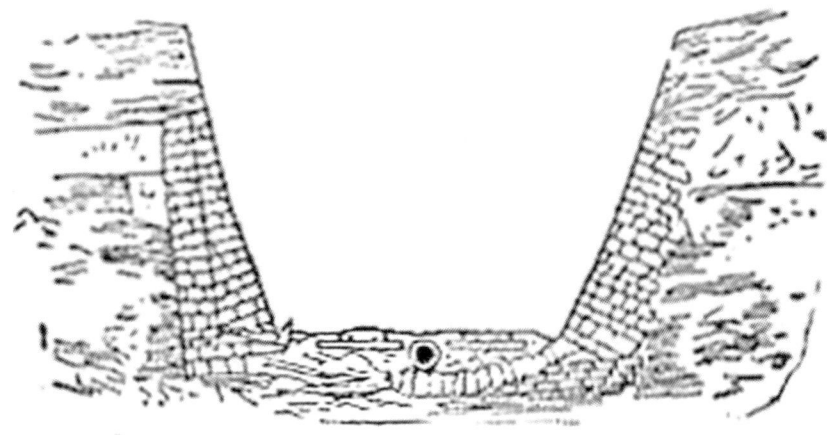

Cutting section
(Encyclopaedia Britannica 9th Edition 1902)

During the initial excavations, a labourer working in an area known as Mr Faulkner's Close, near The New Inn, discovered a skeleton two feet eight inches below the surface. The remains were face down and it was determined that the figure had been considerably over six feet in height. Laid out alongside the skeleton was a dagger and brace of pistols. A further discovery of human remains was made during the construction on the line between Roade and Ashton. At a place known as Ashton Warren the skeletal remains of a female were reported to have been uncovered by William Hughes, the contractor supervising the navvies.

Work progressed 24 hours a day, 12 hours per shift, while one shift toiled the other slept. Sunday was the only day off. The excavation and building of the towering retaining walls required men of the highest calibre, with each man required to shift over 20 tons of earth, rock and spoil per day.

The first 18 months of construction were beset with problems and progress was soon hampered by severe flooding. Samuel Smiles wrote: 'for a year and a half the contractor went on fruitlessly contending with these difficulties and at length he was compelled to abandon the adventure.' Lecount, the Assistant Engineer of the railway, was much less sympathetic: 'During the first year and a half the progress was extremely slow, owing to the want of proper energy on the part of the contractor, combined with general bad management.' Such was the seriousness of the situation that Stephenson resided in the locality to supervise the works personally.

The impact of the watercourses being severed as a result of the Cutting excavations presented problems to local landowner Sir William Wake; these were recounted by the late Sir Hereward (the 14th Baronet, who died in 2018), who stated that it 'caused ditches and ponds on the Courteenhall Estate to dry up'.

In June 1836, navvy Thomas Denton was taken to the infirmary at Northampton after a wagon had run over his foot. The *Northampton Mercury* stated that his condition was improving and he was out of danger. Serious injury and even death were an ever-present risk to the men engaged on the excavations, and although manpower was at times short, labour was viewed as an expendable resource. Few initial records were kept by the builders of these accidents and incidents, and were it not for reports in the *Northampton Mercury* and other publications, no insight into the perils of the endeavour or the monumental impacts on the community would remain.

Another insight into the nature of the navvies and how they were viewed by the town and county residents was reported in the *Northampton Mercury* in June 1836. In a lecture given to the Northampton Mechanics Institute, the Revd Claudius Sandys had the following to say –

> *It is known that the excavators who worked on the railway were generally ignorant in the extreme and their habits accordingly were most sensual and debasing. At Roade part of the men had recently been engaged from Scotland, where education was much more general than in England.*
>
> *The habits of these men were frugal, steady and sober, they were laughed at by the others, but they did not mind that, they kept to themselves, they were laying by money, and when the profitable work was over, they would return to their homes and families with their savings.*
>
> *The others on the contrary spent in reckless prodigality the whole of their earnings, and good wages only had the effect of enabling them to become more profligate and demoralised. This difference was the consequence of education and the want of education.*

Lawlessness was rife, and the local courts and assizes declarations reported in the Northampton newspapers throughout the period record incidents which must have been horrifying for the local residents. One example of such an incident at Kilsby reads: 'One of those disgraceful exhibitions, a prize fight, took Place at Kilsby, in this county, on Monday last, between two men named John George, from near Cheltenham, and Charles Manning, of Braunston, in this county'. Reported the *Northampton Mercury*: 'An immense number of people assembled, but 'the sport', we believe, was but middling.'

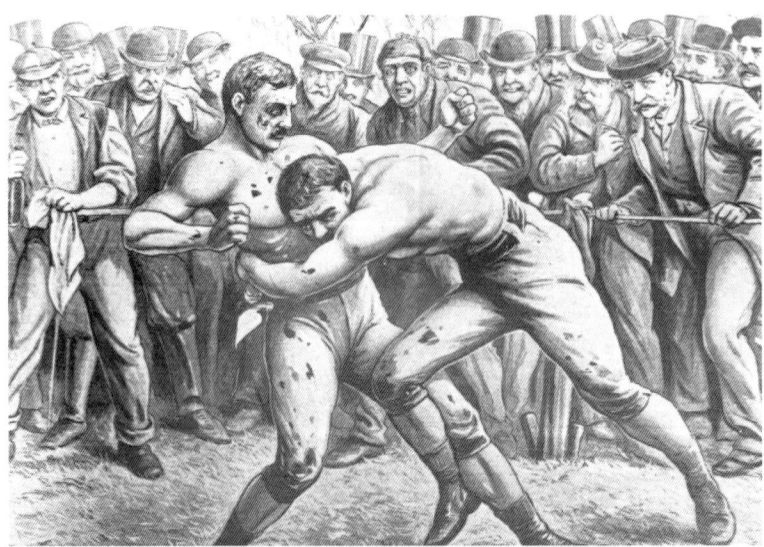

Bare knuckle prize fighting
(fighthistoryextra.com)

Making the Cut – The Navvy Invasion

The *Northampton Mercury* reported that on 4th August, railway navvy John Scott had attacked William Travil of Roade, robbing him of one shilling and sixpence and attempting to steal his watch. Scott, who was drunk at the time, wanted the money in order that he and his colleagues could buy more beer. The events were witnessed by Samuel Downing whose evidence in court saw Scott sentenced to one month's hard labour. In October, another railway labourer, George Booth, pleaded guilty to the theft of a watch from the house of Mary Gawthorn of Roade. He was sentenced to one month's hard labour, with a further month of solitary confinement.

Local people were intimidated, robbed and threatened
(reframingthevictorians.com)

As the excavations continued, the railway company was greatly concerned with the lack of progress. This was due to the lack of local resources to meet the demands of the task and a letter was sent to the contractor dated 1st September 1836, requesting that agents be posted around the roads of the district with instructions to offer any male pedestrians employment. William Hughes, the contractor, went bankrupt, and from December 1836, the railway company was forced to take on the work in-house, and seek alternative contractors in order to overcome a six-month loss of construction time.

In addition to the continuing construction problems, the London & Birmingham Railway Company meeting minutes reveal that they encountered great difficulty in obtaining the required land at Wolverton from the Radcliffe Estate, essential for its Central Station and Works. Such were the concerns, Roade was suggested as a more suitable site as the land would be easier to acquire. It can only be speculated what impact this proposal would have had on the locality if this alternative had come to fruition. As a consequence, Richard Dunkley, a local builder from Blisworth, together with George Wills, were successful in being awarded the contract for the bridge, N°212, over the then main road between Towcester and Northampton at Blisworth. This magnificent stone and brick structure, preferred to a five-arched viaduct which was originally planned, has stood the test of time and is testament to their skills.

CUTTING REMARKS

Bridge N°212 on the Towcester to Northampton road
(Young's Postcard)

Dunkley went on to undertake major infrastructure work for other railway companies, building some of the original workshops at Wolverton Works together with workers' housing and the Mechanics Institute. He was also the builder of the Blisworth Hotel and, in Roade, the Station, School and Rectory building (site of the current Bowls Club). He also built many other buildings and structures in the county of Northamptonshire and beyond.

The Cutting also severed highways, bridleways and trackways, which required bridges to be built over the excavation. The Assistant Engineer, Peter Lecount, was to describe these thus: 'The excavation is crossed by five bridges, some of which are to be of a considerable span, and will present a fine appearance from the Railway; they are to be composed of a mixture of stone from the Cutting, and brickwork'. A specification by Samuel Charles Brees details the requirements –

Bridge for the road from Hardingstone to Old Stratford (A508, N°207)

This bridge is for the railway where it is 33'3" Cutting and must be built at an angle of 53 ½ degrees to the railways direction. The span of the Arch will be 53'6" upon the shown face and its rise 8'10". The height from the rail to the soffit will be 26'2"; the thickness of the arch (which will be entirely of stone), at the key will be 3' and the springing 4'. The width, in the clear, between the parapets, 20'. The Shale & Marle marked 'A', upon which the rock from which the bridge spans will be required to be faced with Ashlar work, extending 10' on each side of the bridge, and of the thickness shown on the drawing. The invert 'B' of rough stone must be made across the railway, between the facing walls, and extend a certain distance on each side-line of the bridge as shown in the drawing. The course of stone composing the invert will be built square with the line of the railway; but the courses of stone composing the arch of the bridge will be laid in a spiral direction, as usual skew bridges, and is shown in Drawing No10, Fig2. Re the Bridge for the road from Ashton to

16

Making the Cut – The Navvy Invasion

Roade and where they inserted the springing of the rock must be cut-toothed, as shown in Fig5, Drawing No10 to receive them. The whole of the remainder of the bridge will be built of stone.

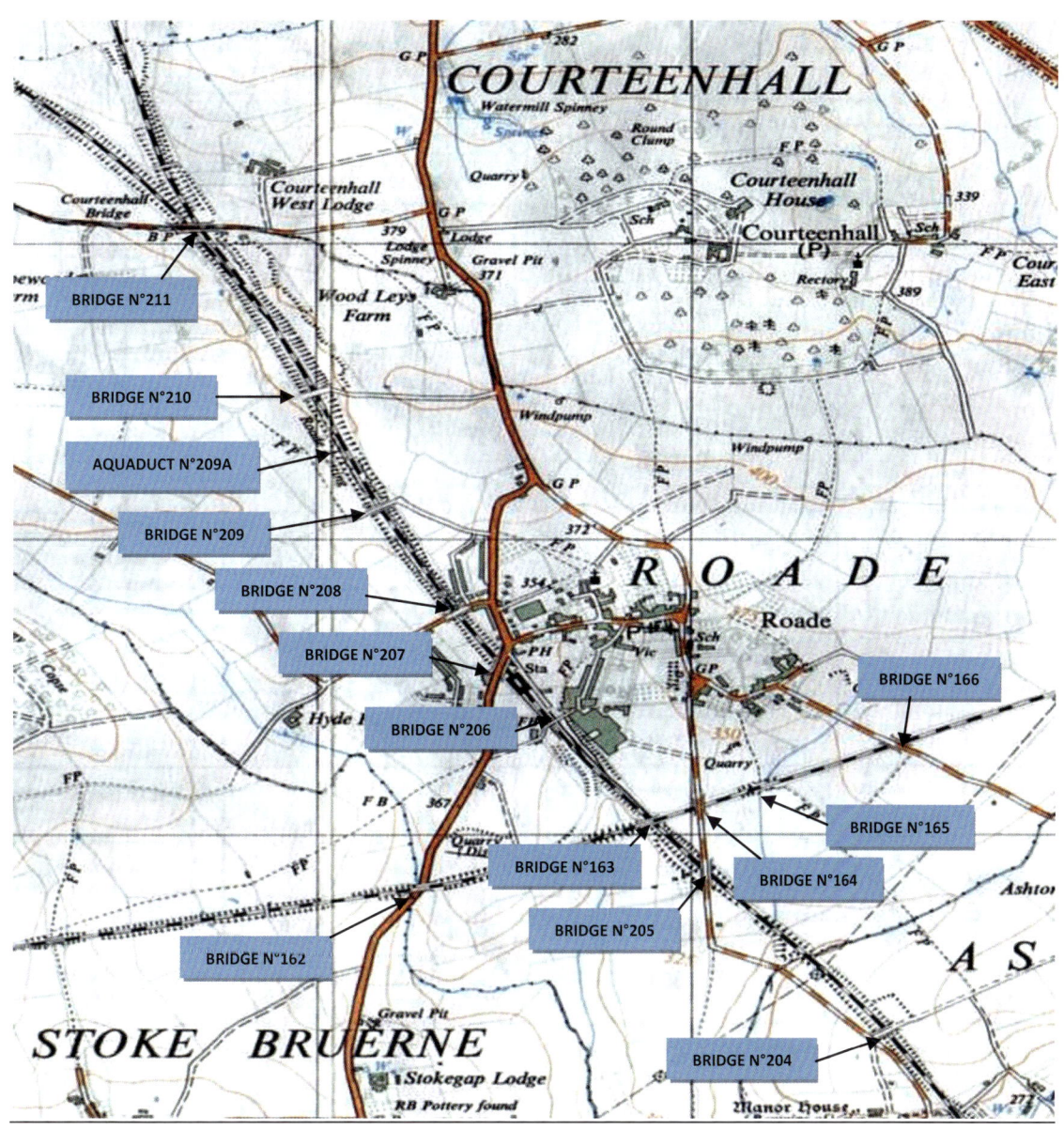

Bridge identification (L&NWR 1882 & S&MJR 1890)
(Ordnance survey SP75 1961)

Bridge for a road from Roade Hyde to Spinney Lane, (Hyde Road Bridge, N°208)

This bridge is on part of the railway where it is about 35'9" cutting and will be built square to the direction of the railway. The span of the Arch will be 45'2", rise 10', thickness at the key 2'6", and the springing. 3', width between the parapets will be 15' clear. The whole of the bridge will be of stone, the dimensions are shown on the drawing.

CUTTING REMARKS

<u>Bridge for the road from Roade to Plain Woods 'A'</u>
<u>Dirty (Muddy) Lane Bridge. (Bailey Brooks, N°209.)</u>

This bridge is on part of the railway where it is about 46'4" cutting, and will be built square to the direction of the railway. The span of the Arch will be 45'2", rise 18', thickness at the key 2'6", and the springing 2'9", width between the parapets 15' in the clear. It is intended to be built entirely of stone. The dimensions and forms of the various forms are shown on the drawing. [Note: The aqueduct, (Listed building, Structure N°209A), required to channel the water from the severed watercourses, is sited between this bridge and the following structure].

<u>Bridge for a road from Roade to Plain Woods 'B'</u>
<u>Thorpe Wood. (Accommodation Bridge N°210)</u>

This bridge is in part of the railway where it is almost 52'4" cutting. The Arch will be of a semi-circle of 46' span, thickness at the key 2'6", thickness at the springing 3', width in the clear between the parapets 15'. The bridge is intended to be entirely of stone. The dimensions and forms are shown on the drawing.

At this point the specification details two further bridges. However, in reality there is only one, that being the one at right angles to the line on the road between Blisworth and the A508 at the point of access to the Wake Estate. The location for the unbuilt bridge specified remains a mystery to the author.

<u>Bridge for a road from Roade to Blisworth, (Blisworth/A508, N°211)</u>

This bridge is on part of the railway where it is in about 53'6" cutting, and will cross at right angles. The span of the Arch will be 48'4 ½", rise 18' 9", thickness at the key 2'6": width in the clear between the parapets 15'. The bridge is intended to be built entirely of stone. The dimensions and forms of the various parts are shown on the drawing.

The methods adopted during the construction were observed by interested parties and engineers alike, who would later recount their observations in publicity guides produced after the line's eventual opening.

A regular army, upwards of 800 strong, and consisting of stone masons, miners, labourers, boys, etc., headed by experienced engineers, and aided by steam and horse power, with "all appliances and means to boot," were brought up to the attack.

One of the most striking features of the work was that of blasting the rock. This operation is performed by first boring several holes into the stone; when this is done a fuse is inserted into each hole; they are then partly filled with gunpowder, and their mouths stopped up firmly; the fuses are then lighted, and the signal being given, the men withdraw till the explosion has taken place. Upwards of twenty-five barrels of gunpowder were consumed weekly for this purpose. The blasting of the rock sounded like a continued firing of mixed arms; there were heard sounds like the heavy boom of the cannon, the sharp crack of the rifle, and the report of the musket and the pistol. Before each explosion, on the signal-cry, fire, the men were seen bustling away to a safe distance, or screening themselves behind projecting portions of the rock. As soon as it had taken place, the clatter of falling stones disrupted from the mass might be heard, when the labourers hastily returned to their position, and resumed their arduous work.

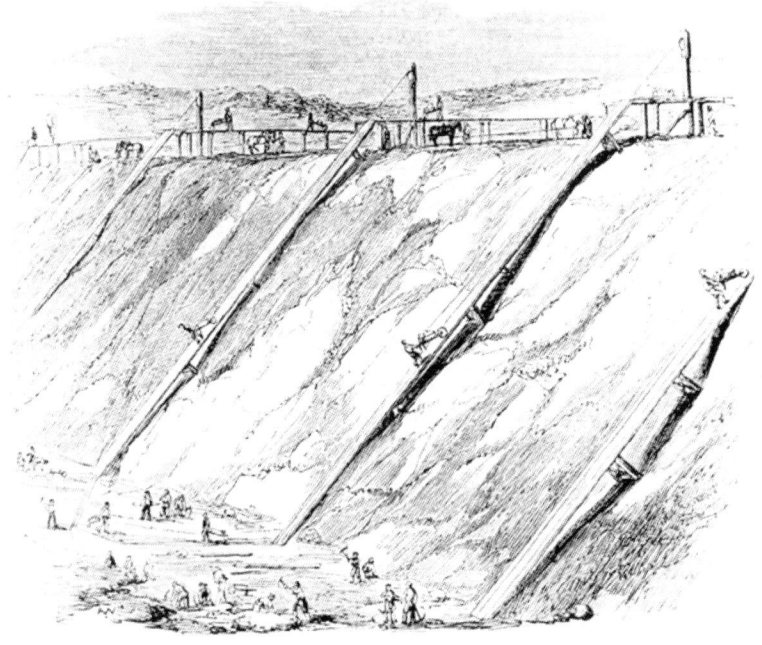

Horse-drawn barrow runs
(victorianweb.org)

Up the precipitous sides of the Cutting were numerous runs, as they are technically called, composed of wood planks, up and down which numerous wagons and barrows were plied, to remove the earth and stone from the Cutting, to heaps called spoilbanks on the tops of the precipices.

Strenuous efforts
(www.havershamvillage.co.uk)

CUTTING REMARKS

The wagons were worked by horse power, applied with suitable machinery, and the barrows were wheeled up and down by stout young men. Round each of their waists were fixed strong belts, attached to which was a rope that went up the side of the Cutting along the run, and having turned on a wheel, was fastened at the extremity remote to the man to a horse in the field above the Cutting. This animal when the signal was given was led into the field a set distance, and thus drew the man up the acclivity, wheeling before him a barrow loaded with stone or clay.

This was speedily emptied on arriving at the top, and then the man galloped down the run, drawing the empty barrow behind him. The appearance of this process of wheeling barrows up and down a nearly perpendicular plane, was singularly striking to those who were strangers to railway feats.

A stationary steam engine named 'Hercules', fired by Robert Billingham, was kept constantly at work, pumping out the water from the Cutting. Numerous locomotives were ever plying backwards and forwards, taking trains loaded with the matter excavated from the Cutting to the neighbouring embankments at Ashton & Blisworth, where the blocks of stone and masses of clay were tumbled down for the purpose of forming the mound, and bringing back the empty wagons to be reloaded.

Lecount recorded that 25 x 100 pound (45 kilogram's approximately) barrels of gunpowder were used each week.

In January 1837 the London & Birmingham Railway Company placed an advertisement in the *Northampton Mercury,* offering a 100 Guineas Reward for information leading to the conviction of offenders who had deliberately placed a cast-iron pedestal upon the rails at Ashton on the 18th. This action, the company stated, would have caused the throwing of engine and wagons off the road, endangering the lives of the attendants and other workmen.

Lawlessness continued to be a problem and the local populace became enraged by the serious increase of criminal activities in the surrounding area. In desperation the following notice was placed in the *Northampton Mercury –*

In consequence of the numerous depredations which have been committed in Roade and several adjoining parishes in which the works of The London & Birmingham Rail Road are now in progress:–

A PUBLIC MEETING

Will be held in the Cock Inn in Roade, on Wednesday next, the SEVENTH of JUNE at 11 o'clock in the forenoon, for the purpose of taking into consideration the propriety of appointing one or more POLICEMEN or SPECIAL CONSTABLES for the better protection of the property and protection of individuals during the progression of the said works.

Making the Cut – The Navvy Invasion

Pursuant to the notice, the meeting was chaired by the Revd W.M. Butlin and was numerously attended by gentlemen living in Roade and the neighbouring Villages. Three resolutions were duly passed –

> *This meeting through the Chairman W.M. Butlin to make representation to the Directors of the London – Birmingham Railway. That in consequence of the works now being carried out at Roade, and neighbouring Villages, crime has increased by a very great amount and it has become absolutely necessary to take some measures to prevent it increasing further. They (the meeting) hope the Directors will establish some kind of Policing to protect the persons and property of individuals living in the parishes bordering the line between Ashton and Blisworth.*

> *To adjourn the meeting to the 23rd June to consider the response of the Railway Company. [There is no record of the adjourned meeting or the Railway Company's response.]*

> *To put a report and the resolutions of the meeting in three Northampton papers, The Mercury, Herald and Chronicle.*

The Revd Gentleman having left the chair, the thanks of the meeting were unanimously voted to him.

On 6th May 1837, the *Northampton Mercury* reported on the inquest into the death of James Vennimore, a stonemason, aged 46 years. The deceased was employed upon the Railway at Roade in dressing stones. A triangle, consisting of three poles, used for the purpose of raising large stones, for some unknown cause gave way and fell with some considerable force on the back of the deceased killing him instantly. The article continued by informing readers that fellow workmen of the deceased had been liberal enough to make a subscription for his widow. Vennimore's mortal remains were interred in the churchyard of St Mary's at Roade, his tombstone paid for by fellow workers carries the following inscription – 'This stone is erected by his friends and fellow workmen of Courteenhall Bridge as a token of regard'.

This newspaper recorded three further incidents during the same month. On the 13th a navvy suffered a broken leg after a wagon hit a stone which lay across the rails, the jerk throwing out several men. The second resulted in another labourer being sent to the infirmary with little hope of recovery. He had lost his footing, slipped, and had fallen with his back across a wagon axle, the impact crushing his spine. On the 24th, Thomas Blunt, a boy of 13, was killed whilst unhooking a horse; he had slipped and a wagon had run over him. George Henman was engaged in undermining on the 29th when the earth gave way and upwards of two tons fell upon him; he died in excruciating pain over three hours. The newspaper reported that the inquests into his and Thomas Blunt's demise were held at Roade in early June.

In June, two inquests into the deaths of railway navvies were held at Ashton and Blisworth respectively, both following tragic accidents. One of the unfortunate individuals involved in the accident at Ashton was John Addington, 29, from Grafton

CUTTING REMARKS

Regis, who died whilst working on the embankment on the 2nd. The incident, which saw the fall of several tons of undermined earth collapse from a height of 14 feet, was witnessed by John Mills and Duncan Camp. Addington was buried under the fall for ten minutes before being dug free. He was attended by a surgeon from Roade and taken thereafter to the Infirmary with a fractured left leg and a severe concussion to the brain. He was not to recover and died shortly afterwards, leaving a wife and two small children. Accidental death was recorded.

The second inquest was upon George Baldwin who lost his life whilst propelling a wagon laden with spoil. He tripped over a sleeper and fell beneath the wheels, suffering a broken left arm and severe internal injuries. He was rushed to the infirmary accompanied by a colleague, his last words being "Bill, I shall die in five minutes". His death was recorded as 'died by accident'.

On11th of the month, a young girl named Mary Ann Hodges was walking on the railway between Ashton and Roade, when an engine caught her dress. Her arm was mutilated, requiring its removal from the socket; she also sustained other severe injuries. Mortification took place within days. The most horrific aspect of this case was that medical attention took place without anaesthetic.

The New Inn, the navvies' watering hole, was not exempt from the attentions of the marauding labourers. In October, Robert Hammerway, 37, and John Gooding, 22, were found guilty of destroying seven apple trees belonging to the landlord, Robert Beckett. Both were found guilty and sentenced to six months jail terms with hard labour.

In early September the following notice of an auction was advertised in the *Northampton Mercury*, to be held on the 28th at The New Inn, Roade, near the great Cutting where steam engines are daily at work.

The proprietor, Mr Robert Beckett, who has declined 'Horseing' the works on the railway offers upwards of 20 valuable strong horses and mares; 20 sets of cart horse gearing nearly new, with extra weight of chains; several sets of gearing for barrows; Chaff cutting machine, Chaff boxes and bean mill, all nearly new; portable mangers, rack and mangers 40 feet long; excellent broad-wheeled wagon, ditto broad-wheeled cart, narrow-wheeled ditto; one light Scotch cart, with frame; one corner box for stable; a handsome Alderney cow, in full profit; upwards of 20 ewe and wether lambs; a valuable brown cob horse, five years old, 15 hands high, and quiet in harness; neat gig and harness, nearly new; one three-year-old horse pony, and one four-year-old ditto, quiet in harness; additionally several other lots of useful household furniture and other effects.

Why Mr Beckett should be disposing of such a large quantity of horsepower and excavating apparatus a year before the Cutting's completion can only be speculated upon.

As the year drew to a close, the 4th November edition of the *Northampton Mercury* reported upon two further incidents with tragic consequences for the individuals

Making the Cut – The Navvy Invasion

involved. In the first, a railway navvy drowned in the canal at Stoke Bruerne whilst in a state of intoxication, a companion narrowly escaping a similar fate. The second occurred at Gayton, where a young man named Chamberlain suffered terrible injuries to his arm and side after his clothing became caught in the wheel of a moving wagon. Such was the extent of the damage to his arm, it had to be amputated.

In January 1838, a young boy named George Clark was severely injured when he fell whilst unhooking a gangers-wagon. His leg and thigh were reported to have been so seriously lacerated that he was taken to the infirmary. In the same month Richard Hayes, 22, for no discernible reason, endeavoured to run between a moving locomotive and 15 wagons which were linked by a length of chain. He fell and all of the wagons passed over his chest, killing him instantly. Accidental death was recorded. Also reported in the *Northampton Mercury* that month were the deaths of navvies named Gawthorn and Thomas Gregory, who both died as a result of injuries sustained on the works. Such was the frequency of what the press called '*Railway Accidents'* that the Northampton Infirmary refused admission of the unfortunate victims.

On the 24th, a large ember from an engine working on the line between Roade and Ashton fell upon a thatched barn occupied by Mr John Weston. The roof immediately set alight and fell upon a horse, which suffered a terrible death. The adjoining stable, a hovel and a piggery were also destroyed; three pigs and 19 sheep were saved. The event was witnessed by two local railway labourers, Dennis Warren and Joseph Clark, the premises were the property of the Duke of Grafton.

In February, the *Northampton Mercury* reported on a serious disturbance which occurred at Blisworth. A band of navvies led by a 'job master', Thomas Richardson, 36, arrived at the village seeking out a contractor named John Brown for payment of wages for work carried out on his behalf. They located Mr Brown taking lunch at The Royal Oak and confronted him with their claim. Brown, it would seem, had doubted Richardson's intent to do the work and had, in the interim, engaged others to undertake the task. However, Richardson and his colleagues insisted that as the arrangements had been previously agreed, the payment was in their opinion still outstanding. The demand was accompanied by threats to Brown's continued wellbeing if they were not satisfied.

Under much duress, Brown was forced by the navvies to proceed with them to the office of the railway engineer, Mr Farrell, where arrangements were made for the payment to be made later. However, as it was a Sunday and no cash was immediately available, the penniless navvies were dissatisfied, to such a degree that the unfortunate Brown was assaulted and robbed of his personal money and possessions. After dividing the gains of eight shillings and nine pence, the navvies dispersed. One of the ringleaders, William Stamp, 25, was subsequently taken into custody by the police and taken to be held at The Royal Oak. Upon learning of their comrade's arrest, in excess of a hundred navvies proceeded to the public house to effect his rescue. In the interim, police reinforcements of six men plus the local constables had arrived in the village just in time, preventing them gaining access.

A major riot ensued resulting in much damage being caused to the establishment. Every window was broken in the building, as were those at the engineers' office, such was the anger of the mob.

The navvies caused serious local disturbances
(nationaltransporttrust.org.uk)

The police were eventually successful in quelling the disturbance, and apprehended ten of the rioters including Richardson and Stamp, whose rescue had been foiled. They were all taken to the county jail to await trial. John Richardson, who had also been involved in the sharing of money taken from Mr Brown but subsequently returned it to him, was acquitted in the interim.

At the trial, William Stamp, James Dawson, 23, and Richardson were charged with having violently assaulted and robbed John Brown of two purses, a five-pound note, three sovereigns and about 15 shillings at Blisworth, (inflation?!). John Tate, 23, William Dart, 21, Robert Johnson, 35, John Harrison, 25, John Bramley, 23, and Thomas Darkins, 40, were charged with assaulting James Watson and other constables and attempting to rescue from their lawful custody William Stamp, he being charged with others of having robbed John Brown. All were sent to the county jail.

Poaching bothered the landowners throughout this period. Navvies were good at it (the best in the world, they boasted), and since they roamed about in gangs, nobody dared to challenge or attempted to apprehend them.

Making the Cut – The Navvy Invasion

The Poacher
(nsimblog.wordpress.com)

Setting the Snare
(burtonlatimer.info)

As the excavations progressed, flooding continued to be a major issue due to the water-laden shale layer, accompanied by the continued flow of a number of streams which had been severed by the works. In an effort to prevent the run-off from these continually compounding the problem, a cast iron aqueduct, still is use today, was built on sandstone piers.

Aqueduct over the Cutting. Structure N°209A Listed Building 1294250.
(John Farebrother)

CUTTING REMARKS

In his report to the directors of 17th February 1838, Stephenson describes how he planned to expedite progress in extending the line from the temporary terminus at Denbigh Hall, near Bletchley, to Roade, by forming the embankment – presumably that at Ashton – using the technique known as 'side cutting'.

An extract from his report reads –

The Blisworth Contract, which consists of an extensive cutting is progressing favourably; but the character of the excavation is now more difficult than at first, and as it gets deeper, the space for employing men gradually becomes more confined. The material is increasing in hardness, and there has also been a greater quantity of water. In order to facilitate the completion of this part of the line, an arrangement has been made for throwing an additional quantity of earth into spoil from the centre of the excavation, and supplying the deficiency in the embankment by a corresponding quantity of side cutting at the southern extremity of the contract. The object thus aimed at is the completion of the south portion of the contract in May, nearly at the same time with the Wolverton and Castlethorpe contracts, at which period an extended opening may be made from Denbigh-hall to the village of Roade, situate on the turnpike road leading from Stony Stratford to Northampton, and only five miles from the latter town. This position appears highly advantageous for the next temporary terminus, which must remain the terminus for the London division until the opening of the whole railway.

In the Roade Cutting there now remains 100,000 cubic yards of materials which will be disposed of in the following manner:-

30,000 cubic yards to Ashton Embankment;
35,000 cubic yards to Blisworth Embankment
35,000 cubic yards to spoil.
The first quantity is that which relates to the opening of the line as far as Roade, and reckoning the south end of the Cutting to yield at the rate of 10,000 yards per month this may be effected in three months, allowing necessary time for joining the permanent road.

Embankment construction
(victorianweb.org)

Making the Cut – The Navvy Invasion

With reference to the 'side cutting' technique referred to in the report, Lecount mentions in his publication, *The History the Railway connecting London & Birmingham*, several major slippages of the embankment at Ashton during its construction. One of these slips was close to one of the two bridges; it enveloped and destroyed two cottages, despite the company's best efforts to save them.

On 13th March, the home of Mr Turland of Milton Malsor was the scene of a robbery where two silver watches and other items were stolen. Superintendent Ball of the police investigated the case, and three months later received intelligence that four silver spoons had been offered for sale at a beer house in Northampton by two railway workers from Milton. He proceeded to the venue and searched the premises and found one of Mr Turland's timepieces which had been left against loans of 18 shillings and 4 pence, and a quantity of beer. Two of the suspects, George Henson and James Hurst, were apprehended and their residence searched, and the other watch was recovered. Returning to Milton, Superintendent Ball took into custody Henry Hurst who was also implicated. Subsequently Henry Hurst and George Henson were committed to the county jail, while James Hurst, who was also suspected of robbing the Church at Milton, was released through a lack of evidence.

Some of the navvies were
opportunist thieves and
vagabonds
(transporttrust.com)

Although the end of the project was in sight, manpower was still in great demand. George Hooton, a resident of Bozeat, came to Roade seeking work and was immediately taken-on, undertaking labouring duties. Soon after beginning work, he was approached by a navvy named James Hafford who asked him the time. When Hooton produced his watch it was snatched away by the navvy. Hooton reported the theft to the constable, who promptly arrested the thief. The suspect told the constable that he had given the timepiece to the landlord (Robert Beckett) of a local beer-house (The New Inn), where it was recovered by the constable, it having been set against the provision of three shillings worth of ale.

At the trial, Hafford stated in his defence that it was the custom among the navvies that 'newcomers' stand three shillings worth of drink as a fee for acceptance, and as Hooton did not have the money, the watch was taken instead. To back his claim, he called a fellow navvy named Perkins to verify the practice. Unfortunately, Perkins was found by the court to be drunk and insensible of giving an intelligent response. Undeterred, Hafford called a further navvy to back his claim. This fellow, named

CUTTING REMARKS

Bates, and described as a man of 'extraordinary dimensions', was asked by the judge to 'Kiss the book', prior to giving his account.

At this request the witness gazed at the publication with a perplexed expression, and addressing the bench asked, "Kiss the book?" It was with some difficulty that he was made to believe that the bible was to receive a bona-fide kiss. He was asked if he was acquainted with the nature of taking the oath, to which he replied, "No, I am sure I don't". However, he did understand that the court required him to tell the truth. In his evidence, he corroborated the evidence of the prisoner and stated that it was the custom of the navigators to *'colt'* a fresh man. The accuser, Hooton, admitted to the court that he had drunk some ale after the watch was taken, but did not know that it was the produce of his timepiece, he had been told that he would be 'colted', (a form of initiation), on the following Saturday night. On reviewing the evidence, the jury acquitted the prisoner!

On 14th April, the *Northampton Mercury* reported an incident involving a group of navvies who were riding upon open wagons from the Cutting to the Ashton embankment. The loose coupled wagons jolted, resulting in a concussion which saw Welshman Henry John being thrown onto the rails. One of his feet was run over causing horrible injuries. He was taken to the infirmary where his condition was recorded by the paper as being 'in a very precarious state'.

On the 23rd of the same month, as work to join the two extremities of the line continued, a correspondent was to witness a further tragic accident during his visit to the Ashton construction site. His commentary was subsequently published in *Osborne's London and Birmingham Railway Guide* –

> *At dinner time, the men used to ride down from the Blisworth works [to Ashton] on the loaded trains, and if a wagon slipped from the rails, its contents of stone and workmen would be precipitated in a heterogeneous mass upon the ground, when, of course, the most rueful consequences resulted. An instance of this kind happened at the time when the editor of this work was engaged in collecting matter to form its contents, which was strikingly illustrative of the recklessness of life and daring hardihood of the British labourer. A few days prior, a severe accident, accompanied with loss of life, had occurred in this place, yet, nothing daunted, the men, instead of walking to their dinner, they came riding down on the trains. A similar catastrophe was the result; several wagons were thrown off the rails; one man was completely buried under the masses of limestone, and several partly so. One stalwart navigator disencumbered himself from the heap, and feeling his arm, said, addressing a more fortunate comrade, "It's broke, by G-d ! I must go home."*

> *He waited for a short time to ascertain the amount of evil inflicted on his fellow-sufferers, and then, supporting his broken arm with his sound one, accompanied by a friend, strode off homewards to his cottage which was six miles off! A fine, handsome youth, who had his foot pulverised into a*

shapeless mass of flesh and bone, bore his fate with less fortitude, and cried bitterly. A rough-looking fellow, who stood by, and seemed to be a sort of foreman among the workmen, took his pipe from his mouth, spat out, and in a blunt advising tone said, addressing the boy, "Crying 'll do thee no good, lad; thou'dst better have it cut off from above the knee!" A number of the village women came upon the bank, each evincing a great desire to touch with their fingers the mangled limb. The man who was buried under the heap, on being taken out, asked for a little cold water, and soon showed symptoms of internal bleeding, that gave the bystanders the conviction that his organisation was incapacitated to sustain life much longer. In the course of a quarter of an hour, a cart was obtained to convey these two poor victims to a neighbouring hospital.

Removing the limestone
(pinterest.com)

This incident was also reported in the *Northampton Mercury,* which named three of the accident victims as John Yarrel, Joseph Anton and Matthew Faulkner. Yarrel sustained an extensive fracture to his left hip; Anton suffered a double compound fracture to one arm, and Faulkner a compound fracture of the left leg. Yarrel, who was 18, was later to die of his injuries, accidental death being recorded at the inquest.

Safety of men engaged upon railway construction had, due to the large numbers of deaths occurring, come to the attention, somewhat belatedly, of the government. The surveyor Robert Rawlinson was summoned to give a report to the House of Commons Select Committee on Railway Labourers in 1846 on the fatalities which had resulted from the Cutting's construction. He had this to say about the excavations at Roade –

CUTTING REMARKS

Question:"A very severe cutting?"

Rawlinson:"The heaviest open cutting and largest work in its character, excepting the Kilsby tunnel, on that railway.

Question:"Were those works attended with a considerable loss of life?"

Rawlinson: "There was a considerable loss of life, and very many accidents upon the work; I kept no account of the number."

Question: "In what way did those accidents occur?"

Rawlinson: "At that cutting there was a top lift of from 10 to 12 feet of gravel and clay, and marl of various consistencies; the bottom of a portion of the cutting was composed of limestone rock, but a portion of that rock at each end founded itself upon the clay again. The top lift was taken off in the ordinary method of working excavations, by means of wagons, and a great portion run out into spoil by barrow runs. The bottom portion was cut off with picks and wedges, and an immense quantity of gunpowder was used. I believe as much as 100,000lbs in weight; the top portions of the excavation were brought down at each end of the cutting by inclines to the ordinary level of the railway, and those inclines were the cause of considerable accidents from the temporary wagons; the men would sometimes, through carelessness, put more wagons on the incline than the brakeman could hold, and they would overcome him, and sometimes a wheel would break, or a rail would get out of place. I have seen as many as 20 wagons broken up at one time. Frequently accidents would happen in this way: the men would get upon these temporary wagons to ride from their work, and I believe six or seven men had their arms and legs broken at one time, though the contractor told them to get off the wagons at the top of the incline, and they disobeyed him".

On 19th May, the *Reading Mercury* reported –

The Works on the line of the London and Birmingham Railway, although rapidly proceeding, there remains much to be done at Roade in Northamptonshire, where the rock is blasted in a process which consumes weekly, no less than 1½ tons of gunpowder.

In June, James Offord a railway labourer was accused of stealing a shovel belonging to Peter Kightley of Roade, a charge which was subsequently dismissed. Not so fortunate was William Hull also a railway worker who received three months hard labour for the theft of a watch and a key from local resident Job Hillyard. George Goode, another railway labourer, was convicted of stealing three silk handkerchiefs, the property of James Marsh of Roade.

Goode, who had been held in custody since committing the offence, was found guilty and sentenced to one further month of confinement. John Bunney, thought to have

Making the Cut – The Navvy Invasion

been a railway labourer, was convicted of stealing a pair of stockings from John Phillips, and William Darby and Robert Newsham were found guilty of a violent assault on the unfortunate Constable Smith during the execution of his duties.

One of the major events that preceded the public's access to the new railway was the ceremonial insertion of the last brick in Kilsby Tunnel on 21st June 1838. Coinciding with this, the crossing of the Ouse valley at Wolverton was completed, as was the extensive embankment between Roade and Ashton, at the end of the month.

Lithograph of Kilsby Tunnel
(John Cooke Bourne)

Wolverton Viaduct & Embankment
(John Cooke Bourne)

CUTTING REMARKS

British History online describes the 'London and Birmingham' railway Station at Roade as sited "immediately to the south of a bridge carrying the London road over the line". The company, eager to exploit every opportunity to the maximum, duly advertised the opening of 'The Roade Station', heralded as 'The Station for Northampton'; this notable event took place on 2nd July. The Station was designated 'First Class', and was complete with refreshment rooms, in the charge of a Miss Johanna White.

The size of the excavations at Roade, according to the original estimate, would have totalled 800,000 cubic yards. However, as a result of the need to lengthen the wide part of the Cutting and numerous slips in the upper part, the total removed was approximately 1,000,000 cubic yards, apart from additions required to form adjoining embankments. The popular writer Samuel Smiles recorded that 3 million bricks were used in the construction of the restraining walls.

It is difficult to imagine the sheer magnitude of the work undertaken; however, the words of the renowned railway civil engineer Thomas Brassey (1805-77), help to portray the scene –

> 'I think as fine a spectacle as any man could witness, who is accustomed to look at work, is to see a cutting in full operation, with about twenty wagons being filled, every man at his post, and every man with his shirt open, working in the heat of the day, the gangers looking about and everything going like clockwork'.

The original estimated cost of the works was £112,950; delays, landslides and necessary additional works took this figure to over £310,000; equivalent in purchasing power to about £34 million in February 2020.

When almost complete, enthusiastic local horticulturists, including the Duke of Grafton, planted the Cutting's towering embankments along their entire length with shrubs and saplings. These would eventually mask the spoil heaps and scars in the once rural landscape. Built at a huge cost to life and limb, this monumental excavation through the formidable Blisworth Ridge had by this time become known as 'Roade Cutting', a name which would become notorious in later years as additional works were undertaken. Future events in its evolution would ensure its lasting local, national and international significance.

In August, as the number of navvies declined, local youngster was charged with stealing 210 lbs of iron, the property of the railway company from their yard at Roade. This theft was witnessed by Jane Richardson whose house at Mill Orchard overlooked the yard, where she observed the felon picking up the iron and placing it in a cart. Constable George Smith was summoned and questioned the suspect who informed him that he had collected the metal from 'houses in the village', a statement which upon investigation was found to be false. Smith escaped from custody during the evening, returning to give himself up the following day. He was convicted two months later. Crime continued to be rife in the area and the theft of iron seems to

Making the Cut – The Navvy Invasion

have been a popular pastime. Samuel Hodgkins of Ashton was also charged with the theft of iron belonging to the London & Birmingham Railway Company. The same offence was committed by Richard Taylor and John Telfree who, between them, stole some 20 pieces.

Excavations complete
(John Cooke Bourne)

Despite continued local unruliness, the national interest in the railway's imminent opening was making the headline news. *The Staffordshire Advertiser* reported that on Monday 20th August, a large party of directors and proprietors had breakfasted at the Birmingham Station, and at half-past six they left, with one of Mr Bury's engines, to make the first excursion along the entire line to London. From a lengthy report of the journey, the following is extracted -

> *The rocky excavations at Blisworth, extending through a considerable extent of country, astonished the visitors as much as any other part of the line, and must be seen to enable any person to form an adequate idea of its character. The jaunt gave much satisfaction.*

At the completion of the works Robert Rawlinson, the contractor who had been involved in surveying the land prior to the excavations beginning, was presented with a brace of partridges by Sir William Wake on the day the first train ran. Rawlinson recalled that when he first went to Blisworth to survey the works, he counted 50 hares in a single walk across Sir William Wake's estate. "I'd have brought you a hare," said the disconsolate Sir William, "but I don't believe I have one left on my estate; I have not had one in my house for the last two years" One of the remaining navvies later told Rawlinson "There isn't above one, and we'll have that this week."

Three and a half years after the first sod was cut, and shortly before the railway was to be officially opened, a relative calm descended upon the locality as the majority of the navvies moved on to find work and income elsewhere. In an anonymous letter to the *Northampton Mercury* a correspondent observed –

> *… as they now gradually withdraw from the works, leave bills unpaid in all the villages where they could obtain credit with trades people or those who let lodgings; the losses sustained are in many areas severe. And not only does*

the district suffer in a pecuniary way from the visits of these freebooters, but fellows have taken many women from the neighbourhood, and in some instances the wives of decent men and mothers of families, who have been induced to rob their husbands and abscond ….

Although the majority of the navvies had left, five of the Wesleyan Methodists remained with their families and in subsequent years a rudimentary Chapel was built between two cottages on the Ashton Road.

The magnitude of the accomplishment was commented upon by author Thomas Roscoe, who wrote the following in his *London & Birmingham Railway Guide*,

> *Viewing the work altogether, it affords one of the finest specimens of engineering this country can boast of. It is a spot beset with difficulties of every kind, and the bold and effective manner in which it has been executed, is a bright example of the talents of the Engineer in Chief.*

CHAPTER 3

The Train Now Departing

The completed line of railway from London to the Birmingham terminus at Curzon Street was officially opened on Monday 17th September 1838, reported the *Worcester Journal* –

The first train started from Euston Square Station at seven o'clock, having in the carriages the proprietors of the undertaking and their friends. Roade was reached at 17 minutes past 11; the train stopped ten minutes at this Station, which is 60 miles from London.

LNWR Colour Postcard issued 1907
(RLHS Images).

The popular press was also quick to report the conclusion of the line's construction and the sites to be witnessed by travellers. The *Penny Magazine* reported on a train's passage through the Cutting thus –

Immediately after entering Northamptonshire the line of the Railway is obstructed by the Blisworth ridge, which forms the division between the valley through which we have come, and the valley of the Nene, a stream which rises in the high lands near Daventry and runs east to Northampton. The Grand Junction Canal is carried through a tunnel at Blisworth 3,080 yards in length. The Railroad avoids a tunnel but is carried through an open cutting of limestone resting on a stratum of rock. The rock has been 'blasted' with great labour and expense.

CUTTING REMARKS

Wyld's *London & Birmingham Railway Guide* in its accolade, described the scene that passengers could expect to encounter as they journeyed through Roade–

> *….proceeding by this village we pass beneath a handsome brick bridge which marks the commencement of a long deep cutting. This is the first specimen of rocky cutting which has occurred, and which, therefore, excites our admiration on beholding it. The blue limestone rocks which frown upon us as we proceed, appear to have been rent asunder by some mighty convulsion of nature. The bridge, which crosses the line at the termination of this rocky trench, is much admired for its spacious span and elegant lines of masonry.*

Tragically, on 26th September, only nine days after the trains began running, the *Northampton Mercury* reported that a 'policeman', had been knocked down and killed at Roade. Evidently he had mistaken the line upon which the train was travelling and was struck. The death of this unknown individual was possibly the first recorded fatality since the line was opened.

These servants of the company were stationed in military style sentry boxes at defined intervals, and gave instructions to drivers both verbally and via basic hand and arm movements. This was the fledgling practice which would become the 'absolute block system', and ensured that trains were kept apart by safe time intervals. Mechanical signalling, semaphore, began to be installed from 1841. This evolved whereby all the required notifications to a driver could be given visually over a greater distance from one location, the signalling box. These were manned by signalmen who kept the trains apart by safe distance rather than time, with the policeman's role redefined to signalman.

SIGNALS.

RED is a Signal of DANGER–STOP.

GREEN   „   CAUTION–PROCEED SLOWLY.

WHITE   „   ALL RIGHT–GO ON.

These Signals will be made by **Flags** in the Daytime, and by **Lamps** at Night.

In addition to this, any Signal, or the arm, **waved** violently, denotes danger, and the necessity of stopping immediately.

London & Birmingham Railway Signalling instructions for Policemen
(Unknown)

The Station clock was 12 inches in diameter with converse plates in a mahogany case, and was provided on 3rd October by Thwaites & Reed of Clerkenwell, London, at a cost of £6, plus £2 and 10 shillings to cover the expense of carriage and fixings at both Roade and Weedon Stations.

As Roade's Station was the preferred destination for travellers bound for Northampton, the local economy continued to benefit. Alternative employment avenues also became available to the locals and opportunities to 'travel' were afforded the population.

The identity of the first Stationmaster is uncertain, although Elliott Sewell is recorded as an early Booking Clerk (born 1801). The original Stationmaster's house ('The White House') was said to have been designed by Stephenson, which supports the local legend that he resided within the village during his stay in the area.

From the map below it is evident that the original Station buildings were positioned at the bottom of the existing Station Road, in the vicinity of a footpath, locally known as 'The Gravel'. At the time of the line's construction, it is believed that no footbridge existed; crossing the line being via gates both sides and a footway over the two running lines.

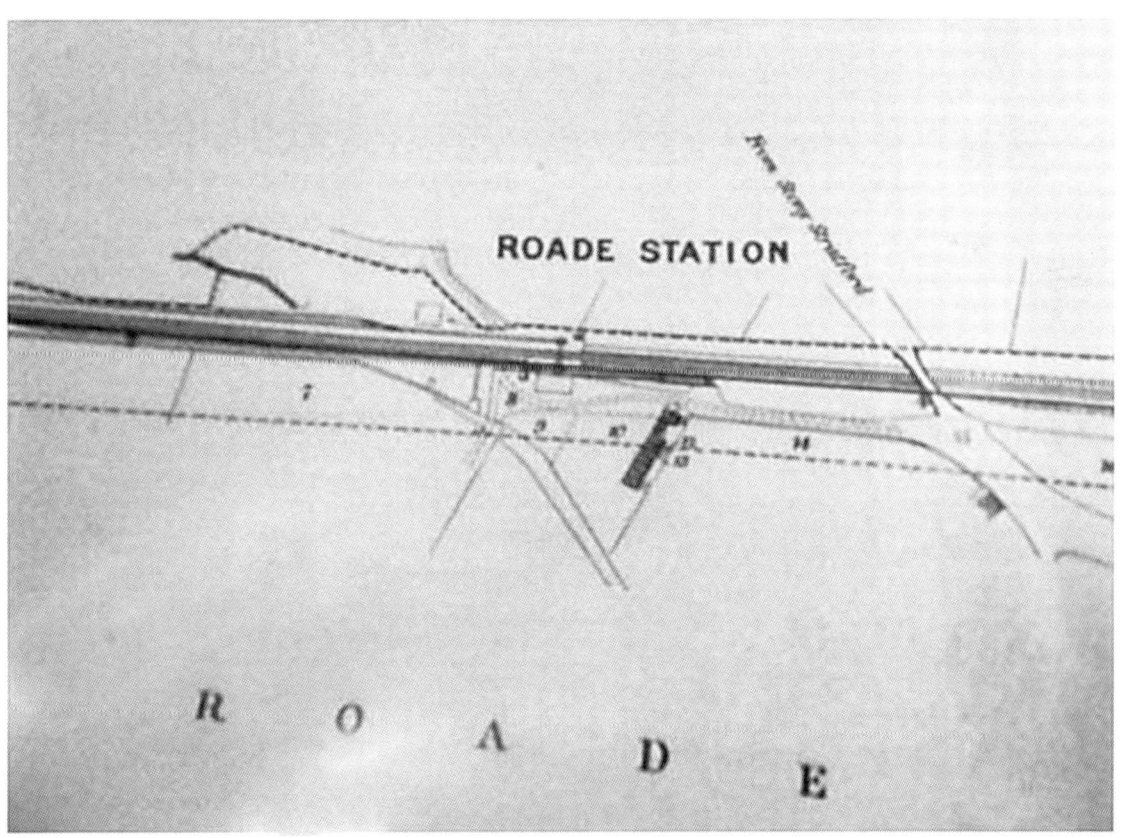

The original Roade Station location
(Chris Hillyard Collection)

Mr Thomas Shaw, a Coach operator, advertised a branch office adjoining Roade Station, bringing inquisitive folk – who could afford the fare– to the village in order to experience the new railway. On 13th October, an advertisement appeared in the *Northampton Mercury* for a daily coach, called 'The Rising Sun', running from

CUTTING REMARKS

Kettering at 8.15am, through Northampton to Roade Railway Station in time to meet the First Class train to London at 11.00am. This was scheduled to arrive in the capital at 2.00pm. A similar service operated daily from Market Harborough to Roade Station.

On the platforms, the passengers would board or detrain for the capital and beyond to Birmingham, or for the county town, a five-mile carriage journey from the top of Station Road, where the 'Stephenson Coaching Inn' thrived. It was built in 1839 and had been renamed 'The George Inn' by February 1842.

Upon boarding the train and leaving the station, those travelling
in the Mail portion or First Class carriages were very comfortable
(Illustrated London News)

Second Class passengers soon discovered that in the open carriages the best
position was with their backs to the engine, to avoid being hit by cinders
thrown from the engine's chimney, or a cold blast of air
(Illustrated London News)

Initially, only First and Second Class passengers, along with parcels, were conveyed; bulk goods traffic commenced on 12th November. Third Class customers would have to wait until 5th October 1840!
(Illustrated London News)

The London & Birmingham Railway Company issued strict timetables and rules and regulations with which the commuters had to comply.

Distance from Birmingham.	**BIRMINGHAM** TO **LONDON.** STATIONS.	* *Mixed Short.* 6 20 *a.m.*	*Mixed Class.* 6 *a.m.*	* *Mail.* 8½ *a.m.*	*Mixed, calling at 1st classS. 10 a.m*	*Mixed Class.* 12 *p.m.*	* *Mixed Class.* 1¼ *p.m.*	* *First Class.* 4 *p.m.*	*Mixed Class* 5 *p.m.*	*First, calling at Mail S.* 6 *p m.*	* *Mail, Mixed.* 12 *p.m.*	FARES. 4 in. car. by day, or 1 class 6 in. by night	1st class carriage, 6 inside, by day	2nd class carriage, closed, by night	2nd class carriage, open, by day
Miles		H. M.	H. M.	H. M.	H. M.	H. M	H M.	H. M.	H. M.	H. M.	H. M.	S. D.	S. D.	S. D.	S. D.
	BIRMINGHAM	..	6 0	8 30	10 0	12 0	1 15	4 0	5 0	6 0	12 0				
12¼	HAMPTON	..	6 25	..	..	12 25	1 40	4 25	5 25	6 25	..	3 6	3 0	2 6	2 0
18¼	COVENTRY	..	6 50	9 17	10 45	12 50	2 0	4 45	5 50	6 45	12 53	5 0	4 6	4 0	3 0
23¼	BRANDON	..	7 5	..	..	1 5	..	..	6 5	..	..	7 0	6 0	5 0	4 0
29¼	BUGBY............	..	7 25	..	11 15	1 25	2 30	5 15	6 25	..	..	8 6	8 0	6 6	5 0
37	CRICK	..	7 50	..	..	1 50	..	..	6 50	..	..	11 0	10 0	8 6	6 6
42¾	WEEDON	..	8 5	10 26	11 55	2 5	3 10	5 55	7 5	7 55	2 9	12 6	11 6	9 6	7 6
49	BLISWORTH	..	8 25	..	12 15	2 25	3 30	6 15	7 25	..	..	14 6	13 0	11 0	8 6
52¼	ROADE...........	6 20	8 40	..	..	2 40	..	..	7 40	..	..	15 6	14 0	11 6	9 6
59¾	WOLVERTON	6 45	9 0	11 11	12 40	3 0	3 55	6 40	8 0	8 40	2 58	17 6	16 0	13 6	10 6
	BLETCHLEY	7 5	9 20	..	..	3 20	..	..	8 20	..	..	19 6	17 6	15 0	12 0
71½	LEIGHTON	7 20	9 35	..	1 15	3 35	..	7 15	8 35	..	..	21 0	19 0	16 0	12 6
80¼	TRING	7 45	10 0	12 11	1 40	4 0	4 55	7 40	9 0	9 40	4 3	23 6	21 6	18 0	14 6
84¾	B. HAMPSTEAD..	7 55	10 10	..	..	4 10	..	..	9 10	..	..	24 6	22 6	19 0	15 0
87¾	BOXMOOR	8 5	10 20	..	..	4 20	..	..	9 20	..	..	25 6	23 6	19 6	15 6
94¾	WATFORD	8 20	10 35	..	2 10	4 35	5 25	8 10	9 35	..	..	27 6	25 6	21 0	17 0
101	HARROW	8 45	11 0	..	..	5 0	..	..	10 0	..	..	29 6	27 0	22 6	18 0
112¼	LONDON	9 30	12 0	1 30	3 30	6 0	6 45	9 30	11 0	11 30	5 30	32 6	30 0	25 0	20 0

There is a *Mixed Train* from Aylesbury to London at 11 *a.m.* and one from London to Aylesbury at 3 *p.m.*

SUNDAY TRAINS.—Times of Departure, Mixed (from Roade) 6 20 a.m, *Mail 8½ a.m, *Mixed 1¼ p.m, *Mail, Mix. 12 p.m

The First Class Trains consist of First Class and Mail Carriages, carrying four inside (one compartment of which is convertible into a Bed Carriage, if required) and of Carriages carrying six inside,—The Mixed Trains consist of First Class Carriages, carrying six inside, and of 2d class carriages *open* at the side, without linings, cushions, or divisions in the compartments.—The Night Mail Train consists of First Class Carriages carrying six inside, and of Second Class Carriages *closed*, and entirely protected from the weather.—Each Carriage has a small roof lamp by day and night.

Passengers are especially recommended to have their names and address, or destination, *legibly written* on each part of their Luggage, when it will be placed on the top of the Coach in which they ride. unless it be in a bag, or such other small package as may conveniently be taken under the seats inside, opposite the one they occupy. If the Passenger be destined for Liverpool or Manchester, and has booked his place through, his luggage will be placed on the Liverpool or Manchester coach, and will not be disturbed till it reaches its destination; and to prevent mistakes, the Passenger should shew his ticket to the Porters, and *see* that his luggage is placed on the proper coach.

A Passenger having paid his fare, and taken out a ticket, may go by any of the Trains of *that day*, but the ticket will not be available on the following day, unless under special circumstances, when it may be exchanged for a new pass for the day required

The Trains marked with an asterisk (*) are in conjunction with those of the Grand Junction Railway; sufficient time being allowed at the Birmingham Station, where refreshments are provided, and waiting rooms, with female attendants.

Railway Fares
(tringlocalhistorymuseum.org.uk

CUTTING REMARKS

REGULATIONS.

Note.—Attention is particularly requested to the Company's Public Notices exhibited in each Office.

A charge of 1*d*. per lb. is made for Luggage accompanying a Passenger, exceeding the weight of 100 lbs. for each person.

The Company are not responsible for Luggage left for the convenience of Parties, or till called for; nor for Luggage which has not the Passenger's name and destination legibly marked thereon.

Passengers are requested to claim their Luggage, after having passed through the Office, to insure its correct disposal; and if this precaution be omitted, the article will not be forwarded until application is made, and will then be charged as a booked parcel.

Each Passenger's Luggage, as far it can conveniently, is placed in or upon the Coach in which he has taken his place.

Carpet Bags and small Luggage are placed underneath the seat *opposite* to that which the owner occupies.

Each Passenger's ticket for the First Class Train is numbered to correspond with the seat taken.

The places by the Mixed Trains are not numbered.

Passengers' Tickets are only admissible with the Train expressed thereon; but if parties are desirous of transferring their seats to a succeeding Train, on the same day, their Tickets will be exchanged.

The doors of the Booking Offices are closed precisely at the appointed time for starting, after which no person can be admitted.

Passengers can only be Booked at the Road Stations, on condition that there is room, on the arrival of the Train.

Smoking is strictly prohibited in the Carriages, even with the consent of the Passengers, or upon the Stations.

No gratuity, under any circumstances, is allowed to be taken by any servant of the Company.

No persons are permitted to sell Liquors, or any other articles, upon the Line or Stations.

Every Guard, Porter, or Policeman, employed by the Company, bears a distinguishing number on the collar.

Ten minutes are allowed at the Wolverton Central Station, where a female attendant is appointed.

Railway regulations
(tringlocalhistorymuseum.org.uk)

Employed as porters were William Kightley (born1810), and Henry Wilding (b.1823). The tracks in the section were maintained by platelayers John Dodd (b.1811), William Hillyard (b.1812), Daniel Jones (b.1806) and Thomas Clarke (b.1798). The Policemen (the initial term for signalmen) were William Hick (b.1796), Gordon Thomas (b.1801), Samuel Chater (b.1801) and Thomas Byrns (b.1801).

Roade had been irreversibly changed by the coming of the railways. This former rural community now lived with fire-breathing dragons belching steam and smoke into the heavens on a daily basis. The following appeared in a journey guide –

A PROPHECY ABOUT ROADE

In a "Handbook for Travellers along the London and Birmingham Railway" published in 1839 at the price of 2/-, when the line had only been opened to traffic for a year, there is an interesting reference to the village of Roade. After describing the course of the line from London to Hanslope, the book proceeds:

> "About this spot we leave the county of Buckingham and enter that of Northampton and, passing rapidly over a lofty embankment of about a mile in length, which divides the village of Ashton in two parts, shortly arrive at the Roade Station.
>
> The little village of Roade, which lies close to the railway, has suddenly been invested with all the bustle and activity of a town; and will, no doubt, enjoy increasing consequence and prosperity from its locality to this great line of communication. This is one of the numerous instances which could be adduced, of the great benefit which a Railway confers upon the towns near which it is formed; and amidst the changes which are thus originated, many places that heretofore have been comparatively unknown will become towns of considerable extent."

Mogg's Handbook for Railway Travellers 1839

In October 1838, the *Northampton Herald* reported that navvy Thomas Clark had been killed by Joseph King, 29, in a fight which began in a place near the Courteenhall pits. He had received a severe beating to his head and throat and died of his injuries. The fight arose out of what the railroad men called 'drinking out', whereby some of them who were in the habit of illegally selling ale and spirits to other workmen, arranged a party, entered a house and consumed all the ale and spirits they could find. The newspaper's opinion was that it was a great pity that the managers should suffer such illegal practices and that the Excise officers were not more alert to their duty. At the inquest held at Roade, King was charged with feloniously killing and slaying Clark. At the following Northampton Lent Assizes he was found guilty in his absence, having absconded in the intcrim.

The railway's popularity and the public demand were such that, on 3rd November 1838, Robert Beckett, the landlord of The New Inn (former den of iniquity of the navvy 'Banditti', now Woodleys Farm), notified friends and customers that his establishment had undergone a thorough repair and he would be most happy to accommodate them and others passing through, to or from Roade Railway Station.

He offered potential patrons –

Well Aired Beds
Wines and Spirits of the Purest Quality
Home Brewed Ale & London Porter
Dublin Stout - Scotch Ale, Lemonade & Soda Water
Good Corn, Hay and Grass Keeping
Stalled and other Stabling

CUTTING REMARKS

Former New Inn in 1953
(Fred Blincow Collection)

The completion of the Cutting did not end its civil engineering problems as unstable clay continued to make its presence felt. Shortly after the opening of the line, several slips occurred, a problem which would trouble the company over the next decade and require them to deploy watchmen to continually patrol it, 'in order to guard against falling masonry fouling the line'. The solution to these slippages was to build 'counterforts' – in this context, five-feet wide trenches, dug at 20-feet intervals into the slip (i.e. at right angles to the rails) and then filled with well-compacted gravel or crushed stone. The counterforts thus divided the slip area into segments, acted as drainage channels and applied frictional force to the body of the clay to prevent it from sliding forward. Drifts were also driven into the sides of the Cutting behind the retaining walls to drain off the excess water and maintain stability.

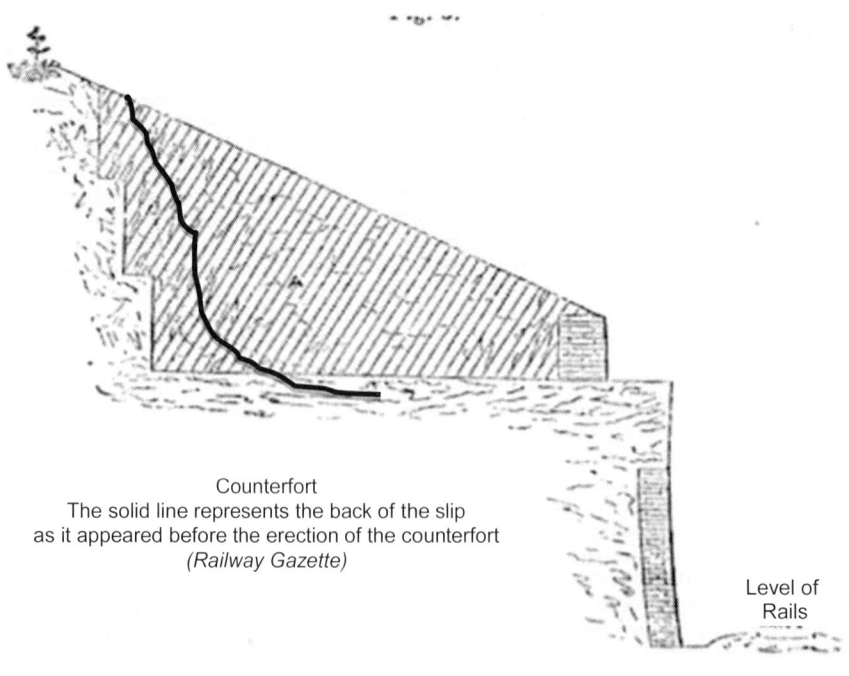

Counterfort
The solid line represents the back of the slip
as it appeared before the erection of the counterfort
(Railway Gazette)

Level of
Rails

THE TRAIN NOW DEPARTING

These additional works required a contingent of navvies to remain and, as a consequence, crime continued to be troublesome throughout their extended stay.

During the Cutting's construction, Stephenson had become concerned with the perpetual dampness and its effect on (untreated) wooden sleepers on which the rails were mounted. To mitigate the risk, he opted to mount the rails on stone sleepers. As a consequence these had the effect of giving the early passengers an uncomfortably rough and noisy ride. This was greatly improved when a method of protecting wooden sleepers was established by a process called 'Kyanising' and the stone sleepers were replaced. The original stone sleepers were subsequently sold to the Grand Junction Canal Company; some may still be seen at Stoke Bruerne, where they were used as coping stones.

In winter, frost was to become a major issue, contributing to the erosion of the sides, and at severe low temperatures enormous icicles would be caused, threatening the safe passage of trains.

In early March 1839, the *Northampton Mercury* contained the following notice of an auction of properties. These premises had evidently served their function, and were now surplus to the railway company's requirements –

BUILDING MATERIALS OF 46 COTTAGES
Near to the London and Birmingham Railway
TO BE SOLD BY AUCTION
BY RICHARD GRIFFITHS
On Friday 22nd March 1839

This was the entirety of the materials for 40 recently-erected cottages, situated in a field near the Stony Stratford road and nearly adjoining the Roade Station House; comprising hard burnt bricks, Best Bangor Countess slates, ridge tiles, foreign deal joists, rafters, floors, ledge doors, two light frames with lead lights and crown glass, an iron oven, boiler and grate, etc. Other railway-built cottages at the northern end of the Cutting were similarly auctioned.

In June, Roade Station was the site of the first ever recorded passenger train accident in Northamptonshire. The passenger train collided head-on with a ballast train which had been shunted onto the line from a siding. A report in the *Northampton Herald* on 6th June said that – 'The engines were sadly dented'. Of the unfortunate passengers, it was stated –

> the face of a young man came into contact with the head of a lady in front of him, and all his front teeth were knocked out, the whole of the passengers were thrown from their seats and more or less injured. Had the train not been slowing down to stop at the Station, the accident may have been considerably worse.

43

CUTTING REMARKS

In January 1840, following heavy rains and severe frost, a slippage occurred in the Cutting. Situated on the embankment in the area of the slip was a pumping station, located upon a wooden staging. John Clark, 69, was working the apparatus at the time. Both he and the equipment tumbled to the bottom of the Cutting; he suffered six broken ribs and died of his injuries. The same month, Thomas Willett, a local lad of 19, was convicted of stealing the iron rim of a railway wagon wheel, the property of the London & Birmingham Railway at Roade.

In February John Paggett was charged with stealing a wheelbarrow from the railway company at Roade, and with it he then stole three pecks of Barley from the local Vicar, the Revd William Butlin.

The railway company's newspaper advertisements, dated 17th September 1840, advised that Third Class trains for the conveyance of passengers (in open carriages) between London and Birmingham would commence on the 5th October. The London bound train arriving at Roade at 5.45pm, and 12.15pm for the Birmingham service. The notices in the press stated that, 'Ample time will be allowed to passengers for refreshments at the Roade Station, distance 60 miles from London'.

It was also advertised in the *Northampton Mercury* that Mr Beckett, Landlord of The New Inn, having 'declined the inn keeping business', was to auction its contents (removed for the convenience of sale) at The Hare & Hounds, near the Railway Station at Roade on November 20th 1840. It is thought that The Hare and Hounds was a misprint for The Fox and Hounds.

Heavy rain in September 1842 caused an embankment slippage at Roade, reported the *London Weekly Dispatch,* resulting in the lines being blocked. As a consequence passengers on a London bound train from York were required to walk from Roade to Wolverton in order to resume their journey, with northbound passengers doing likewise in the other direction. Initially it was feared that many persons had been injured, but these concerns were unfounded. The newspaper reported that 100 men had been sent to repair the damage; however, it informed its readers that great secrecy was being observed by the management, with the servants of the company being cautioned to be silent.

On 12th August 1843, the *Northampton Mercury* reported upon the death of a railway labourer two and a half miles south of Roade Station. The 'Down Mail' train was proceeding at 23 mph in darkness on a moonlit night when the driver saw an object ahead of him on the line. Getting closer, he realised it was man, apparently asleep, sitting on the rail. The driver made every effort to stop his locomotive but, such was the momentum, the man was struck by the engine's buffer and both it and several carriages passed over the unfortunate individual. Upon stopping his train, the driver hurried back on foot to investigate, he found that the man's legs had been virtually severed from his torso. Remarkably he was still alive. The injured man was conveyed in one of the carriages to Roade, where he was removed to the platform, one of his legs falling off in the process. Unbelievably still alive, he was recognised by a signalman as a railway labourer called Robbins, who had been engaged upon railway work for the previous ten years. He was a married man with six children, and was currently in the employ of contractors Pele & Gissell, who were engaged upon major building works at Wolverton. He expired on the platform, the report concluding that he had been 'drinking freely, became overpowered and sat down on the rail to rest'.

The London & Birmingham Railway Company, which had made the costly investment in a carriage 'fit for a Queen', were rewarded on 28th November when Queen Victoria, accompanied by Prince Albert, travelled in a specially constructed coach, described by George P Neale as 'handsome and luxurious'. It was in the centre of a train which departed at 11.00am from Watford, in Hertfordshire, travelling to Tamworth and passing through the magnificent earthworks of Roade Cutting at around 12.30pm.

It is not known if the impression Her Majesty had upon viewing these tall excavations was ever recorded, however, the *Wilts & Gloucestershire Standard* reported that at Roade her passing was met with vociferous cheering of loyalty. She returned by the same route a few days later, reported the *Northampton Mercury*, leaving Weedon at 2.55pm. The Royal Train passed Blisworth at 3.09pm, through the 'heavy cutting', passing Roade Station at 3.14pm. The newspaper stated that at both these Stations a considerable number of persons had assembled to loudly cheer Her Majesty.

Her Majesty boards the train
(agefotostock.com)

1843 London & Birmingham Railway Royal Train
(The English Illustrated Magazine July 1897)

Her Majesty's second journey through the Cutting was a year later, on 12th November 1844, when she travelled with Prince Albert from the newly opened London Euston Station. The Royal couple again used the handsome coach, which George P Neale reported to have been richly embellished and altered for their journey to visit The Marquis of Exeter at Burghley House. In the weeks preceding the visit the national and provincial newspapers; including the *Morning Post*, *St James Chronicle* and *Norwich Mercury;* printed articles speculating upon the regal travelling arrangements. Roade, Blisworth and Weedon Stations were all reported to be the place where the Royal couple would alight and join royal horse-drawn carriages forming a cortege to their local destinations.

CUTTING REMARKS

Blisworth was soon discounted due to the poor state of the highway between that place and Northampton. Roade however was still believed to be the preferred location, as it was revealed that Mr Higgins, of the George Hotel, had been requested to provide a number of horses for the visit. Additionally, fourteen horses from the royal stud were to be sent to stables in Northampton in readiness.

It is uncertain as to when the final decision was made, but ultimately Weedon was decided upon, perhaps because of it being closer to Burghley House. Roade however played its part, when, two hours prior to the Royal Train's passing, a special train conveying the Royal Household suite arrived at the Station where carriages awaited on Station Road to allow them to precede the royal party to the Queen's destination.

The *Yorkshire Gazette's* report on Her Majesty's progress includes: 'At Roade Station, which was reached at eighteen minutes past eleven, the special train passed the ordinary passenger train, which had left London for Birmingham at nine o'clock'. It was also reported in the *Leamington Spa Courier* that at Roade 'the lineside was thronged with anxious groups of well-wishers'.

At Weedon, the locals welcomed the Royal couple by erecting an 'unpretending arch, composed of evergreens' over the principal street. The couple returned south three days later from the same Station, where the inhabitants 'joined in loyal vociferations'.

Whenever the London & Birmingham railway through Roade is discussed in earnest, reference is always made to the dispute as to why the original route missed out the County Town. The debate centres on the differing and shifting interests of the railway company, the landowners, and the town's civil advocators and objectors. The issue became what would later become known in some quarters as 'The Northampton Legend'.

The proposed route of the line was contentious from the outset, with plans to include Northampton becoming a topic of much debate in the town's newspapers. Letters of opposition to the railway from both titled landowners and the common Council of Northampton, equally opposed by the colourful efforts of the Town Assembly and townspeople who were in favour of it, were a weekly occurrence.

When finally the railway's route was decided upon by the engineers, opinionated correspondents continued to fill up the letter pages of the county's publications. After the line's opening, with the benefits of hindsight and/or the realisation of the missed opportunities, letters in condemnation of the decision makers appeared with ongoing regularity.

Although the town would eventually be connected to the network the debate continued, as evidenced in a 1964 contribution to *Northamptonshire Past & Present*, Volume. III, N°5a, where reference is made to: 'much nonsense continuing to be written in spite of the exposition of the truth by Miss Joan Wake in *'Northampton Vindicated'* (or *'Why the Main Line missed the Town'*), published in 1935. Which is substantiated by further evidence in *Northamptonshire Past & Present* Volume II, by Mr Victor Hatley, *'Northampton Re-Vindicated'*, (or *'More Light on Why the Main Line missed the Town'*). Published in 1959.

As previously mentioned, the gradient factor was probably decisive from the engineer's viewpoint in determining the route taken, and this can assist in arriving at the truth in spite of much conflicting evidence. For example, Stephenson, writing to Samuel Smiles, biographer of George & Robert Stephenson, in 1857, said that Northampton had: 'distinguished itself by being rather more furious than other places in its opposition to railways, and begged that the line might be kept away from them'. In his article (referenced above) Mr Hatley condemned the effrontery of this statement and suggested that Stephenson might have wished to divert attention from his own part in the disastrous undertaking at Kilsby. Thus, it could be argued that for over a century, Northampton became the whipping boy for Stephenson's errors. However, Miss Wake clearly demonstrated that public opinion was vociferously divided in the County Town.

On balance, it is plausible that Stephenson and his engineers, although it was never publicly stated, did not intend to include Northampton as a waypoint from the outset. The limited power of early locomotives, and the steep descent through the Nene Valley (from Roade Cutting) and then the long climb through Althorp, Long Buckby, and Crick being beyond their capabilities, hence the route with less demanding gradients was chosen. To substantiate this conclusion, Sir Richard Moon (Chairman, L&NWR) in his address at the shareholders' meeting in 1881, is quoted as saying: 'I do not believe it was the intention of Stephenson to go through Northampton'.

Further evidence of Stephenson's intent was to surface many years later, in the form of a letter to the *Northampton Daily Chronicle* in August 1895 from a Mr William Law who wrote –

> The late Mr T Robinson-Rice has often related to me a conversation that took place between the late Mr Grundy at his house in Spencer Parade and Mr Stephenson the engineer of the line. Mr Stephenson said that the real cause of its being taken by Blisworth was 'that he feared if he got down into the valley of the Nene he would never get out again'.

One further consideration is important, namely that the principle desire of those who wished to promote the construction of the railway was to connect London with a provincial city (Birmingham in this case), and the intermediate traffic was a secondary matter. This apparent indifference to local traffic and populations illustrates why apparently large settlements suffered from badly situated and poorly provisioned Stations, together with inconveniently timed trains, from the outset.

CHAPTER 4

London & North Western Railway – All Change

London & North Western Railway Armorial device
(Chris Hillyard Collection)

The London & North Western Railway company (L&NWR) was formed in 1846, consisting principally of the amalgamation of the London & Birmingham, the Grand Junction and the Manchester & Birmingham Railways. It also absorbed the Northampton and Peterborough branch line which served Northampton from Blisworth. The company initially had a network of approximately 350 miles (560 km), connecting London with Birmingham, Crewe, Chester, Liverpool and Manchester. The L&NWR thereafter continued to expand and in its heyday had an operating network in excess of 2,000 miles.

On 18th April 1848, a serious accident occurred south of Roade Station, resulting in three persons sustaining injury, the subsequent enquiry revealed the following –

The Peterborough had mail had passed the Roade Station at its usual speed, and when about half a mile south from it, the engine-driver (Thomas Richardson) and the guard (N B Cambridge), who had travelled on the engine, N° 98, in consequence of the driver having only lately been employed as such by the Company, remarked that the engine beat in an irregular manner. The train continued its onward course for a distance of 1¼ miles, but the engine was unable to maintain its speed and was stopped by the driver shutting off the steam.

Immediately, the guard sent out signals with great promptness, to endeavour to stop the train which he knew to be due. The under-guard, who ran back with the signals, hearing the coming train, placed a detonating warning signal on the rails, and continued to run back with his lamp showing "red" to signify "danger". When he was about 150 to 200 yards from the rear of his own train, the York mail passed him. The driver of engine N°188, immediately shut off his steam and attempted to reverse, but failed in doing so, and the guard who was with him blew the whistle. Their endeavours to arrest the progress of their train were of no avail, and it consequently ran into the Peterborough train, completely destroying the post-office van and crushing one compartment of a first-class carriage.

Railway accident
(Illustrated London News)

This accident happened during strike action by regular footplate staff, and both driver Richardson and his contemporary, William Cumberlidge, the driver of the York Mail were strike-breaking fitters, employed at Wolverton Works, with little or no experience of driving on the main line. Primary causes were found to be driver error; the enquiry found that driver Richardson, with only nine days experience, and Cumberlidge, who could demonstrate no knowledge of how to operate his engine, were both incompetent to drive and had no training in working practices in foggy weather.

Documentary evidence notes the Stationmaster and Goods Clerk at Roade in 1849 as Mr Blamire Porteous Shaw who was born in Tongland, Kirkcudbrightshire, Scotland, in 1815, and who may have moved to England as part of the Scottish Lowland clearances which continued into the 1830s. The emigrants travelled south seeking work and prosperity in the industrial towns of Newcastle and Liverpool. He was married in Liverpool in 1839 to Mary Kitson before moving south. Three children were born in Tring/Leighton Buzzard and it is surmised that he was engaged upon railway work at these locations prior to taking up his position in Roade.

In the first week of January 1850, a coal train departed Rugby for Wolverton, accompanied by Thomas Underwood, a shunting porter. Upon arrival at Roade the train was signalled into a siding to permit the midday express to pass. With the train in the siding, Underwood left his van and crossed over the line beneath the wagons between the coupling chains. As he emerged on the other side of the train, he was struck on the head and instantly killed as the guard's van of the express passed by.

London & North Western Railway – All Change

In dense fog, on the 28th of that month, the Newcastle mail train was derailed in the Cutting due to a track defect, which threw the engine, N°102, and it's tender off the rails and severed the telegraph wires. The first carriage, which was fortuitously empty, came to rest on top of the tender, thankfully no fatalities or injuries were reported. The passengers, loaded with their impedimentary luggage, were required to struggle back to the Station, and subsequent company reports recorded 100 men were brought in to unload the mail sacks and clear the line.

An eight-hour delay resulted, with no fewer than 10 passenger trains held south of Roade. In freezing temperatures, the host of passengers on both sides of the blockage gave vent to angry remonstrations that arrangements could not be made allowing them to proceed with their journeys, being kept shivering in the cold and half-starved by their protracted detention.

Depiction of a similar Cutting accident at Winchburgh Scotland 1862
(fineartamerica.com)

In her (unpublished) account of *The History of Wesleyan Methodism in Roade*, covering the period from around 1834 to 1924, Mrs Sarah Caswell recorded the following incident, c1850, which involved one of the Chapel's worshipers. –

> *John Inwood was a Platelayer on the railway. When at work one day he suddenly looked up and saw two trains coming, he could not get out of the way of either, so, commending his soul to his God he lay down between the rails and let the express train go over him. His fellow worker came to pick him up, as he thought him to be dead, but no, nothing more than shock. A draught of water from the spring, and, he said, "Let us kneel down and thank God", which they did'. (Edited).*

CUTTING REMARKS

During this period the Station porter is recorded as Henry Wilding, who would have witnessed the building of improved Station facilities. From artists' prints it appears the new buildings were built with an overhanging roof and would have included waiting rooms, toilets and possibly a porters/parcels room. By this time, Roade's status had been reduced to third class, with only seven stopping trains per day and the once popular refreshment rooms removed.

Correspondence from the General Manager's Office at Euston on February 9th 1850 includes mention of an engineer's report on the state of the track-bed within the Cutting. It suggests that due to severe frosts the condition of the ballasting had deteriorated to such an extent that six men per mile were required to maintain the integrity of the running lines. The introduction of wooden sleepers, in addition to the existing track supporting blocks, was suggested as a possible solution.

Also, the continued instability of the Cutting walls and frequent incidences of slippage are evident from the following correspondence from May of that year, giving details of the actions being taken to safeguard the travelling public.

SIR, *May* 20, 1850.

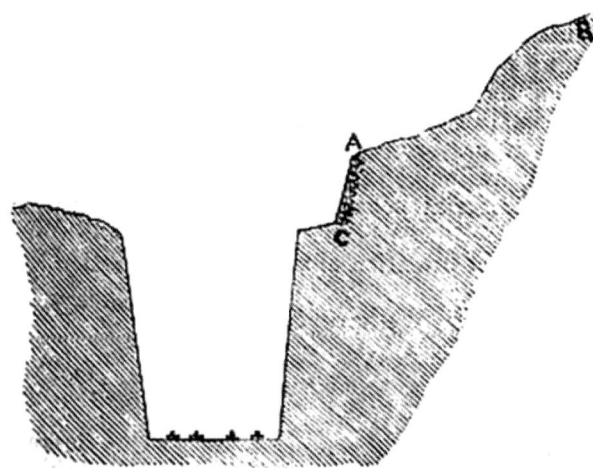

THE Commissioners of Railways having by their Minute of the 17th instant referred to me a letter dated 16th May, from the London and North Western Railway Company, requesting authority to take temporary possession of a piece of land belonging to Mr. John Markham, in the parish of Roade, in the county of Northampton, containing 2A. 3R. 10P., the same being "rendered necessary in consequence of a slip having occurred in the Blisworth cutting," I have the honour to report, for their information, that I this day proceeded to the spot, and found that in a deep cutting of the annexed section, the upper part A B is sliding forward, and has thrown down about 70 yards of the retaining wall A C. To arrest the farther progress of the slip, the Company propose running a number of dry stone counterforts into the part that is slipping, and if necessary, to remove some of the stuff. The ground on which the Company propose entering is already covered to a depth of some 20 feet with the spoil originally taken from the cutting.

I am of opinion that it is essential for the public safety, and for the proper maintenance of the Railway in a state of efficiency for the public service, that the Company should be empowered to enter upon the land described in the letter referred to me, for the purpose of repairing the said slip and preventing its further progress, and to do such works as may be necessary for the purpose.

I have, &c.,

Capt. Simmons, R.E.,   GEO. WYNNE,
   &c.   *&c.*   *Capt. Royal Engineers.*

(Parliamentary Papers, House of Commons and Command, Volume 30)

London & North Western Railway – All Change

A serious case of 'Abaction', (the stealing of cattle on a large scale), was reported in the *Northampton Mercury* on Saturday 14th June 1851. The offence involved the removal of seven bullocks from a field near Wootton on the outskirts of Northampton. A man named Shipp was suspected of the theft of the beasts which he had subsequently sold at Leighton Buzzard market, further intelligence suggested that the offender was known to be making his way to London.

Inspector Thomas of the Northamptonshire County police was dispatched to search for the felon whom he successfully apprehended in the early hours of Thursday 12th at Boxmoor. Handcuffing himself to Shipp, described as a big and powerful man, the Inspector boarded a compartment of the nine o'clock Down train to return to the county. Passing Cheddington the prisoner, who until this point had been quiet and reserved, leapt out of his seat and made for the carriage door, dragging Inspector Thomas by the handcuffs in his wake. With the train travelling at full speed he managed to open the door and push the policeman out. They both fell from the speeding train, Shipp landing uppermost on top of Thomas. Remarkably Shipp was uninjured; Thomas however was incapacitated, suffering a badly broken leg. Under threat from Shipp the officer was forced to hand over the key to the handcuffs from which Shipp disengaged himself and made off.

The injured and exhausted Inspector Thomas was discovered by employees of the railway company who hastily made arrangement for him to be conveyed by train for medical attention. At the Elephant and Castle public house, near Wolverton, he was attended by two doctors who deemed it necessary that amputation of the injured limb should be performed. Inspector Thomas, the newspaper recorded, refused to give his permission for the procedure to be undertaken, and he remained in a precarious state.

It was further reported that the escaped felon, Shipp, was well known to the constabulary of the North Western railway, who considered that he would be unable to elude justice for any lengthy period.

In its edition of the 21st the newspaper reported on the condition of Inspector Thomas. He was said to be 'going on as well as the severe nature of his injury would allow; but not yet out of Danger'. The Inspector had served the force since its establishment, and been recently promoted.

No further progress was subsequently reported on the search for the escaped felon, who seemed to have disappeared without trace. Of the unfortunate Inspector Thomas it is known that he did lose his leg, but remained in the service of the police force.

Eighty years later in September 1931 an article appeared in *The Northamptonshire County Magazine* on the subject of the offence of 'Abaction'. The article attracted the attention of one of its readers who responded under the pen-name of 'A Roade Boy'.

The correspondent identified the Christian name of the felon as Job. At the time of the crime Job Shipp's father Thomas, was employed as a platelayer on the railway.

CUTTING REMARKS

He also kept a small public house near Roade Station, The Swan. Shipp it was claimed, once released from the handcuffs and freed from his apprehension, quickly made his way home to Roade, where he was secreted somewhere in the village until arrangements were made for his escape.

The manner of this escape was in itself quite remarkable. A big oak cask was procured and into this with plenty of straw and some food and drink, Shipp was securely fastened. At night when the Down goods train stopped at Roade the cask was put in a wagon for Liverpool. At the docks it was transferred to a steamship and in a day or so the vessel, the cask and Shipp were on the way – to America!

The correspondent informed the magazine that sometime after setting sail, Shipp 'discovered himself', and upon being released from his confinement he made up such a tale, possibly helped out by money, that he was not prosecuted nor suspected of any crime on arrival in New York.

Thomas Wickens, a resident of Ashton and married with one child, was tragically killed south of Roade Station whilst engaged upon relaying the tracks, reported the *Stamford Mercury* in its edition of 25th June 1851. Two trains, one containing mail and the other luggage, passed simultaneously, and it was thought that he stepped out the way of one, directly into the path of the second. The paper stated that he was 'torn to pieces', and could only be positively identified by his clothing.

The same year a local merchant, Mr S.Wickins, operated from the 'coal wharf' in the goods yard serving the local villages, while William Edward Butlin advertised in the *Northampton Mercury* throughout the period that he could despatch quality coal to any location on the L&NWR from 'Roade Coal Wharf'. George Hallam from Northampton, who also advertised in the *Northampton Mercury,* offered delivery of coal to the town from the same wharf.

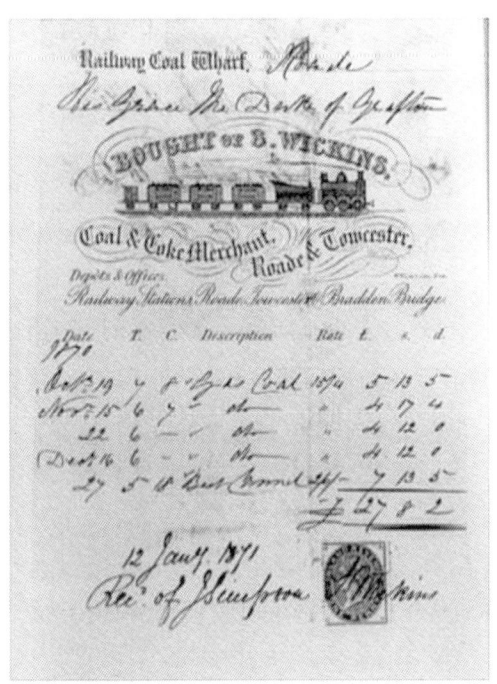

Duke of Grafton's Wickins Coal Invoice
(Charles FitzRoy *Collection)*

London & North Western Railway – All Change

In November 1852 the *Northampton Mercury* reported on numerous incidences around the county of damage caused by recent persistent heavy rain. Roade Cutting was one location mentioned –

> *Due to the heavy rain the piers of Courteenhall Bridge gave way in part, and the thin threads of water which usually trickle down the gullies in the Cutting were swollen into absolute cascades, but the way remained unimpeded and traffic has gone on as usual.*

In addition, the *Illustrated London News* reported in its edition of the 27th that on the 13th the 9pm mail train from the Euston Square terminus was stopped in the Cutting by a subsidence, caused by water cascading with destructive force over its lofty banks. It stated that the guard was sent back to stop the following luggage train, and the clearing of the fallen earth caused an hour's delay to services.

Embankment slip in Roade Cutting
(Illustrated London News)

The February 1853 *Northampton Mercury* reported that Lionel Gomez Da Costa had been released on bail, charged with assaulting Mary Ann Story in a railway carriage at Roade. At the following Lent Assizes he was released without trial, the case against him being discharged by proclamation, due to the absence of witnesses and the lack of evidence against him.

In the summer of that year a boiler tube burst on a locomotive, N°269, as it passed through the village on the 3rd of June. As the train slowed the fireman of the engine, Wallace, jumped clear, and was run over and killed by a passing express. The driver of the stricken locomotive, Micklethwaite, whose actions were deemed to be the cause of the tube failure, was subsequently dismissed. A further incident occurred on the 9th August involving a special train which ran between Wolverton and Northampton on Saturdays. This service was to give the railway employees of the former place an opportunity to avail themselves of Northampton market. Approaching Roade it ran into the rear of a luggage train and derailed, several of the passengers were injured and the line blocked for several hours, fortunately no lives were lost. This latter incident was investigated by Mr David Stevenson, a senior manager of the company, and is mentioned in his memoirs, *Fifty Years on the L&NWR,* published in 1891.

In February 1854 Joseph Wilcox, a bee-hive maker from Roade, was found guilty of trespassing in search of rabbits on land owned by the L&NWR. He was fined £1 and 13 shillings, the alternative being 21 days imprisonment.

A railway signalman was to make a gruesome discovery in the course of his duties on the 1st September 1855. Between the rails of the Up line within the Cutting beneath Dirty Lane Bridge, he found the mortal remains of Job Lyman, 27, who was employed as head groom to Mr Baxter, a local horse dealer. At the inquest into his death, held at The George, the jurors learned that he had been suffering a low bilious fever for a number of days, was suffering a depression of spirits and feared that he might lose his position. It was found that he had thrown himself off the bridge and died as a result of the fall, other injuries inflicted on his body being caused by a train hitting the corpse. Death through temporary insanity was recorded.

On 29th October 1856, a major incident occurred south of Roade which resulted in the total closure of the line for 36 hours, the longest ever closure recorded on the southern division of the railway. The train consisted of coal wagons and two 'dead' engines, N° 55 and N° 22 'BILSTON', destined for Wolverton Works for repair. At the inquest, the driver, Jonathan Oscar, reported that the fog was so dense he could not see above the length of his engine, N° 277, and upon realising that his train had 'broken away' he stopped and drove slowly backwards to look for it. The broken away portion consisting of the two dead engines and 27 wagons was at this point rolling down a 1 in 300 gradient towards him. The subsequent collision, described as 'an inextricable mass' saw all three engines and the coal wagons derailed.

The driver's unfortunate fireman, Benjamin Pike, was killed. The inquest, held at The Globe at Hanslope, found that the driver's failure to signal for the guard to brake led to the collision. One consequence of the collision was that all the telegraph wires were severed, with just one exception, this being the communicating link between Northampton-Blisworth-Wolverton. Blisworth telegraph office, under Thomas Whitney, became central to the recovery efforts and such was the efficiency with which that office dealt with the situation, the Chairman of the L&NWR, the Marquis of Chandos, travelled from London to give his personal thanks to Mr Whitney

CHAPTER 5

R ͟EYNARD ͟, R ͟OUGH ͟-S ͟HUNTS ͟ & M ͟YSTERY ͟

By the 1860s, the railways had become an integral part of daily life, communities having settled back in the most part to the routines and regular pursuits embedded in the fabric of the countryside over generations.

Fox hunting 'the Sport of Kings' was one such activity. In a talk given to the Blisworth Heritage Society, Sir Hereward Wake, 14th Baronet, commented that the building and excavation of the Cutting had resulted in 'a disruption to fox hunting'.

The previously unhindered free rein of the huntsmen had been restricted by the railway passing through their long established 'runs'. Not that this was to deter the more determined pursuer. In his *Railway Reminiscences*, published in 1904, George P Neale records that the aqueduct passing over Roade Cutting was no barrier to the huntsmen, and that he was 'positively advised by Mr Henry P. Bruyeres, superintendent of the line, of an instance of a fox, pursued by a liveried huntsman on horseback, who had succeeded in safely crossing the line along the unprotected watercourse at that giddy height'. This was to be one of many instances in which the activities of Railwaymen, Huntsmen, and 'Reynard' the fox were to be in conflict.

Melville's *Directory of Northants 1861* records two coal merchants operating from the coal wharf in the Station yard.

In its edition of Saturday 8th February 1862, the *Northampton Mercury* featured a report on a meeting of the Architectural Society of Northampton. At this meeting, the Vicar of Roade, the Revd Maze W. Gregory, presented a collection of several fragments of human bone, fragments of lignite, bituminous shale, ammonites and other fossils and shells discovered during the Cutting's excavation. He also submitted a hand drawn map, and a paper on the History of Roade, in which he described Roade as it was at that time. He tells of a village of 178 houses, principally for the labouring class, in which 669 people resided, the most northerly building in the village being St Mary's Church.

Of the railway, he mentions only seven trains stopping per day, lamenting that Blisworth's prominence has led to the demise of Roade as a railway waypoint. He notes that the old refreshment room walls had been removed one or two years previously and the Station had sunk to its lowest ebb, superior only to those wayside halts where the Stationmaster, signalman, points-man and porter are all one. However, he states that –

> *Still, the effects of the railway are visible - men made their fortunes, the houses built for the accommodation of the railway people are there, and, worse than all, the public-houses and beer-shops thought necessary are, with one exception, still in existence, and we have now six to 669 people.*

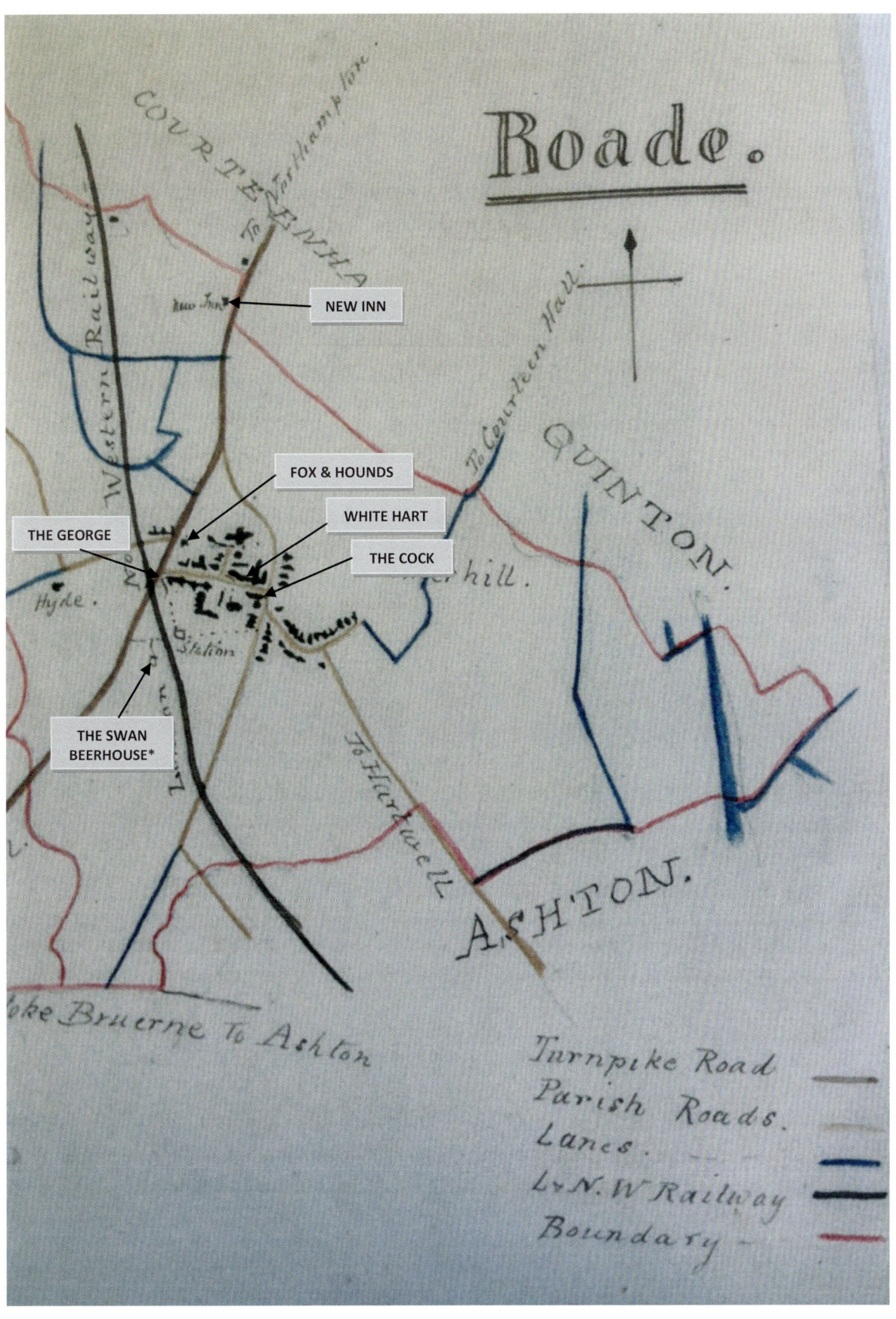

Details of Revd Maze W Gregory's sketch map of Roade 1862.
Annotated with information from the 1861 census. The *Swan Beerhouse is
thought to have been on or near the site of the Swan Inn which closed in 1959.
(RLHS Image)

REYNARD, ROUGH-SHUNTS & MYSTERY

The same year, William Marriott and Joseph Wilcox, two locals, were to be charged for being drunk in breach of the Railways Act (the latter being the same individual who was fined for trespass eight years earlier). They had arrived at the Station drunk and causing annoyance, smoking in a carriage and using abusive language to Mr G. Mobbs who took out a summons against them. Following what were considered ample apologies being made by the miscreants, Mobbs asked the Magistrate to withdraw the charge and the case against the two inebriates was withdrawn.

In February 1864 the *Northampton Mercury* reported that George Frost, a cellerman to Messrs. Higgins, had been pitched from his cart over a Cutting bridge parapet when his horse shied at a passing train, He was taken to the infirmary suffering from a severely fractured skull.

The following month the residents of Roade assembled at the Station wearing badges of mourning. The mortal remains of the 'kind hearted squire', Sir Charles Wake, 10th Baronet, who had passed away whilst in Brighton on 25th February, were returned by rail for his funeral. The coffin was taken to Courteenhall with his family and a large throng of locals marching in respectful solemnity behind.

The *Newcastle Daily Chronicle* in November headlined an article – THE SUPPOSED MURDER IN A RAILWAY CARRIAGE – THE MISSING MAN FOUND. It reported upon a bizarre incident involving a sailor named Apter from Liverpool, who it appeared had been the subject of ill-treatment in a railway carriage and disappeared. He had been travelling with four others, taking with them several bottles of gin and rum from which they drank so freely that on arrival at Wolverton they were all insensibly intoxicated. When the train approached Roade at express speed Apter went missing in unexplained circumstances. Foul play was suspected and a man called Murphy, who had no explanation for his companion's disappearance, was, upon arrival at the Merseyside Station, placed under suspicion. Whilst Murphy was being interviewed, a telegram was received from Detective Eccles at Rugby:-

> *The men you have must be liberated, they have, no doubt, all been drunk. I send him to you on the first train.*

When Apter arrived in Liverpool he went directly to the Detective Office, apparently no worse for his misfortune, though thoroughly ashamed of himself for being the cause of needless alarm. He was unable to give any clear account of what had taken place, but he had an indistinct recollection of falling from the train. He was rendered unconscious for some time and awoke in a ditch at the bottom of a high embankment. Disorientated he first took shelter in a signalman's hut before he found his way to the Station and presented himself to the Stationmaster. The report concluded that the trouble and anxiety occasioned to the railway authorities by the drunken vagabond could scarcely be overstated, various officials of the company having been laboriously engaged until some hours after midnight in a fruitless search for what had been reported to be the body of a murdered man.

CUTTING REMARKS

In mid-December of that year, two platelayers were killed whilst working to maintain the Up line between Blisworth and Roade. William Cotton and Joseph Smith were struck by an express travelling at 30/40 mph on the Down line. They had stepped away from the Up line due to the approach of a coal train, but were unaware of the approach of the express on the Down tracks. Although Cotton was killed instantly, Smith who, from the engine driver's evidence had seen the approaching train at the last few seconds before being struck, had tried to jump clear, but was caught by one of the engine's buffers. He survived the blow, but died of his injuries shortly after arrival at the infirmary. A verdict of accidental death was subsequently recorded on both individuals.

Maintenance of the roadways in the Roade area was under the charge of the Hardingstone Highway Board whose representative, Mr Love, inspected the railway over-bridges above the Cutting during October 1865. In his report, he stated that the bridge parapet on the 'Dirty Lane' bridge was only three feet four inches in height, and he expressed his serious concerns that an unwary pedestrian could fall from it. He made the same observations at Victoria Bridge, (also known as Coronation Bridge), in Ashton Parish; his recommendations were passed to the L&NWR and the parapets were raised accordingly.

At Roade during early December, John Wright Timbs, 40, of Ashton, a railway platelayer, was killed whilst returning home from his labours. He was reportedly struck by a train and decapitated whilst working on the line in the locality.

It was reported in the *Northampton Mercury* of 11th August 1866, that the Petty Sessions Court had received an application to summons Blamire Shaw, the Stationmaster at Roade. The summons was for allowing trucks, which had previously been laden with sheep, to leave the cattle dock without being disinfected.

At the subsequent trial, the company was represented by a Mr Adcock on Mr Shaw's behalf. Police Superintendent Chambers represented local Police Constable, William Abbott, Inspector of Nuisances, who had sought the conviction for contravention of the Board of Trade's regulations against the spread of cattle plague. PC Abbott stated to the court that, on Friday 20th July, he had visited the Station, and during his inspection in the sidings he observed two trucks which had not been properly cleaned. The following day, he again went to the Station and noted that the wagons had been moved, one of which was being loaded with sheep. In observing the loading, which was being overseen by Mr Shaw, he noted that the truck was still in a dirty condition. PC Abbott drew Mr Shaw's attention to the unfit state of the wagons, to which Shaw replied: "Oh yes they are", further stating that the wagon being loaded had been disinfected. PC Abbott responded by stating: "no it has not been, Sir".

In response, Shaw ordered the porter, Thomas White, to sweep out the wagon, which thereafter was despatched to London. The second wagon was duly brought to the loading dock and swept out by the porter prior to being loaded. Cross-examined by Mr Adcock for the company, PC Abbott stated that he was convinced that neither of the wagons had been properly cleaned prior to being loaded. Mr Adcock reminded the court that this case was one of those in which 'the informer' got half of the fine, and consequently the police were enthusiastic to ensure compliance. He further stated that in this case the police had been 'too sharp'.

Mr Adcock then proceeded to call witnesses in the company's defence. The first witness was porter White, who had held that position for 12 years. He stated that both trucks had arrived at the Station with the interiors newly whitewashed and fresh sawdust scattered upon the floor. Cross-examined by Superintendent Chambers, he confirmed his previous statement and added that there was no need to repeat the cleaning as the wagons had arrived in perfect order. White confirmed that he had swept out both trucks, as instructed by Stationmaster Shaw, and applied further disinfectant against the wishes of the owner of the beasts, Thomas Capon, who feared the lime dust particles would get in the eyes of his sheep. Thomas Capon, a butcher from Blakesley was then called to give evidence.

Capon stated that he was at the Station to observe the loading of his animals into the wagons, which were perfectly sweet and clean, and fit for anything to go in. So clean in fact, that he could have sat down to eat his dinner off them. He also confirmed that it was against his wishes that porter White further applied disinfectant for fear of killing his sheep or rendering them unfit for sale. He concluded his evidence by stating that he had been bringing his animals to the Station for the past 15 years and had never had any reason to complain.

The magistrates retired to consider their verdict. After deliberations, they concluded there was not sufficient evidence to justify conviction against the company, but the police had undertaken their duty very properly.

However, from the evidence presented, they did not think that the trucks were in such an overly dirty state to secure a conviction against the Board of Trade regulations. They concluded that any allusion to the police doing their duty for the sake of monetary reward would be much better left unsaid!

Between Blisworth and Roade in late January 1867, another incident with fatal consequences occurred on a goods train. The train had two locomotives hauling it due to the severe cold weather conditions. James Ford was driving the leading engine, accompanied by his fireman Elias Davies, the latter being a resident of the Far Cotton area of Northampton. Joseph Hadfield was at the controls of the second locomotive. Approaching Roade Cutting at 10/15mph, driver Ford turned to speak with his fireman only to find himself alone on the footplate. Quickly looking back, he noted the second engine lurch. Immediately, Ford slowed the train to a halt and investigated, only to find fireman Davies mangled beneath the wagons. The inquest recorded accidental death as the cause, determining that the unfortunate man had inadvertently slipped to his untimely death.

CUTTING REMARKS

South of Roade on 5th July the same year, a mechanical defect caused an accident to occur as reported in the *Croydon Weekly Standard*: 'A very singular and alarming accident occurred on the London and North-Western Railway near this place late on Friday night the 5th instant, to the limited mail from London to the north.

The train left London at its usual time and when near Castlethorpe the engine and tender became detached from the carriages. The train was running at its usual speed – about 40 miles an hour – when this took place, and neither the driver nor fireman perceived the separation; indeed, they had never anticipated anything of that sort, and no noise of any description accompanied the separation. They continued to look ahead and drive on in the ordinary manner. Neither of the guards who were with the train noticed any indication of what had happened.

Eventually noticing the separation, the driver slackened his speed with the intention of allowing the train to come up. However, he had either miscalculated the speed of the carriages or had backed his engine too much, for immediately afterwards the train came rushing up propelled merely by its own impetus and crashed into the tender. The collision was very violent and the passengers, who happened not to be as numerous as usual by this train, were thrown about in all directions. A guard's van was in front of the train, and it was much smashed and portions of it were driven through the end of the post office van, which was directly behind it. The post office clerks were thrown down, the boxes were overturned, the letters were scattered about and the lamps were broken.

After this abrupt stoppage of the train, the first inquiries made were naturally whether any personal injuries had been sustained. It was found that all the passengers had sustained a severe shock and that one of them, a gentleman who was travelling to Glasgow, had his leg broken. One of the guards was so severely injured that he had to be left at Rugby, with two post office officials who also had to remain there.

Fatal accident at Rednal near Birmingham 1865
(Illustrated London News)

Recovery of injured passengers
(Unknown)

A second guard was also hurt, but he travelled forward with the train. In addition to the post office officials mentioned, two others were present; one of them, Mr James Dewhurst, of Preston, who was severely shaken and had his head hurt, went forward home.

A clerk named Flannery, who was among the injured, had only resumed duty a few weeks ago, having previously been hurt by another railway accident. Neither the driver nor fireman was hurt. The tender was considerably broken and some of the carriages were also damaged. Nearly two hours elapsed before the train could proceed. The gentleman who had his leg broken went on to Glasgow'.

As Roade Stationmaster Blamire Shaw was about his duties on the morning of 2nd April 1868, he was suddenly struck above the right eye by a stone hurled from the outside platform of a travelling horse box attached to a passing goods train travelling at 25mph. The train was subsequently stopped and the culprit arrested for the assault. At the trial, Robert Sexton, 17, a groom in the employ of racehorse trainer Mr Saxon, pleaded guilty and apologised to Mr Shaw. The court determined that such was the dangerous character of the offence, which could have caused more serious injurious results, the maximum fine should be imposed; five pounds plus costs. The sum was duly paid.

On the 8th of the same month, a gang of platelayers was working beneath a bridge north of the Station and upon finding that they were in need of further equipment, John Dodd, 54, returned to the Station stores to collect what was needed. He returned via the Down line and was cut to pieces by the 8.47am mail train from

CUTTING REMARKS

London. The train was travelling at 25mph and the driver told the inquest that he had sounded his whistle several times. Accidental death was recorded.

The New Inn public house, navvies' den-cum-travellers rest, finally closed its doors in 1870, its closure probably due to declining trade, its convenience for travellers as a waypoint on-route to the county town having greatly diminished.

Within the village, Blamire Shaw, the former booking clerk/ticket collector, who had subsequently been elevated to Stationmaster 22 years earlier, had become a pillar of the local community. On 8th January 1872, he was killed in somewhat strange circumstances whilst on duty. The inquest was held at The George public house the following day under the direction of the Coroner, William Terry Esq, and witnesses to the circumstances of his demise were assembled to give evidence. A report of the proceedings was published in the *Northampton Mercury* on the following Saturday, 13th.

Shaw, 57, was struck by a northbound express mail train which had departed London at 9.00am, passing through the Station at 10.30am at a speed, from the driver's testimony, of 45mph. Shaw's death was instantaneous, his body being scattered and mutilated. William Smith, a platelayer who did not see the accident, informed the inquest that he was summoned to collect the dismembered and unrecognisable mortal remains. His statement was later verified by Surgeon W.P.Knott of Blisworth, who was acquainted with the deceased by virtue of being his medical attendant on previous occasions. He had viewed the remains which had been kept in the stables at The George overnight.

John Knot, the porter, told the inquest that Shaw had passed him on the Up platform at 10.15am whilst he was awaiting the arrival of a goods train, and instructed him to provide a ticket to a customer, a Mr Hasker, who was descending the steps to the platform.

As he proceeded to undertake this request, he heard the approach of the express and turned to see Mr Shaw crossing from the Up to the Down platform by means of the footway at the platform end. He called out in vain a warning to Shaw, whom he witnessed being struck by the locomotive.

Another eyewitness, John Butlin, told the inquiry that he and Shaw had spoken barely two minutes before the incident, exchanging greetings, with Shaw asking about his health. He next saw the deceased walking on the Down line with his back to the approaching train, then turning to face the engine; he was caught by his heel and dragged under the speeding train. Butlin further stated that Shaw did appear to be trying to get out of the way before the impact. Asked if he had heard the driver sound a warning whistle he stated that he had not.

The driver, Robert Steel, and his fireman, John Hawkins, were both in attendance at the inquest. In his evidence, Steel stated that his train passed Roade at 10.31am. He was on the right-hand side of his engine's cab (No 1006 'PROSERPINE') and he sounded his whistle at the signal before the platform, but not as he passed through as this area was deserted. He then saw the deceased at the north end of the Up platform, 20 yards from the policeman's [signalman's] hut. He saw nothing else until informed by his fireman that they had run a man over. He slowed his engine and informed a gang of platelayers of the incident, proceeding without stopping to Rugby, where he noted bloody remains on the wheels and a hat wedged between the buffers and locomotive body. In his evidence, the fireman stated that the warning whistle was sounded on the approach to the Station, and at about 60 yards from it he saw a man standing at the north end of the Up platform, with his face towards the train. He then moved between the running lines and proceeded to step onto the Down line in the act of running. The witness stated that he could not say what the deceased's intentions were, whether to get out of the way or not. He further stated that he lost sight of the man for an instant and it was at once evident that he had been run over, and he applied the brake immediately.

PC William Abbott of Roade told the inquest that he had searched the clothing of the deceased and found a purse containing £1, 6 shillings and 2 pence, together with a key, two receipts and two third class tickets for journeying between Northampton and Blisworth, dated for the day of his death. Abbott also stated that he had been requested by Mr Shaw to look for a missing watch; Abbott did not however mention when this request had been made. One further item was found during his search, this being correspondence from the Superintendent's Office, Euston Station, dated 1st January 1872, which read –

> *With reference to the investigation made by Mr Entwistle at Roade on the 27th December last, I regret to inform you that I have this day received notice from the general manager that you are to be dismissed from the service of the Company. W.J.Bruyeres.*

During his disposition, the porter John Knot produced the watch belonging to Mr Shaw which he had found in the Station's money safe. Why Mr Shaw was not in possession of this vital and essential piece of Stationmaster's equipment at the time of the incident can only be speculated upon.

In addition, Knot produced a further memorandum found on the Stationmaster's desk

> *To Mr Shaw, Roade, 6th January 1872. T.Clarke from Bicester has been appointed to succeed you, and will arrive on Monday morning when an audit inspector will be in attendance to transfer accounts. W.J. Bruyeres*

Under the direction of the Coroner, the jury were required to come to a verdict as to the cause of Shaw's demise. The jury consisted of Thomas Williams (Foreman), George Goodridge, William E. Butlin (father of one of the witnesses), Benjamin Foddy, Charles Howes, William Jones, William Hands, Thomas Watts, George Smith, Thomas Smith, George Checkley and John Lucas. The newspaper reported that from the memoranda produced before the jury, it was evident that some of those assembled considered that Shaw had premeditated his own destruction.

CUTTING REMARKS

However, the report contended that the evidence adduced by the Coroner during his questioning did not support the suggestion of suicide, and that any doubt that existed would be subsequently dispelled by the verdict of the jury. Accidental death was the verdict duly recorded.

Details of the investigations which resulted in Shaw's swift dismissal, following many years of service to the company, including 22 years at Roade, have not survived. However, other events in the latter part of his life may have had some influence on his state of mind. Blamire Shaw and his wife Mary had three sons, the eldest also being employed as a servant of the L&NWR. Three years prior to his passing, his second son James Oswald had died at home at the Stationmaster's house following a long illness. The following year the *Northampton Mercury* had recorded on 27th February 1869 the death of his youngest son Arthur, who had died on 14th January. Arthur was serving in the 60th Regiment of Foot of Her Majesty's forces in the East Indies and died at Ramamdroog. It can only be imagined what effect these tragic circumstances had on the Shaw family, particularly Blamire, whose faith and soundness of reason must have been sorely challenged.

On19th January 1874, The Grafton Hunt was out, the hounds picking up the scent near Plain Woods close to Roade. After a successful chase which concluded near Potterspury, the hounds again took flight at Easton Neston Gardens leading the huntsmen past Shutlanger and Stoke Bruerne across the fields to Roade where the fox ran into the Cutting. More than half the hounds pursued and only the alertness of a driver, who stopped his train in time, prevented a dreadful carnage; the cunning fox escaped to fight another day.

'Hold Hard There'
(By J.H.Englehart 1850)

REYNARD, ROUGH-SHUNTS & MYSTERY

A special cattle train departed Northampton for London via Blisworth on 28th November 1874. Upon arrival at Roade, it was shunted into a siding to permit a Scottish express to pass. The driver climbed out of his engine to check his train only to discover that half of his wagons were missing. An urgent telegraph was sent to Blisworth, from where an engine was despatched, accompanied by the Stationmaster to find the missing wagons. They were found stationary, deep in the Cutting where, upon investigation, the guard was found to be fast asleep in his van, blissfully unaware of his circumstance. The engine shunted the wagons forward to Roade to re-join their original train where, upon arrival, it was concluded that the guard was drunk and incapable of performing his duty. In the interim, the Scottish express had sped through Blisworth at full speed, hauled by two engines, towards the stranded wagons and only the quick thinking of the signalman prevented a catastrophe. The unfortunate guard of the cattle train was returned to Northampton where he was locked up.

At just after 11.00am on Saturday 12th December, a further incident involving a guard occurred. Driver Thomas Terle, accompanied by fireman Henry Lane, departed Rugby with a coal train; this service was stopping at Stations and sidings down the line, dropping off consignments of wagons. In charge of the shunting of these wagons at the required locations was guard David Burrows.

Wagons were dropped at Crick, Weedon and Heyford as the train progressed down the line. Upon leaving Heyford, the train slowed at Blisworth to pick up water, continuing to Roade where five coal wagons were to be shunted into the coal wharf, where George Hillyard worked from the goods yard as the L&NWR carrier. Upon arrival, the train stopped in order to drop the wagons into the sidings. However, guard Burrows did not appear and driver Terle, upon investigating his absence, found the brake van to be empty.

The Station staff assisted in moving the train into the siding where it remained for two hours, eventually continuing its journey with one of Roade Station's porters acting as the brakeman. George Robinson, a platelayer at Roade was subsequently sent with two others to search the line over which the train had travelled, and discovered Burrows's body on the line-side three-quarters of a mile from Blisworth. The inquest returned a verdict of accidental death, concluding that he had fallen from his brake van in uncertain circumstances.

Kelly's Directory for 1874 records Samuel Tew and John Clarke as coal dealers supplying from the goods yard; they would both continue in business for in excess of 50 years. With the imminent upgrading of the line the goods yard would see activities multiply over the following decades.

The duplication of the lines from Bletchley to Roade commenced in 1875, and the eventual widening of the Cutting for the construction of the Northampton line was eagerly awaited by residents of the County Town.

CUTTING REMARKS

At Towcester, Stationmaster Mr Edmund Stanton would have ensured that his Station was spic and span in early March 1876 for the arrival of Her Imperial Majesty, the Empress of Austria, accompanied by Her Majesty the Queen of Naples.

Her Imperial Majesty, Elizabeth, Empress of Austria *(Wikimedia.org)*

Her Majesty Maria Sophie the Queen of Naples *(Wikimedia.org)*

Whilst staying at Easton Neston, Her Imperial Majesty joined the Grafton Hunt escorted by Huntsman Frank Beers, HM The Queen of Naples and Austrian Princes in attendance. Near Grafton Regis, the hounds picked up the scent and pursued 'Reynard' to Stoke Bruerne and onward to Plain Woods where the beast turned the Hunt and headed for the Cutting. On reaching the railway the exhausted fox ran beside the line with the hounds and huntsman in full-cry behind, passed the Station at Roade and met its fate near Ashton. Frank Beers had the honour of presenting 'the brush' to Her Imperial Majesty and he commented in his diary: 'the Empress rode beautifully, and expressed her great delight to me, and thanked me very much for the good sport'.

CHAPTER 6

Wider and Deeper – Navvies, the Second Coming

By 1877 work on the L&NWR's doubling of the tracks from Bletchley northward had reached Roade. Thomas Clarke, who had succeeded the unfortunate Blamire Shaw as Stationmaster three years earlier, witnessed the beginning of the next major engineering challenge to affect the Cutting and impact on village life, and the initial widening of the Cutting commenced. These major works saw the return of the navvies in their hundreds, impacting once again on the inhabitants of the local villages. Blisworth, as well as Roade, would soon be disturbed by their presence.

On 6th May Thomas Lee, landlord of The Royal Oak at Blisworth was violently assaulted by navvy William Barker after he refused to serve him more beer due to his drunkenness. A village of shanties was once again erected close to the former New Inn at a location which would subsequently become known as Fiddlers Green.

The *Northampton Mercury* reported at length on the progress –

> The exploitation of the new LNWR line to Northampton is being pushed forward with great energy. The course of the line is staked out all the way from Far Cotton to the point where it will branch off, and where workmen there are already levelling and filling up the hollows. Workmen in fact all along the route are vigorously attacking the more difficult portions of the undertaking as, for instance, the rock cutting at Roade, the cutting at Milton and the tunnelling at Hunsbury Hill. Bricklayers and Masons are also erecting bridges where needed, in order to facilitate the conveyance of materials from one point to another.

Spoil removal
(leominster1941.tumblr.com)

CUTTING REMARKS

The Northampton Courts heard two cases during May relating to the illicit sale of intoxicants in the village. In the first, the *Northampton Mercury* reported that Jacob Shipp had been charged with having his beer-house, The Swan, open during prohibited hours for the sale of beer. PC Thomas Swingler stated that on Sunday 7th May, at 4.30pm he had visited the establishment and found a large number of navvies and labourers drinking. Of these men, 30 lived in Roade, the remainder being from Shutlanger. Mr Brown, foreman of the navvies, stated that he gave each man a beer on Sundays, paid for by him on behalf of the contractor for the new railway.

Navvies Shanty
(Unknown)

In his defence, he pointed out that an Act of Parliament allowed the sale of refreshments at railway Stations, and suggested that as the beer supplied by him to Jacob Shipp was delivered to, and supplied by the Station, he was not in contravention of the law, as the Station was the nearest house here-to. The bench fined Shipp one shilling plus costs! The chairman stating that in his opinion the law relating to this issue was a hardship, and granted a case of appeal.

In the same issue, it was reported that Thomas Oxenham had been summoned for selling beer without a licence at Roade from an illegal beer house on 9th May. Evidence was given by William Brigden who claimed that he managed 'the shanty' erected by the railway for Oxenham, who possessed a number of similar premises in various places around the country.

The defendant stated that he held a wholesale licence which permitted him to sell beer in 4½ gallon measures. However, John Willowby of Roade stated that he and another had been served pint measures, for which they had paid, and he had also witnessed others being similarly served. This was also claimed by a man named Tite. The busy PC Swingler stated that he had visited the premises and witnessed men drinking quarts and pints. He asked Brigden if he had sold beer, to which Brigden confirmed he did. He also stated that he was unaware if Oxenham held a licence. Inspector Williamson and Superintendent Norman had also visited and found full, part-full and empty barrels on the premises and had seized three 36-gallon barrels. The court found the defendant guilty and fined him £5, plus costs of two shillings and eight pence, the maximum fine for the offence at that time being £50.

Also during May 1877, Roade Stationmaster, Thomas Clarke, transferred to Sudbury near Harrow. His successor was William Pearson who had held a similar position for the company at Stanbridgeford in Bedfordshire.

The *Northampton Mercury*, in its edition of 8th June, reported on the circumstances of the death of labourer George Dow, 30, who had been killed working on the Cutting widening excavations on the morning of the 1st. Fellow workman William Hood testified that on the day of Dow's demise he had overseen a horse which was hauling a wagon up the side of the excavation.

Once the wagon had crested the rim of the Cutting, it was his task to run with the beast and unshackle the rope prior to the wagon reaching the tipping point. Unfortunately, he slipped and was run over, breaking his right thigh. He died in the infirmary that evening. The foreman of the works stated the wagon would have contained three tons of material and that the deceased would have been quite sober at the time.

On Thursday 12th July, an inquest was held at The Fox and Hounds, Roade, into the deaths of Thomas Smith, 25, and James Cross, 67, who were both killed by a fall of earth within the Cutting on the previous day. Cross had been engaged on the work for three weeks; in the case of Smith it was only the second day of his employment.

The men were engaged upon 'holing', a procedure which involved digging into the embankment to a certain point where the weight of the overhanging mass would cause it to fall. In between the falls, the spoil was removed in a process referred to as 'chambering'.

James Smith, the sub-contractor for the work and a resident of 'The Huts', Courteenhall, was called to give evidence. He stated that the structure of the work-face was mostly clay but contained a thin layer of limestone, the height of the embankment being undermined he estimated at 10-11 feet. He explained that the normal practice was for a group of four men to work as a unit, one of whom would act as look-out for any signs of cracking with the duty to warn the men to move away accordingly. Accidental death was recorded on the unfortunate pair.

CUTTING REMARKS

The Fox & Hounds Public House, now the village surgery.
(RLHS)

A further inquest was held on 26th of July 1877 under the charge of Coroner Terry. Evidence was given by Foreman Albert Batt on behalf of the contractor Mr Nelson. The jury were to hear of the death on the previous day of 46-year old Robert Hospital from Derby, who had arrived at the works a few days previously. At 5.40pm, at the conclusion of his first day of work, he had attempted to climb upon a train of empty wagons being moved in readiness for the following day. He fell between the third and fourth wagon and was run over and killed. Henry Thomas removed his body from the rails and with others took it to the Station to be attended by local surgeon Richard Orpen. He found the deceased had suffered a broken and dislocated left shoulder, the right shoulder torn from the body and the chest crushed, breaking several ribs. Accidental death was recorded.

Construction of the Northampton Loop
(Northants Record Office)

Wider and Deeper – Navvies, the Second Coming

The *Northampton Mercury* reported in August that John James Badby, a railway labourer from Croughton, had been found guilty of the theft of two hens from Mr Butlin of Roade. He had been caught by PC Swingler and was sentenced to two months hard labour. Also that month, Thomas Oxenham made three licence applications for canteens at various places along the new works in the Parishes of Roade and Courteenhall, where 60 men were employed at the latter. Superintendent Norman objected to these on a number of grounds and the magistrates adjourned the cases until the following month, the outcome is unknown.

In October the overseers of Roade applied on behalf of the parishioners for a Special Constable in consequence of the building of the new railway. They had received a large number of complaints and the parish had come to the conclusion that one was quite necessary. They also reported incidences of six cases of larceny since 7th July. The application was granted and George Brownlow was duly appointed.

Following the initial railway construction boom, John Francis, in his *History of the English Railways* wrote, –

> *The dread of such men as they spread throughout the rural community was striking, They injured everything they approached, from their huts to the parts of the railway they were working on, over corn and grass they tore down embankments, injured young plantations, made gaps in hedges with no regard to damage of the property invaded. Game disappeared from the most sacred preserves, game keepers were defied, and the country gentlemen, who had imprisoned country rustics by the dozen for violating the law, shrank in despair at the railway navigator. They defied the law, broke open prisons, released their comrades and slew policemen.*

The lawless navvies
(Police Gazette)

CUTTING REMARKS

Barely a month was to elapse before the overseers of the village returned to the authorities and reiterated the need for additional police supervision in the neighbourhood, again in respect of the impact the navvies were having on the community. The Magistrate himself was in full agreement and determined that one should be sworn in without delay. Superintendent Norman asked the Magistrate to make an order to the railway company to bear the £8 expense of outfitting the constable, and also the 26 shillings weekly wage. With the threat returning, the local authorities, conscious of the civil disruption and disobedience that had accompanied the initial excavations, eventually employed 12 special constables to be in attendance 'around the clock', to keep order. It was also at this point that many of the former railway houses known as 'the sixty', built close to the Cutting's edge, were demolished as they stood directly in the way of the widening works.

In addition to the troubles faced by the local authorities and the men engaged upon the new works, the railway company's train services continued to be beset with operational incidents throughout the Cutting's widening. On 2nd March 1878, a special meat train was stopped upon arrival at Roade Station. The driver was instructed to take his train to the sidings as a late running up-express was due and no further delay should impede its progress. The signal was given and the train crossed the points to the designated siding. However, also in the sidings was an engineers' train, being used by the contractors engaged upon the work in the Cutting. Due to insufficient clearance, the engine of the meat train struck the brake van of the contractor's train and pushed it off the rails. With the meat train unable to use the sidings, it was through a lengthy set of manoeuvres that it was eventually transferred to the Down line, which further delayed the express.

The death of John Barker, 45, a resident of Far Cotton, was reported in the 25th May edition of the *Northampton Mercury*. He was foreman of the navvies engaged upon the installation of a five-ton girder at Ladybridge when the derrick poles collapsed upon him; accidental death was subsequently recorded. Note, Ladybridge is situated south of Hunsbury Hill tunnel, close to the Towcester Road, in the area of a small brook which is crossed by the railway. Local legend suggests that it is haunted, and the ghost of a woman can be seen walking over the bridge on certain nights of the year.

Coroner William Terry presided at an inquest on 22nd June into the death of George Whitlock, who had been engaged upon the excavations filling wagons from an elevated 'bench'. He had fallen from a height of 20 feet, receiving a severe head wound, breaking his neck and dislocating both shoulders; accidental death was recorded.

Poaching continued to be a major inconvenience in the area, and the Wake estate was a popular target for the navvies' nocturnal activities. Following complaints from the gamekeeper, both he and PC Swingler patrolled the area regularly. On 23rd August they found a group of three navvies netting rabbits and when challenged, the navvies attempted to flee. John William Brookes was caught and found to have a rabbit in his pocket and four more close by wrapped in a rag. When brought before

Wider and Deeper – Navvies, the Second Coming

the court, presided over by Sir Herewald Wake, 12th Baronet, he received two months hard labour with the addition of being required to provide two further sureties of £3. Failure to provide the latter, he was told, would result in a further six months imprisonment.

In December, Henry Case was taken to the infirmary at Northampton after being inadvertently struck with an iron crowbar by a fellow workman whilst engaged upon works in the Cutting.

On Thursday 30th January 1879, the *Northampton Mercury* reported upon another tragic event at Roade. A navvy named Smart, who was accompanied by his wife carrying a small child, were walking beside the main line towards Ashton. They were seen by the driver of a Manchester to London train who sounded a warning whistle. Smart stepped into a siding, but his wife stepped directly into the path of the express and was cut to pieces. The child however was thought to have escaped injury and was taken to The George where, upon arrival, it was also found to be life expired.

On 8th February 1879 Benjamin Lovesey, 23, of Syresham was killed when his horse stumbled whist hauling a heavily loaded wagon. In an effort to save himself he was run over and both his thighs severely lacerated.

Later in the month, Joseph Skears, the landlord of The White Hart, was forced to summon PC Swingler to his premises as a band of over a dozen navvies was causing trouble. One drunken individual, John Williams of Rhymney, had been ejected from the building after threatening Mrs Skears, who had refused to serve him as he was 'too much in his cups'. As PC Swingler arrived, Williams re-entered the pub and in attempting to arrest the drunkard, the officer was assaulted, suffering a bloody nose for his trouble. The Welshman's friends then joined in and tried to prevent his apprehension. PC Harnett was summoned and Williams was arrested. The judge sentenced him to two months hard labour, to which the defiant man retorted: "Thank you sir; I am much obliged to you".

The White Hart Public House Roade c.1900
(Northamptonshire Record Office PBP78)

CUTTING REMARKS

During the second week of April, two men engaged upon the works, Robert Gibbs and William Griffin, a driver and stoker, travelled from Long Buckby to Roade to have a drink with fellow navvies at The George. Jacob Shipp the landlord welcomed them in at 3.00pm. Later that evening, they enquired if beds were available and having no luck they left the inn at 9.45pm, both very much the worse for drink. They made their way to a signalman's hut at the Station and asked that they may 'lodge with him' for the night as it was raining heavily. Robert Attfield, the signalman, refused as it was in breach of the rules. Having no luck, the two inebriated fellows decided to sleep in the engine shed, which was presumably in the area of the goods yard. Attfield guided them both safely over the lines aided by his lamp and returned to his duty. At 12.30am, Stationmaster William Pearson was summoned from his bed to investigate an incident south of the Station. Within 100 yards, he found an overcoat, half a skull covered in brains, an arm, a leg and the mortal remains minus the aforementioned limbs between the tracks. The body was identified as that of Robert Gibbs; accidental death was recorded.

On 23rd May, William Jones, a special constable, was called to stop two navvies who were fighting furiously in the area of the works. Upon reaching the scene he broke up the quarrel and the two desisted from their aggravated fracas. Charles Jones, another navvy, originating from Chepstow, then challenged Constable Jones, asking: "What have you to do with it?" following up with a violent strike with his fist to the constable's eye. PC George Arnett was summoned and immediately attempted to apprehend Jones. A violent struggle ensued with Arnett being repeatedly beaten with fists; both were then struggling on the floor, Jones attempting to bite the face of the unfortunate policeman. The two were eventually separated and Jones arrested. At the trial the chairman asked PC Arnett: "What is the general condition of the navvies in Roade?" Arnett replied: "It is very bad, and getting worse as the weather is getting better, and they are getting more money, I have had occasion to speak with the prisoner before". Jones was fined £1 for each offence and costs of £38 and four pence, against six weeks hard labour. The chairman stated that the fine would, he hoped, be a major deterrent in stopping the conduct which the prisoner and his fellows were prone to indulge in around the railway works and nearby villages. He hoped it would serve as a warning. Having no money, Jones was to suffer the six weeks hard labour.

The following month the *Northampton Mercury* reported that Joseph Crossland, a navvy from Oxford, had been arrested for the theft of a shovel belonging to John Watts of Hartwell. Watts had left the implement at his place of work ready for the next day's endeavours. The theft was witnessed by Henry Williams who saw the accused take it to 'the shanty' and try to sell it to Sarah Oxenham, wife of the notorious Thomas. Not wishing to buy the shovel, she allowed Crossland to set it against food and drink to the value of 1 shilling 1d. The following day PC Swingler investigated, tracking the accused to The Wagon & Horses public house in Bridge Street, Northampton to make the arrest. Crossland was found guilty, receiving one month's imprisonment with hard labour for each of his offences.

Wider and Deeper – Navvies, the Second Coming

In July 1879 at the Northampton Quarter Sessions, navvy John Phillips, 24, was convicted of indecently assaulting Susannah Beers, 16, on 21st June. The jury recommended that the court show him mercy on account of the girl's previous conduct towards him. He was found guilty and imprisoned for ten months with hard labour.

Navvy Charles Robinson was found guilty of drunkenness in November, charges were proved by Special Constable George Arnett, and the defendant was fined 2 shillings and 6 pence with a further 12 shillings 2 pence costs.

Later in the month, the body of a soldier, Sergeant John Cambell, 35, of the 48th Regiment, based at Weedon Barracks and Militia Store, was found deep within the Cutting under the Hyde Road Bridge. Recently returned from India, he was reported as missing by his wife the following day. It appears that following his training he had travelled to Roade, possibly on foot, and spoken with various individuals about staging an event for the children of the Barracks in fields close to the village.

On two occasions that day he frequented The George Hotel. During his first visit, he borrowed three shillings from the landlady, Mrs Shipp, against the value of his ring. His second visit concluded with him stating that he was going to walk home, presumably along the railway. His remains were found the following morning. Stationmaster Thomas Clarke and PC Swingler recovered the much mangled corpse and found a walking stick and bayonet close by. The verdict of the inquest was recorded as 'found dead on the railway'.

Image of the navvies
(*New York Public Library on Flickr*)

CUTTING REMARKS

In August navvy Benjamin Challender was working below Dirty Lane Bridge. He was engaged upon filling wagons with rock and spoil from the excavations with fellow navvy George Smith. By 3.30pm, 14 wagons had been loaded and were in the process of being removed. Smith then witnessed Challender attempt to jump up into the seventh wagon, but tragically he missed and fell beneath the train. The wagons were halted and Challender's body was recovered, the wheels of one of the wagons having evidently run over his head. A verdict of accidental death was recorded at the inquest.

On the August Bank Holiday 1879, Thomas Oxenham, the proprietor of several shanties, organised sporting events for the navvies. These were held in a field close to Courteenhall Bridge and lent for the occasion by a Mr Young. The first event was a match for one sovereign between James of Milton and J. Smart of Greens Norton. The distance was 200 yards, and the race was easily won by James. A 150 yards open handicap was then run, the prize being a timepiece valued at £2 and 10 shillings. Ten took part in the race which resulted in favour of Parker, of Northampton, the scratch man. A navvy's race (150 yards) for a gallon of beer and sixpence was won by Scann, who also secured the first prize of £2 and 6 pence in a blindfold wheelbarrow race. Considerable amusement was occasioned by the attempts to climb a greasy pole, at the top of which a 10lb leg of mutton had been placed. About 20 men had a try and a navvy named Williams in his first attempt succeeded in securing the leg of mutton. In the evening there was a display of fireworks, and a band for dancing was provided.

Beer, the Navvies' drink of choice, at work, rest & play
(Unknown)

Wider and Deeper – Navvies, the Second Coming

During October, Stationmaster William Pearson was transferred to Gamblingay; he was succeeded by Mr James Adams. In the autumn of the following year, Adams was, for reasons unknown, transferred to Rugby. He was moved by the company into the position of a wages clerk at the Goods Department, though he resigned before taking up the role. Arthur Williams, previously at Blisworth, was appointed as the new Stationmaster at Roade.

Yet another navvy perished during the closing month of the year. William Fuller, 60, lodged in Roade with John Marshall, whom he had known for over 20 years. He set off from his lodgings at 6.00am on the morning of 5th December and by 6.10am he was engaged on the works with William Warren of Hartwell. A train passed and Warren turned to see Fuller kneeling between the tracks of the Down line. He went to him and helped him to get up; Fuller told him that he had been hit by the engine. Warren took him back to his lodgings noting that he had a smashed hand and a large laceration to his forehead. Fuller was subsequently taken to the infirmary where it was also found that several ribs had been broken and such was the damage to his hand that it required amputation. He was not to recover from the extent of his injuries, and he died a few days later.

Tragedy struck again at Roade on Christmas Eve 1879. At the inquest held at The George, Coroner William Terry was told that as a group of navvies were walking on the Up line a train approached. As the men moved out of its path some stepped onto the Down line. Unfortunately another train was also approaching the gang from the opposite direction. Despite warning shouts, William McDonald, 72, was struck and killed instantly; his feet were found detached from his legs. Accidental death was recorded.

As the year ended, William Glenn, 41, a resident of Ashton, who was engaged upon the widening works, was tragically killed. Whilst walking to his work on the morning of his death, he was being followed by Walter Fern and Joseph Mills, also railway labourers from Ashton, who were some 40 yards behind him. Fern stated that the deceased was walking between the tracks of the Up line when an empty coal train passed on the Down line. At that point an express passed him on the Up line and he lost sight of Glenn; he and Mills found his dead body 80 yards further ahead of the place he had been struck. Jacob Shaw, foreman of the contractors, went to the site and found the deceased cut to pieces, one leg being 20 yards away from the torso, which was almost cut in two; one hand was missing. A verdict of accidental death was recorded.

On the evening of 3rd February 1880, PC Thomas Swingler, accompanied by Special Constable Arnett, was investigating complaints of drunkenness in the Roade neighbourhood. Upon passing a barn frequented by the navvies, Swingler overheard someone ask for a quart of beer. He crept up to the window and witnessed ale being dispensed for which money was paid. He and Arnett retreated to continue to watch and shortly afterwards another navvy entered, ordered his quart and produced a florin which he passed to the dispenser, Thomas Lockett. Lockett returned one shilling and sixpence in change. As the two policemen continued to observe, a night watchman arrived and he also indulged in a libation, though no money was proffered on this occasion. Swingler and Arnett swooped and charged Thomas Lockett (alias William Lockett) with selling beer without a licence. Two barrels, equating to ten gallons of beer, were forfeited. Lockett was fined £50 by the chairman of the court; such was the seriousness of the case. Not having the money, Lockett opted for one month's hard labour.

The sheer physical effort exerted by the average Navvy would require an intake of around 8,000 calories daily, the bulk of this consisted of bread and meat, washed down with five quarts of ale. This sustenance was available at purpose built tuck, (or Tommy), shops provided by the contractors and paid for with goods or with tickets issued by them. The Tommy-shops extracted a surcharge from which the contractor benefitted; these provisions were noted for being overpriced, short-weight, and poor of quality. This diet was supplemented by locally sourced sustenance either gleaned or illicitly poached.

To keep the men refreshed during their labours scores of young boys, termed 'nippers', would roam the works supplying cold tea in a tea bottle or brewed on site in a drum. A drum was any vessel such as an old tin, and making the tea was called drumming-up.

Lunchtime
(alamy.com)

Wider and Deeper – Navvies, the Second Coming

The structure of the railway hierarchy was such that chaplains were employed to look after the moral and spiritual well-being of company employees. The *Grantham Journal* of 19th February 1880 publicised the recent book by the Revd Daniel William Barrett, *Life and Work among the Navvies*, including the following extract –

> *And as the Chapel bell was then going, we gave our usual invitation to them to accompany us to the service, reminding them at the same time that it was Sunday. One of the group, who took upon himself the office of spokesman, in reply, said to us, "Ah! us chaps doesn't know Sunday from workaday, only thinks it sometimes when that there bell goes." Of course that was only an excuse. So I said to him, "You shall know another Sunday in good time what day it is, if you will look out at the hut door towards the Chapel, for I will have a flag put up."*

Early In March navvy William Parish was arrested by the busy constable for being drunk and disorderly. He was subsequently fined ten shillings, with ten shillings and eight pence costs reported the *Northampton Mercury.* The same newspaper reported in its edition of the 10th that navvy Thomas Whittaker had been knocked down and seriously injured whilst at work on the new railway.

During the same month at the Divisional Petty Sessions court, Thomas Beers was summoned for selling ale without a licence. PC Josiah Teet, accompanied by PC Mabbutt, had visited the defendant's 'shanty' on two consecutive occasions the previous December and witnessed the defendant's wife and daughter dispensing drinks for which only the defendant was licensed.

Mrs Beers gave evidence, telling the court that her husband had been ill at the time and had not been expected to live, and she was ignorant of the fact that she too was required to be licensed. The court did not accept her excuses and fined her £5 plus costs. In addition, following the offence, Superintendent Norman visited the 'shanty' with a warrant and removed two 36 and one 18 gallon barrels of beer which were forfeited.

(Unknown)

CUTTING REMARKS

In May 1880, PC Swingler discovered that the hares on the Wake Estate were once again under threat. Patrolling his beat at 6.00 o'clock one evening, in the company of Gamekeeper John Whiting, they challenged William Hood, a navvy who was in possession of a hare concealed in his bag. Hood was charged with being in breach of the Poaching Prevention Act. He initially claimed he had found the animal on his return from his work, which he had finished at 5.30pm. On being challenged further he admitted his misdemeanour and said he was sorry and it was the first he had caught that year. He was found guilty of poaching and trespass and fined ten shillings with 13 shillings and two pence costs.

William Hood was to be in trouble again later in the month when he and fellow navvy Charles Williams were charged with stealing timber belonging to the contractors Messrs. Meakin & Deane. The charge was subsequently dropped after the works foreman stated that he had given the men his permission to remove the wood.

In the same month John Clarke and a boy named Thomas Beers, probably the son of the 'shanty' owner, were apprehended for poaching. Beers was fined seven shillings; Clarke had absconded in the interim. Also during May, navvy Stephen Wilson was summoned for threatening to kill his wife Harriet, to whom he had been married for only a year; he was bound-over to keep the peace for 12 months. His father-in-law, John Evens, was also brought before the court for assaulting his son-in-law in an attempt to protect his daughter. The case was dismissed. In a further case before the courts, navvy Thomas Sprigg was remanded in custody for the theft of a ham, the property of Jacob Shipp, landlord of The Swan.

The Swan Public House
(Left, Fred Blincow. Right Alvin Barby)

Tragedy would also occur during June. Joseph King, a bricklayer, who was working on the retaining wall between the main line and the new lines to Northampton, was killed by a passing train. Among the gang of navvies was his brother Arthur who identified the body at the inquest. Precautions were in place to warn the workmen of approaching trains; these consisted of detonators placed upon the track to give audible warning and to alert the engine drivers to reduce speed and sound their whistles. In addition, the works foreman William Bradbury, who had shouted in vain to the deceased, and watchers, (look-outs), who were positioned to give additional warnings as a further safeguard failed to alert the unfortunate King. John Emery told the inquest that at 3.45pm, two trains passed on the main lines within moments of each other and that other workmen close by had moved away from the lines. He saw the deceased struck by the second train, and could only think that he had not heard either of the warnings.

The driver of the engine, Thomas Jay, told the inquest that he slowed his train after running over the detonator at Courteenhall Bridge and sounded his whistle. He stated that he saw a man stooping down engaged upon his work in a safe position who suddenly stepped forward and was struck by the engine's buffers. He continued to the Station and reported the incident to the Stationmaster. Dr Harper, Surgeon of Roade who attended the incident, stated that the deceased had been struck in the back and his head split in two and death was instantaneous; accidental death was recorded.

Also in June 1880 a more serious incident was reported in the *Northampton Mercury* under the headline: 'Stabbing Case at Roade'. At the resultant court case the circumstances were described by the witnesses. Thomas Chapman stated that on the 7th he was at The Swan beer house in the company of George Mullen, an engineer of Irish descent engaged upon the new works. During the conversation between the two, Mullen stated that he was going to The George to confront another navvy against whom he had a grudge.

Upon arrival at The George Mullen confronted Henry Wood, an engine fireman who lodged with Alice Dunkley, as he left the premises. An altercation ensued which resulted in Wood receiving stab wounds to a leg. Chapman, who had followed Mullen, together with George Leighton, intervened and restrained the assailant. Questioned by Chapman as to the reason for his assault on Wood, Mullen stated that he had been paid to do it and that he was quite prepared to share his purse with him and Leighton. Village surgeon Richard Orpen attended Wood and PC Swingler arrested Mullen. When asked by the court to explain his actions, Mullen stated that it was a case of mistaken identity. He was found guilty of inflicting grievous bodily harm and committed to the Assizes.

During the same month Roade's busy local constable, PC Swingler, charged Thomas King of Stewkley with the theft of a hammer, the property of Robert Massey, a bricklayer engaged on the works. Massey had sent the hammer to the blacksmith's shop for repair earlier in the day, where it was later collected for him by a boy named David Imiree. Imiree stated he had placed it on the ground whilst he went for lunch and found it missing upon his return. His story was verified by William Campion who had seen the hammer with other tools. King was suspected of the theft and his tool bag was searched by PC Swingler. Two hammers were found, one newly repaired and subsequently identified by Massey as his. King was sentenced to 21 days' imprisonment with hard labour. The theft of tools was a common occurrence and in the same month navvy John Ward was found guilty of stealing a shovel belonging to

Joseph Mason. He also received a sentence of 21 days imprisonment with hard labour.

The navvies essential tool
(blackcablondon.net)

In the week prior to Christmas 1880, the *Northampton Mercury* reported that a man named George Abbott had been found in an unconscious state on the Northampton Road near Blisworth. On recovering consciousness he stated that he had been met by a group of navvies who asked him for tobacco. As he was about to give them some he was struck down and robbed and left where he was found; he could remember nothing more.

CHAPTER 7

Bringing Northampton 'Into the Loop'

Heavy snow storms in January 1881 blanketed the whole country delaying the construction process. The *Northampton Mercury* reported that its depth in the Cutting exceeded 10 feet, and consequently the railway was blocked.

The Newport Pagnell newspaper, *Croydon's Weekly Standard,* reported that the first trains to operate on the 'Northampton Loop', as it would become known, commenced on 1st August 1881. These consisted of goods and mineral traffic operating both ways between Roade and Northampton, although the widening work was far from complete.

During that month on the Main Line, considerable delay was caused one mile south of Roade to a northbound Scottish express when the connecting rod on one of the two engines fractured, bringing the line to a standstill. Help was forthcoming from Blisworth which sent another locomotive to the rescue. This engine had been removed from a train awaiting departure from Blisworth to Northampton, delaying travellers to the county town for one and three-quarter hours.

The following month the body of Thomas Gilbert, 22, was found on the Main Line close to Courteenhall Bridge in the early hours of the 23rd. He was formerly an apprentice to Mr Foddy, a tailor of Roade, but had recently set up business for himself at Flore. The inquest found that he had travelled to Roade the previous evening and was possibly returning home when he was struck, footmarks having been discovered on the embankment where he had gained access to the railway. His body, which was taken to Blisworth where he lodged, was found to have sustained severe head injuries. At the inquest, held at the Blisworth Hotel the Coroner Mr W. Terry Esq. returned a verdict to the effect that the deceased had committed suicide whilst in a state of temporary insanity. He was well known in Blisworth, having frequently played for the village cricket team.

On 20th November, following a 12-hour shift, Thomas Nichols, foreman porter at Roade, accompanied by George Brett, decided to travel to Northampton to view progress on the County Town's Station. They boarded a contractor's engine and proceeded through the Cutting, stopping at Ladybridge to collect some wagons. On restarting, Brett stayed on the engine; however Nichols clambered onto a truck towards the rear of the train. Emerging from the darkness of Hunsbury Hill Tunnel, Brett heard a noise from the rear. He looked back and, realising Nichols was nowhere to be seen, he called to the driver, William Bonmass, "My mate's missing".

The train was stopped and a search made. Very soon Nichols was found, alive but severely injured, both his legs being mutilated. He was taken to Northampton Station, which was in the final stages of construction, but was found to be dead upon arrival. His remains were identified by his son William Nichols who also worked at Roade Station. The inquest concluded that the deceased had been climbing from wagon to wagon in an attempt to join Brett on the engine and been flung off as the train jerked or swayed. He had been in the service of the L&NWR for fifteen years, having previously worked at Blisworth. He left a wife and five children.

The scarce amount of accommodation available for the hundreds of navvies in the area was a constant problem. On 9th February 1882 navvies George Bailey and John Bull were arrested by Sergeant Andrews for sleeping in an outhouse, without having any visible means of subsistence. They were remanded in custody to appear before the court at a later date.

Of the original five bridges which spanned the Cutting, those at Hyde Road, Dirty Lane and Thorpe Wood were already wide enough to accommodate the new line. Whether this was due to luck, good fortune or foresight on the part of Stephenson can only be speculated upon. The highway bridges at the Roade Station and Courteenhall Road ends of the excavation both required widening to accommodate the new lines to Northampton.

Eastern embankment at the Courteenhall Road end of the Cutting
(Northampton Central Library)

With the works on the Cutting complete, the new embankment on the eastern side of the excavation was planted with trees and shrubs to help stabilise the ground and mask the scar on the landscape, in much the same manner as in the initial works. Local horticulturists were once again encouraged to participate in this.

Geologists also recorded their observations –

> *When completed, Roade Cutting exposed an almost complete section through the Great Oolite Group of rocks which rests on the Northampton sand formation and Lias Group. The section comprises two parts; the lower is a steep face in the Blisworth limestone formation and are the older units, whilst the upper is a much less steep matter in the Blisworth clay and cornbrash formations. Towards the Northern end the Cutting divides into two where the*

Bringing Northampton 'Into the Loop'

Northampton lines take their separate line within the Cutting. This section is important because geologically it shows the rhythmic depositional rock units that are typical of the Rutland Formation. From a Geologist's point of view it is unfortunate that extensive portions of the Cutting have had to be faced with brick to prevent landslip.

The *London Daily News* reported that these excavations, which took as long to undertake as the original works, were completed at a cost of nearly one million pounds sterling. The Government Inspector, Colonel Rich, inspected the new works on 22nd March 1882, his examination finding them satisfactory for the route to open. The *Northampton Mercury* reported that the first train, a 'private special', arrived at Castle Station on the 28th conveying Baron de Rothschild and party, followed directly by six excursion trains. Unhindered passenger and goods services to the county town commenced on 3rd April.

To coincide with the widening works the original London & Birmingham Railway Station buildings were demolished, with new facilities located 200 yards north of the former site with platforms serving both the 'old line' and the 'new'. Artists' impressions from the period indicate toilet facilities on the island platform and parcels/goods offices. The platforms, all with waiting rooms, were accessed via a footbridge, which was entered from a new booking office built on the embankment of Station Road. In addition a new over bridge, N°206, was build to replace the former Gravel footpath crossing.

A new Stationmaster's residence, still in existence, was built at the top of Station Road adjacent to the new booking office. Its first occupant would be George Buckle who moved from Cheddington; he had succeeded Arthur Williams as Stationmaster when the former transferred to Castlethorpe when it opened for passengers.

The original Stationmaster's house, The White House, was sold for £1 and removed brick by brick to a new location on the edge of the village. (It is the first house in Roade close to the round-about on the A508 approaching from Northampton. It is still 'White', although its appearance has changed somewhat over the years).

The original Stationmaster's house, 'The White House' prior to major renovation, c.1980
(Peter Mawby Collection)

CUTTING REMARKS

South of the new Station a new signal box was constructed on the western side of the line, facing multiple points and crossovers, which allowed trains to transfer from the 'old line' to the 'new' and vice-versa. It also controlled the access to the additional sidings which were installed on the site of the original Station buildings and the enlarged goods yard. Its design was known as a '64 lever L&NWR Tumbler Frame'. James Ling was one of the first signalmen.

Roade Signal Box c.1900
(Alvin Barby Collection)

Signal Box interior
(Robin Patrick)

Bringing Northampton 'Into the Loop'

On the eastern side of the line, at the southern end of the longest siding, was situated an elevated wooden platform. This supported an apparatus for tipping narrow gauge wagons of limestone into larger railway mineral wagons. The rock had been excavated from pits sited adjacent to the Ashton Road in an area known as 'Pixieland'

Limestone Quarry loading platform 1890
(George Freestone Collection)

Two months after the widening works concluded, the *Northampton Mercury* and *Buckingham Express* reported on a mysterious occurrence at Roade. An 'Alsop's Excursion' train from Burton-on-Trent to London entered the Cutting at Courteenhall Bridge at an estimated 40mph, with a passenger, seen by a platelayer named Malsher, hanging out of a carriage window. As he watched he saw the figure fall, hit its head on the footboard, and roll onto the trackside. Malsher rushed to the body and found a man unconscious and suffering from severe head injuries. He raised the alarm and the injured man was taken to Roade Station where he was attended by Dr Richard Orpen and thereafter taken to Northampton General Infirmary. The newspapers identified the injured man to be Mr Henry Lyes of Burton, the report stating that no account could be given as to why he had fallen, suggesting that that he had probably overbalanced whilst standing by an open window. The articles concluded that it was doubtful that the injured man would recover.

A certain number of navvies remained on-site following the opening and in July they were addressed during their lunch break by the Revd. John Gawthrop, a Wesleyan district missionary. He also conducted a flower service at the village Chapel in the evening.

South of Roade a new Station was built at Castlethorpe. Opened initially to goods traffic the previous year, passenger traffic commenced from there on 2nd August 1882, the *Croydon's Weekly Standard* reported that the inauguration was celebrated with a general holiday full of activities. An account of that day was recalled by local resident Mr Farmer Amos –

CUTTING REMARKS

The first passenger train came in about 8.30 a.m. on August 2nd, 1882, and John (Rocker) Rainbow told the men working on the Station that they could go on the train. Dick Denny had been digging a well for the Stationmaster and came out covered in mud. His mate Tom Panter came on the train as well. When the booking office opened Mr J. E. Whiting bought the second ticket (the railway kept the first) and my father the third. I had the first half ticket.

We all got off at Roade and went to The Swan which was kept by Jacob Shipp. We had some beer (I was only eight but I started drinking beer at five) and caught the train back to Castlethorpe about 11 o'clock.

The opening of the Northampton Loop caused the train timetables to be altered. Certain trains which previously stopped at Roade no longer did so, causing confusion for both ordinary passengers and railwaymen alike. Bertram Delves, 18, was a carpenter employed at Wolverton Carriage Works; he lodged in Roade and would catch a train to and from work as part of his daily routine. On arriving at Wolverton Station one evening in November he was to learn there were no services available to him which would stop at Roade, Blisworth being his closest alternative, from where he would have to walk home. Having no alternative, he purchased a ticket for the latter place and in either confusion or frustration boarded the next train to arrive.

He was subsequently to realise that the train upon which he was travelling was not the Blisworth service, but one bound for Northampton. Having travelled the route regularly, he would have known that the train would cross over from the main line to the loop line just before Roade Station, its speed having been reduced to little above walking pace. With this knowledge, he decided to jump out, with fatal consequences.

Edward Jones, the points-man at Roade, saw the train pass at 9.28pm and did not see anything to raise suspicion or anyone alight. When Joseph Stanyon of Hartwell, also a points-man, reported to the signal box at the commencement of his duty, he saw from the window what he believed to be a body beside the line.

Thomas Swingler, the porter, was summoned and discovered the unfortunate Delves severely injured beside the line. He was taken on a stretcher to the Station and from there to the infirmary where he died of his injuries. The inquest heard that the deceased had upon him seven shillings and four pence half-penny, a flute, pipe and tobacco; accidental death was recorded.

As a consequence of more frequent services on the lines through the Cutting and at the Station, the potential risks for the staff employed in the proximity of the permanent way increased.

Despite the known dangers; in June 1883, the *Northampton Mercury* was to report upon yet another fatality which occurred at Roade Station.

Bringing Northampton 'Into the Loop'

The inquest heard the sorry tale of Herbert Bernard Hobley, 18, a telegraph messenger employed at Rugby, who was on relief duties at the Station. On the morning of the incident, the deceased walked the line through the Cutting accompanied by the night foreman Walter Godden. Upon reaching the crossing at Milton, they both climbed aboard a coal train heading south. As the train approached Roade at an estimated 10mph, both tried to jump onto the platform.

The events were witnessed by Alfred Parish, the Station porter who told the inquest that he was on duty at 11.00am and watched the train approaching. Parish witnessed Godden leap safely to the platform; however Hobley caught his foot whilst jumping and fell backwards between the train and the platform. He sustained dreadful injury, one leg was cut off and the other was held on by a mere thread, and one of his arms was crushed. Despite these injuries, he was still alive. Dr Walter Ryan, the local surgeon, was summoned, and Stationmaster Buckle telegraphed for an engine and coach from Wolverton to transport him to Northampton for attention at the infirmary. He was to die of his injuries during the afternoon. The inquest found that both Godden and Hobley had infringed company bye-laws by their actions, recording a verdict of accidental death on the deceased.

Despite the enormity of the enlarged excavations Reynard the fox was again to cause trouble to both the railways, and on 22nd February 1884 the Grafton Hunt, recounted in his diary by Master of the Hunt, Frank Beers –

> *After a successful pursuit from Stoke Bruerne the hounds picked up another scent at Bozenham Mill. The chase took hounds via Alderton, Shutlanger and Tiffield, where by a quirk of fate a second fox jumped up before them. The confused hounds chased after the fresh quarry who ran them ragged via Blisworth, Plain Woods and eventually the sides of Roade Cutting, whereupon three exhausted dogs went 'over the edge'. The trains were stopped at great inconvenience to retrieve the unhurt hounds whilst the pursuit continued as far as Alderton, where the hunt gave up chase.*

Master of the Grafton Hunt Mr Frank Beers
(50 Years of Foxhunting with the Grafton and Other Packs of Hounds)

CUTTING REMARKS

Accidents and incidents continued with alarming regularity. During maintenance work on Victoria Bridge in Ashton Parish during February 1886, a bricklayer named Faulkner slipped and fell from a ladder receiving serious chest and head injuries. He was taken to Roade Station from where he was sent to the Infirmary.

A short paragraph in the *Northampton Mercury* of 12th March records the extremely lucky escape of Roade Stationmaster George Buckle, who was nearly run down by a train due to dense fog on the previous Friday morning.

On a brighter note, in its edition of 9th April the *Northampton Mercury* informed its readers that following a petition from the residents of Ashton and Hartwell the railway company had opened a pathway, gated at both ends, from The Gravel footpath to Roade Station yard. It stated that this was a great boon, as it rendered it unnecessary for travellers to go all through the village as hitherto.

In the early morning of 3rd December 1887, bricklayer Thomas Sansome, who lodged in Roade at the home of Mary Anne Hillyard, was proceeding to his place of work along the Cutting. He was engaged upon the repair of the face on the eastern side of the Cutting near Courteenhall Bridge. His body was found by local railwayman William Parish between the loop lines 280 yards north of the Station at 6.40am; close by lay his basket and parcel of food. Two trains had passed a few minutes earlier, the 6.32am Down newspaper service and a coal train on the Up line at 6.33am. It was suggested by the village surgeon, Dr Richard Orpen that Sansome was struck by an engine buffer. The deceased had suffered a broken spine, multiple jaw fractures, four broken ribs on the right side of his chest and a broken right arm.

The Grafton Hunt was involved in yet another incident on the edges of the widened Cutting on 14th March 1888. Frank Beers recorded the following (edited) pursuit of Reynard by the horse and hounds –

> *The hunt gathered at Blisworth Station, fox found at Tiffield allotments and hounds away heading for Ropers Gorse. Turned over the railway with Gayton village on the right and heading for Eastcote, to the left as if for Tiffield, over the road for Duncote. Lost him at Bushey Edge, found again at Easton Neston Gardens, at a rattling pace the hounds ran through the first covert, Plain Woods and down to Blisworth ironworks. Chase continued towards Blisworth Station then the village, Ropers Gorse to the right and on to Tiffield allotments. From that covert on to the Northampton – Blisworth road, fox in sight, continued across two fields heading for Nun Wood and back towards Blisworth and across the canal at the tunnel mouth and on to Roade Cutting. Stopped the hounds…*

These events were also witnessed by diarist Abel Hurst, a native of Milton Malsor and employed as a railway platelayer at Roade. He takes up the story –

> *One day when the fox hunters were round our place I saw the fox coming along on top of the brickwork through the cutting. I went to meet him and when he saw me he turned his head and slipped down the brickwork and*

Bringing Northampton 'Into the Loop'

landed on top of the girders, and then he jumped from there into the six foot way (the space between pairs of running rails) and then he trotted off down the line and out of the cutting and up the bank. In this way he beat the fox hunters.

From his diary Frank Beers continued –

…The fox was dead-beat, I saw him walk up the cutting and lie down in the six-foot way and a train came past him of which he took no notice. Two platelayers came and buffeted him with their caps before he would get up, he then trotted before them out of the cutting and up the embankment. When he was half way up he was so tired that he lay down again. I was obliged to have him seen off by the second whipper-in, once off the railway the hounds were able to knock him off his feet as he was so tired he could barely walk.

It would seem that Abel did not witness Reynard's lucky escape after all.

In May 1889, at the end of a decade of increased activity and changes, Stationmaster and goods agent George Buckle transferred to Tring, following seven years of service at Roade. His position was taken over by Thomas Coxon, who had previously been employed at Bletchley.

CHAPTER 8

Roade's Other Cutting & The Cross-country Route

It was at this time in the village's history that Roade's 'other railway' comes into the picture. A line from Towcester across country to Bedford, via a junction with the Midland Railway at Ravenstone Wood, had long been considered. Originally proposed in 1878, as the Towcester, Roade & Olney Junction Railway (TR&OJR), the title was changed to include the quarrying activities of Lord Hesketh, becoming the Easton Neston Mineral, Towcester Roade & Olney Junction Railway, (ENMTR&OJR). The proposals suffered many fits and starts through a lack of investment. Also the name changed once more to Stratford-upon-Avon, Towcester & Midland Junction Railway (ST&MJR), before the 'turning of the first sod' by Sir Thomas Hesketh on 15th December 1887.

Eastwards from Towcester the single line ran to Stoke Bruerne Station which had a signal cabin controlling access to a short goods siding.

Stoke Bruerne Station c.1965, now a private house
(Alvin Barby Collection)

From Stoke Bruerne the line crossed over the Stony Stratford to Northampton highway, A508. In his memoirs, Job Sturgess recalled that the bridge contractor had 'some real good horses' which were used in the building of the embankment in an operation described as Run and Tip. (See bridge location on page 17).

CUTTING REMARKS

A508 Overbridge N°162 c.1955 south of Roade village, since dismantled
(RLHS Images)

Between this bridge and the L&NWR Main Line, a rail connection named Roade Junction ran into a newly constructed bay platform, N°5, at that company's Station. In 1909 rail access was provided from the Junction to Sturgess & Company's limestone quarry workings.

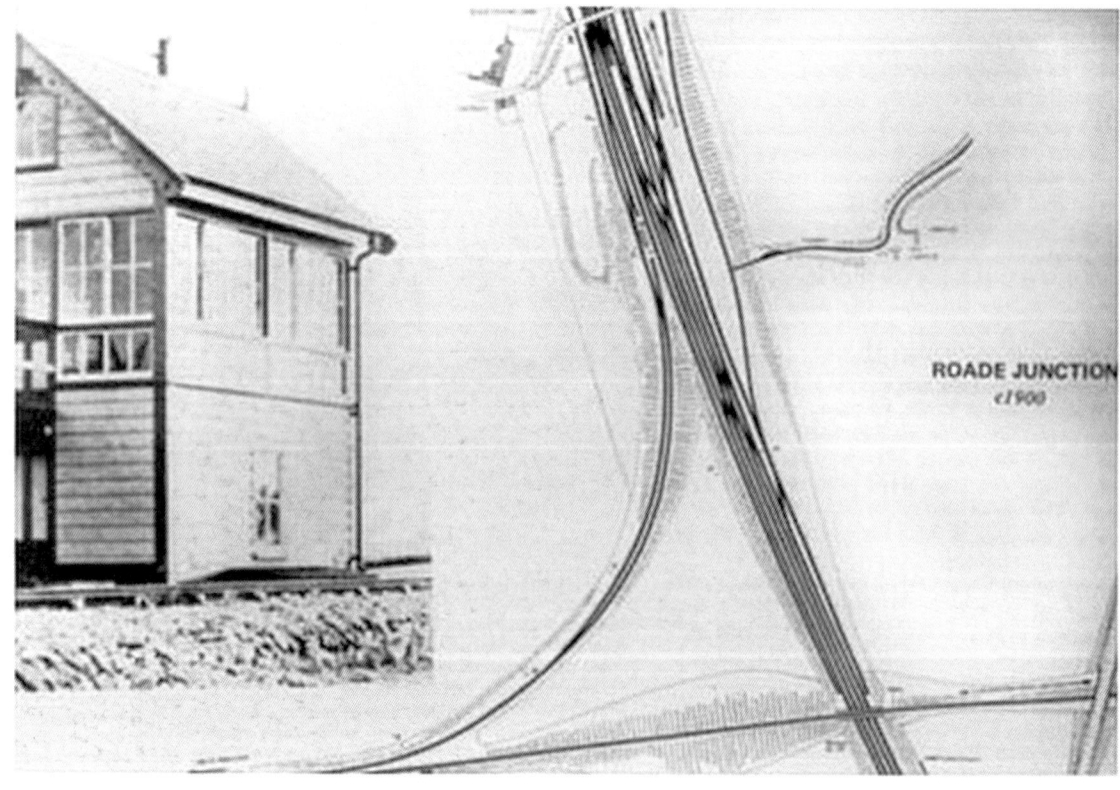

Roade Junction c.1900
(George Freestone Collection)

Construction of Bay Platform N°5, 1890
(George Freestone Collection)

The connection from the ST&MJR 1890
(George Freestone Collection)

The track layout at the Station changed upon completion of the connecting spur between the ST&MJR and the L&NWR. This included a siding running from the bay platform to the northern end of the later company's signal box.

Roade Station 1890
(George Freestone Collection)

CUTTING REMARKS

Work on this cross-country route progressed slowly, with one of the major engineering tasks being the construction of a 73ft girder bridge by which the new railway crossed the West Coast Main Line at 90°. This was under construction during the summer of 1888.

'The Tin Bridge' N°163
(Terry Andrews)

This was followed by an over-bridge for the Ashton Road N°164. It is interesting to note that this was built with a double arch, which may suggest that it was the railway company's original intent to connect a further link line on the eastern side into the L&NWR sidings.

Ashton Road Bridge N°164 & PSL factory water tower on the right c.1963
(Alvin Barby Collection)

From this point the line continued eastwards on a raised embankment to a pair of blue-brick abutments which facilitated another structure, N°165, over a bridleway. In order to build this embankment, material was brought directly from adjacent land being excavated for *'Roade's other Cutting'*. This Cutting extended for 500 yards at a depth of approximately 25 feet at its deepest point.

During these excavations in November 1888, 24 men under direction of Thomas Hall of Towcester were working on raised benching from which they were filling wagons with spoil. Suddenly, without warning, the undermined mass of earth collapsed upon the toilers, three of whom were completely buried.

John Scrivener and John Foster were quickly extricated; however, ten minutes would elapse before Henry Denny of Shutlanger was freed. The unfortunate man was declared dead by Dr Walter Ryan. His skull had been fractured and crushed, as had his ribs and torso. His accidental death was declared instantaneous.

Towards the eastern end of these works the route passed under the Hartwell Road, bridge N°166. This excavation has now been filled in and the bridge removed.

Hartwell Road bridge c.1966
(Alvin Barby Collection)

The line thereafter proceeded up a 1 in 96 gradient over another bridleway, bridge N°167, and by January 1889 work had progressed eastwards close to Quinton village, where further excavations were required. Henry Ludlow of Rainham, Kent, was engaged upon the work. He was positioned six feet below three colleagues who were driving poles into the ground in order to create a fall of earth to be loaded into awaiting wagons. Despite a warning from William Jones that the ground was collapsing, Ludlow was struck by the avalanche and knocked into the edge of the wagon. The inquest was conducted by the Coroner, Mr W Terry, at The Plough at Hartwell. Dr Walter Ryan of Roade stated that the deceased had suffered severe cuts and abrasions to his head, a broken ankle and compound fracture of his lower right leg, and that death was instantaneous. PC James Butlin also gave evidence. A verdict of accidental death was recorded by the jury.

CUTTING REMARKS

Following this was Salcey Forest Station, which in reality was geographically closer to Piddington village. It was built to the same design as that of Stoke Bruerne with a siding and signal cabin. These were somewhat grand facilities for such an isolated location. However, the railway company may have foreseen potential revenue in transporting the thousands of pit props that the forest produced for the coal mining industry. The line thereafter joined the Midland Railway at Ravenstone Wood Junction, three and a half miles from Olney, where a turntable was installed to facilitate the turning of engines for their return journey to Towcester.

Salcey Forest Station c1920's
(Unknown)

Also during 1888 the *Northampton Mercury* recorded that in August the Annual Flower Show and Sports Day at Roade included a tug-of-war contested by railway navvies selected by Mr Davies (ST&MJR*)* and locals under the stewardship of Mr Watts. It reported that amid deafening cheers the natives made several determined attempts to draw their opponents over the boundary, but the navvies prevailed.

On 16th August 1890 the *Bedfordshire Mercury* reported that the L&NWR had sent an inspection train consisting of an engine and two carriages on the Midland line to inspect the works. Upon reaching the junction at Ravenstone Wood, they intended to continue on the Midland route thereafter. However, the points were wrongly set and the whole assemblage was derailed.

During the following month on Feast Monday, a series of games were arranged by Mr Butler, landlord of The George Hotel, on a field adjoining the railway. The *Northampton Mercury* reported that races were held for all ages and a cricket match played between Roade and employees of Mr Noble, the contractor for the ST&MJR.

The George Hotel c1910
(Alvin Barby Collection)

The line opened for goods traffic on 13th April 1891. At Roade trains were able to transfer from one company's tracks to the other's via points sited south of the pedestrian bridge which is still in use. Passenger services from the Station, either anticipated or speculated upon, were never to be realised and no records exist to indicate these ever commenced. However, the memoirs of Job Sturgess recorded that after the opening, 'A great day was had by a party of village dignitaries and local tradesmen who travelled from Roade to Towcester and Olney'.

It is also worthy of note that following an inspection report by the East and West Junction Railway engineer Joseph Burke, undertaken shortly after the opening of the link line, that he considered it *'quite unsafe to run over'*. Passenger services between Olney and Towcester did eventually commence on 1st December 1892 but these were withdrawn on the following 1st of April, the venture being determined as financially unsustainable.

Shortly after the link's opening, a locomotive travelling too fast on the ST&MJR siding failed to stop and destroyed the stop blocks and the external staircase at the north end of the L&NWR box, which resulted in the staircase being relocated internally. Both the L&NWR and the ST&MJR used the siding intermittently for the exchange of goods wagons, the former for its through traffic from London to Bristol.

CHAPTER 9

Landslides! – The Navvies Return

A decade after its Cutting's widening the condition of its lofty embankments were giving company engineers some anxiety, as recorded in 1891 by George P Neale in his *Notes of a Railway Superintendent's Life* –

> *The soil above the rock cutting had shown considerable instability; the water contained in it (however beautiful the resulting icicles, in massive stalactite form, might appear in winter) rendering the super incumbent mass very troublesome and insecure. Temporary measures proving ineffectual, Mr Stephenson decided to close the two new lines while the top surface on the east side of the line was reduced, and a supporting series of girders introduced to guard against future mischief. The traffic between Roade and Northampton was accordingly stopped altogether, and for upwards of three months, February, March and April – the old route via Blisworth was reverted to for running the trains to and from Northampton.*

Shortly after the remedial work commenced John Major of Buckby Wharf became the first casualty, breaking his ribs in a fall. On 17th January 1892, John William Wootton of Paulerspury was run down and killed in the Cutting. The Coroner, Mr C.C. Becke, returned a verdict of accidentally killed, stating that the deceased had no right whatever to have been on the line. Two days later, a navvy named James Delton of Crewe was loading girders on a wagon deep in the Cutting when one slipped, crushing his foot completely. He was conveyed to the infirmary in great haste, his foot being amputated upon arrival.

In February at the Petty Sessions Court at Towcester, navvy Henry Morris of Crick, who was engaged upon the works, was remanded in custody for the theft of a bag of wearing apparel at Blisworth, property of the L&NWR. In the first week of the following month a navvy slipped whilst crossing a plank upon which he was wheeling a barrow of spoil. He fell from a considerable height. He was taken to the infirmary where a broken knee was diagnosed.

In its edition of Thursday 17th March, the *Northampton Mercury* reported the essential remedial work almost complete, resulting in 600 navvies being sacked. The line reopened on 11th April.

Despite the considerable works undertaken to stabilise the Cutting's eastern banks, in November 1892 another major landslip occurred, following shortly after a large gap in the walling was noticed by platelayers. The slip extended 60/70 yards south of the Blisworth – Courteenhall Road Bridge.

CUTTING REMARKS

An eyewitness account was recorded by the aforementioned diarist Abel Hurst.

The big slip came down at Courteenhall Bridge on November 13th, 1892, and the line was blocked until the 11th of April the following year. The slip came down at 12.00 at night. Foreman [Joseph] Eales and I went to Middleton [Milton Malsor] Signal Box to fetch some sleepers up to the slip. I was left at the box to flag for the lorry going up with the sleepers. While I was at the box I heard it fall down. Mr Bellet came up with his coach, I had got 3 detonators on the line and stopped and told him the slip was down, but he had heard it was down. I was at Middleton Box to work hand points to cross the ballast trains with the loads of clay which they unloaded at Ladybridge.

The massive extent of the landslip
(Fred Blincow Collection)

Job Sturgess in his memoir recalled that one of the final trains to pass the site was 'bearing most of the Roade worthies from market, and they were usually pretty merry'.

Local media interest was again sparked, and the following lengthy account was published in the *Northampton Herald* in its edition of 4th December 1892. Headlined 'Visit to the Landslip at Roade'

Seeing that no adequate description has yet appeared of the great landslip (or what have become landslips) near Roade, I determined on Friday to take a ramble as far as the scene of occurrences, and to write upon the subject of the slips and the work that was being carried out. On leaving Roade, and walking along the summit of the very high cutting which runs from the Station towards Northampton as far as Milton Bridge, my mind was carried back to the time the new line from Roade to Northampton was being made, and the strikingly arduous character of the work, and the great difficulties of engineering and otherwise connected with it, not only at the point or points in question but also on almost the whole of the section. At the time the work was proceeding the great depth of the cutting near Roade, and its upright character was much remarked upon, but the idea seemed to have prevailed not only with the railway engineers but with the general public, that the rocky character of the strata would prove to be its safeguard from any slips occurring to interfere in any way with the traffic. That was some 10 or 11 years since, and I remember that only a year or two afterwards when the face of the cutting had been exposed to the weather it began to crumble away.

This proceeded for some considerable time, and with the portion of the section nearest Roade gradually became more noticeable and serious. That the latter term might be applied to it there cannot be the slightest doubt, as some 6 or 7 years since the Company's engineers seemed to have thought it time to protect the cutting in some way, and accordingly began to face it with a wall of brick, several courses in thickness, and of supposed great strength to resist any pressure from behind. This work had been gradually proceeding year by year, and was still being carried out when the unfortunate slip of Saturday, the 14th of November took place. I also remember the frequent slips on the Milton side of the high embankment at the skew bridge at the bottom of Hunsbury Hill, and the difficulty there experienced. Further, the buttresses of the bridge also became affected, and were slightly pushed out of the upright; and in fact, still remain so. About four years since this matter became so serious in the eyes of the travelling public that it was brought to the notice of the Company by letters in the local papers and also privately, and as result steps were taken to secure its safety. This was done by making concrete beds on the Hunsbury Hill side of the embankment and running supporting rods through. Notwithstanding this, the position of the buttress is now often the subject of comment. Again, I recollect the serious slips which occurred near the mouth of the tunnel nearest Northampton, and the consequent great inconvenience with the opening of the section, and the subsequent delay of the traffic. As I said the whole section seems to have given cause for anxiety, and to present difficulties from the time it was opened and Northampton was placed on the main line. Reverting to the object of my ramble I might state that while walking to the scene of the slip along the top of the cutting, the immense height and the enormous weight which had to be kept back was strongly brought before me, and my surprise that such a thing had occurred was considerably lessened. Although the face of the cutting was walled up in the presumably strong manner it was, yet the pressure of matter behind must be enormous, and could not fail to become a source of ultimate danger. Again I observed that the cutting being of such a great depth had for some distance gone below the rock, and on to the bed of clay, and this, I was informed, seems to have been the cause of the slip.

CUTTING REMARKS

Thousands of tons of rock & debris covered the tracks
(Bill Hudson Collection)

The rock, doubtless owing to the great quantity of rain of late, is stated to have slipped off the bed and from its great weight to have toppled over. The slip took place immediately above the Courteenhall Bridge which is said to be between 80 and 90 feet high, and extends some 60 or 70 yards, and there are further signs of weakness beyond it. Some thousands of tons of rock and earth fell into the deep cutting below that of the Blisworth line which runs some 18 or 20 feet higher, therefore affording a degree of safety. The whole of the cutting is still blocked with thousands of tons of rock and earth, some of the pieces of rock being of great size and weight.

Doubtless at first the line could have been cleared in a few days, but seeing the nature of the slip the Company have wisely determined to improve the cutting throughout, and so prevent a chance of any reoccurrence of such slips. I understand they have decided to make the cutting of a sloping character, or rather to carry it back some 30 or 40 yards in the form of landings. For this purpose they have purchased some six or eight acres of land from Mr R.J. Kilburn, of Northampton, and also the house belonging to him which is situate in close proximity to the bridge. Mr Kilburn purchased the land some three years since for £750, and since that time has laid out some £100 in improvements, so that some idea of the cost to the Company in this respect alone can be well imagined. Mr Kilburn has to give up possession of the house and land at Christmas. The cutting will be carried back to within a few yards of the house, and the latter, I understand, is to be formed into two cottages, which will be occupied by two employees of the Company, who will thus be near at hand to keep watch on the cutting. I observed about 100 men engaged in removing the hundreds of thousands of tons of rock and earth which will have to be removed, and it is not anticipated that the whole work will be completed much before midsummer next, although traffic might be renewed in the course of a short time.

Landslides! – The Navvies Return

Clearing the debris
(Bill Hudson Collection)

There are continuous relays of men, and the work is carried on day and night, the light in the latter case being provided by means of several Wells' lamps, which are of great power. I observed that great difficulty is experienced in removing some of the enormous pieces of rock, and I was informed that preparations have already been made in 12 parts to blow up some of the larger pieces of rock on Sunday morning, the time being selected as the best so as not to interfere with the passing trains on the Blisworth line. The fallen rock and earth is being removed by ballast trains, and the scene presented is altogether of an animated character. I was informed that it was fortunate that the immense quantity of rock and earth which first fell came straight out-wards and not at an angle, as otherwise the buttress of the high bridge must certainly have been knocked away, which would have caused a portion of the bridge to come down also, I might state that the traffic on the Blisworth line is not in any way interfered with, and the whole of the trains now go that way. As showing the treacherous nature of the cutting generally I might state that during the last week another serious slip occurred about 300 yards nearer Northampton and midway between the Milton and Courteenhall Bridges.

In this instance the cutting slopes and is not faced with brick. This slip is about 36 yards in extent, and it appears that its occurrence has been kept very quiet and it was only known to a few. A separate large gang of men are engaged at this spot in removing the debris and also in repairing the damage. The men engaged reside at Roade, Blisworth, and Northampton, and those at the latter place are taken to and from their work by ballast trains. I could not glean whether it is thought the line will be so far cleared as to permit of some of the Christmas goods traffic passing that way, but if not the Company will certainly experience some difficulty in combating with the large amount of traffic which prevails at that time. Rumours are current at Roade that the line will not be again opened for passenger traffic until the whole of the cutting is completed to the satisfaction of the Government Inspector. In the course of my enquiries I also heard that the whole of the cutting will be ultimately treated in a similar manner to that portion where the slip occurred, and that other lands will have to be purchased for the purpose of carrying out the work.

Up to 2000 men worked in shifts to repair the damage
(Bill Hudson Collection)

Two months later a further commentary on the landslip, headlined 'The Latest Landslip at Roade – Narrow Escape of a Number of Men', was reported in the same newspaper, including a further life threatening incident.

The work of removing the landslip on the London and North Western Railway between Roade and Courteenhall near Northampton, which occurred some months since, and the further slip of some 2,000 or more tons adjacent to the former which fell on Sunday morning week, has now assumed gigantic proportions, and it is considered the whole of the work contemplated for securing the safety of the cutting will not be completed until next spring, or at least during the ensuing year. At first some 200 or more men were put on, but now there are between 1,600 and 2,000 men to be observed at work, being divided up into gangs of some 70 or 80 each, and the scene presented is of a most animated and surprising character. Some of the men are to be observed at work in the most dangerous positions, but which cannot possibly be avoided, and the greatest care is manifested on the part of the Company by means of numerous watchers and otherwise to prevent accident happening. It will, however, be certainly surprising if we do not hear of some accident before the conclusion of the work, seeing how apparently reckless and indifferent some men are; this, doubtless, being brought about by the very nature of the avocation.

Landslides! – The Navvies Return

Forming the embankment landings
(Bill Hudson Collection)

The whole of the surface of the cutting from Courteenhall Bridge to the bridge some little distance from Roade Station is completely occupied by men using either the pick, shovel or crowbar. The cutting away and blasting operations are proceeding from the immediate front upwards, so that all debris falls below on to the line, or is drawn or carted away to be thrown on to the line at a given spot for removal by the ballast trains. The debris, up to the present, has been tipped into two or three low fields some half a mile or more below the slips, but within the past week some 4½ acres of land near Ladybridge at the bottom of Hunsbury Hill, belonging to the Corporation of Northampton, have been negotiated for, the price being set down at £450, and when the purchase is concluded it will be tipped at those places not only as a means of getting rid of, but also, doubtless, with the view of further strengthening the embankments in the immediate vicinity. We understand it is contemplated removing the whole of the brickwork beyond the slips, and building a retaining wall the whole length 10ft high and 10ft thick, and that the face of the bank will then be carried back in the form of landings, or what might be termed the fronts of batteries. The upper portions of the wall of the whole of the cutting will, however, it is understood, be removed, and replaced in a similar manner, graduating up to the bridge near Roade, and even beyond that.

At first great difficulty was experienced in managing so large a number of men, who had to be put on at the pressure, but when it was found that those who created any objections or difficulties beyond those which were deemed reasonable were discharged, and others quickly found to take their places, matters soon righted themselves, and all credit is now given to the men for the manner in which they carry out their work and their conduct generally. Of course a few black sheep will be sure to be found among so great a number of the men of the classes engaged. The County Police are assisted by special men, and things have as yet gone fairly smoothly. Arrangements have been made for the comfort of the men by the building of shanties, in which they can retire at meal times or for shelter, and in addition, Mr A. Ashby of the Blisworth Hotel, and Mr Perkins have, by permission of the Company, established a canteen for the purpose of supplying tea and coffee and all kinds of edibles, but no intoxicants are allowed to be sold on the work. This canteen is found to be of great convenience and is thoroughly appreciated by the men, who work in night and day shifts, the tea and coffee being carried to them all over the works. On Sunday week and Sunday last some hundreds of persons proceeded to view the district of the slips and the gigantic operations proceeding.

A select group probably taken at the Cutting
(Bill Hudson Collection)

Some score or more of the labourers had a very narrow escape of being seriously or even fatally injured early on Sunday morning. As stated, a retaining wall is to be built ten feet high and ten feet thick, and a portion of the work close to the Courteenhall Bridge has been commenced. About a score of men were working at the bottom of the cutting digging out the foundations for the continuance of the wall, when one of them had the occasion to leave his mates and procure other tools. While doing so he fortunately happened to cast his eyes up to the face of the bank and then saw an enormous quantity of rock just giving signs of breaking away. He at once gave the alarm, and the other men quickly dropped their tools and got out of the way. In the course of a few moments many tons of rock and debris came rolling down on the very spot where they had been working; and but for the fortunate warning received doubtless many of them would have met with instantaneous death, and others have been seriously, if not fatally injured, as some one or two pieces of solid rock which fell were estimated to weigh between ten and fifteen tons. The debris again covered the line, and a clearance had to be made before the

Landslides! – The Navvies Return

trolleys bearing the cranes could be got to work to remove the massive pieces of rock out of the way. Here and there throughout the whole length of the operations pieces of rock and quantities of rubble are continually falling, and, as stated, great danger is attached to the carrying out of the work generally. Instead of the 'weeping' holes, as in the former wall, there will now be headways driven into the rock, and large outlets in the wall for carrying the accumulation of water, which, is thought by some to be the cause of the slips. Not only will the expense to the Company amount to an enormous sum, but great inconvenience is felt by them in conducting their immense traffic, and many delays in the running of the trains are occasioned.

Responsibility for managing the rebuilding work was in the hands of Herbert Goodwin, who had joined the L&NWR in 1888 as a timekeeper at Edge Hill near Liverpool. Over 2,000 men were engaged upon the task.

Herbert Goodwin, Company Overseers & Foremen
(Northampton Mercury/RLHS)

CUTTING REMARKS

The significant landslide caused a major headache for the railway authorities. The initial work was the removal of vast quantities of clay and soil from the slippage. However, they were at a loss to find somewhere to remove it to without incurring great cost.

Their salvation was to come from the Wake family of Courteenhall, as the late Sir Hereward related to the Blisworth Heritage Society–

> *Luckily, in a way, in my grandfather's day a part of the cutting fell in and the lines were blocked to the all-important traffic. The Railway Company begged him to allow soil to be excavated and dumped on his adjoining fields. He readily agreed on condition they put right the loss of water of decades earlier and supplied water free of charge to be pumped up by a ram to maintain two new reservoirs at West Lodge and Woodley Farms and a large one on the highest ground just West of Sharman's Barn which supplied the Hall, Home Farm and eventually Courteenhall Village - all beautifully built by the Railway Company. Much of our water today continues to be free of charge.*

The cost of these remedial works to the railway company was recorded in the Courteenhall Estate records to be £2,000 which included the labour of fifty men employed for the purpose.

Due to the severe disruption that ensued, the L&NWR issued an amended timetable which appeared in the *Northampton Mercury*–

LONDON AND NORTH-WESTERN RAILWAY.
NOTICE OF TRAIN ALTERATIONS.

ON and after Monday, February 1st, the following CHANGES will be made :—

In consequence of the Land-slip at Roade, the Newspaper Train will CEASE running *via* Northampton, but it will call at Blisworth, and a Train will leave Northampton (Castle) at 6.25 a.m. to connect with it.

The 10.40 a.m. Train (Sundays) to Roade, Bletchley, and London, also for Blisworth, Weedon, and Rugby, will leave Northampton (Castle) at 10.35 a.m.

The 11.13 a.m. Train (Sundays) Roade to Northampton will leave at 11.8 a.m.

The 3.32 p.m. Northampton to Bletchley, Willesden, and London, will leave at 3.28 p.m.

The 8.35 p.m. train (Sundays) Roade to Northampton will be discontinued.

The 8.35 p m. Northampton to Blisworth on Thursdays and Saturdays will leave at 8.45 p.m.

NEW TRAINS will run between NORTHAMPTON and BLISWORTH as under :—

From Northampton, 6.25 a.m., 1.38 p.m., and 3.28 p.m. (Week-days), and 10.35 a.m. (Sundays).

From Blisworth, 6.45 a.m. and 3.45 p.m. (Week-days), and 11.25 a.m. and 3.30 p.m. (Sundays).

For further particulars see Company's Bills.

G. FINDLAY, General Manager.

London (Euston), January, 1892.   B653—473

LNWR Notice of Train Alterations
(Northampton Mercury)

109

Landslides! – The Navvies Return

The area where much of the excavated soil and debris was spread would become known locally as *'the roughies'*, situated near Bailey Brook Close and adjacent to the west side of Dirty Lane Bridge.

The works saw the deeper eastern aspect of the Cutting rebuilt with brick facings, these being further reinforced with 100 vertical steel supports with cross-girders to brace the side of the Northampton Loop lines. These were to prove successful and remain to this day almost exactly as built when the task was completed. This structure was nicknamed 'The Birdcage' by railwaymen, a name by which it is still known.

Construction of the 'Birdcage' supporting girders
(Bill Hudson collection)

A driver's eye view
(Unknown)

Foreman platelayer and eyewitness Abel Hurst, was subsequently to reside in one of the two railway cottages at Courteenhall Bridge, mentioned previously, for the following 37 years until his retirement.

Abel Hurst Foreman platelayer & Diarist
(Joan Hedger)

Landslides! – The Navvies Return

Abel Hurst's family home at Courteenhall Bridge Cottages
(Joan Hedger)

CHAPTER 10

Mind the Doors – Situation Normal

Despite improvements in the design of passenger carriages and the implementation of more robust safety procedures for the men employed on the line, fatalities and accidents continued to make headlines.

On the evening of Tuesday 14th November 1893 a train left London for Holyhead, with many of the passengers on the service travelling onward from there to Ireland. The coaching stock was of the type which had no corridor, each compartment being the width of the whole coach. One compartment was shared by five men: Henry Aubrey from Leamington Spa, William Williams from Dublin and three privates from 'B' Company of the East Kent Regiment, based in Athlone.

Approaching Roade, one of the servicemen fell from the moving train and was killed. At the inquest held at The George on the 22nd, both Aubrey and Williams stated that it was evident that the soldiers had been consuming drink prior to the departure of the train, a practice which continued as it proceeded north towards Willesden, whereby they became quite drunk. As the journey progressed, witness Williams noticed one of the doors was open and it was closed by William Bonner, one of the servicemen.

At some point an argument broke out between two of the privates, Richard 'Finch' Hatton and William Day, which developed into a scuffle which saw Hatton strike Day. The aforementioned Bonner tried to break up the melee only to become involved in a three-way fracas. The altercations continued for over half an hour with Day continually striking his fellow until Hatton retreated whilst his fellows struggled with each other across the seats and upon the floor. Hatton was then noted by the civilian witness to go to the window in the door frame and lean out, both his head and an arm being out of the window. In an instant the door burst open and he fell to his death. At Stafford, Superintendent James Perkins, a detective in the L&NWR police who had been advised by telegraph of the incident, arrested both Day and Bonner charging them with causing the death of Hatton. Both made written statements and in Bonner's account he accused Day of pushing Hatton out. The prisoners were held at Stafford whilst initial investigations were made. The Superintendent thereafter accompanied the men from Stafford to Roade for the purposes of the inquest, and to the magistrate's hearing which was to follow. He was supported by the Deputy Chief Constable of Towcester, Superintendent Norman, and Superintendent Webster of Northampton, who were guarding the accused.

Reviewing the statements of both the witnesses and the accused, County Coroner W. Terry further questioned Aubrey and Williams regarding the circumstance which led to Hatton's fall. Both were asked about the door opening and closing incident and both stated that it appeared to have been closed by Bonner. They also stated that the deceased seemed to just step out from the carriage and that the action of his struggling colleagues, in their opinion, could not have contributed to his fall. They did not see either of the men kick the victim.

It was also evident that had one of the accused, by accident or otherwise, struck the deceased, the other would not have been aware with any surety to make an accusation. With regard to the signed statement of Bonner which accused Day of kicking Hatton from the train, Bonner stated that he wished to retract this. He stated that he had been confused when he was initially interviewed while the worse for drink, he only realised his error when awaking the following morning.

The Coroner summed up by saying that, in his view, no one was to blame for the death of Hatton. In his opinion, the previously opened door had not been closed fully, and the deceased's action by putting his head and arm through the open window placed enough pressure upon it for it to be swept open by the force of the wind. A verdict of accidental death was recorded. The Coroner, witnesses and accused then departed for Towcester where the result of the inquest was given to the Divisional Magistrates, Major Price Blackwood and a Mr Watkins. Superintendent Norman stated before the magistrate that following the inquest verdict he did not propose to submit any further evidence against the prisoners. The magistrate duly discharged the men who shortly afterwards continued upon their journey to Ireland.

In early May 1894, platelayers were engaged upon track work at Roade, the group being spread out at intervals of some distance. Thomas Malsher looked along the Down line and saw a train approaching at some distance away. He also saw a fellow platelayer walking towards him between the rails of the same line at a distance of 70 yards from his position. He called warnings and waved at the man to get his attention, however it was in vain and the fellow was struck.

The driver, Alfred Joice, on seeing the frantic waving stopped his engine. The body of Alfred Clarke, 39, of Ashton was found beside the line, he was dead. Dr Walter Ryan was summoned and found the deceased to have broken ribs, fractured left arm and right wrist and a compound fracture to the skull, the latter being the injury which killed him. At the inquest which was attended by Stationmaster Thomas Coxon and PC Avery, driver Joice stated that neither his fireman nor himself had seen the deceased or felt any impact.

A verdict of 'accidentally run over on the railway' was recorded. The deceased left a wife and four young daughters and a benefit concert was held in support of them. It was arranged by William Goode, Thomas Burdett and Herbert Ellard. The local Vicar, Revd Francis William Ames, allowed the Church Institute to loan a piano to use at the concert. The event was well attended by railway colleagues and local parishioners.

Roade was again to hit the headlines of the *Northampton Mercury* on Friday 10th January 1897, which reported –

> *We understand that the Northampton County Police are at the present moment considering the propriety of reopening investigations into the*

mysterious death of Charles Richard Clarke of Bristol, who died from injuries received on the railway near Roade on New-Years night. The jury, it will be remembered, were loath to accept the version of the witnesses that the deceased wilfully jumped through the window of the railway carriage; and after hearing the evidence at the adjourned inquiry on Monday last, they returned an open verdict.

At the adjourned inquest, the wife of the deceased, who saw her husband off at Euston Station, said there were other men in the carriage than the three sailors, and that her husband would have changed carriages before the train started if there had been time. One of the additional men she believed was a commercial traveller.

This gentleman, we are told, is now in communication with the Police; and that it is quite possible, on account of his statement of what took place before he left the train, prior to the occurrence, that a magisterial enquiry will take place. Of course, re-opening the inquest is practically out of the question; and were it possible, no good purpose would be served'.

The outcome is unknown.

Whilst 'walking his length' early on a January morning of 1898, ganger George Tew of Ashton was to make a gruesome discovery. As he approached Victoria Bridge he noticed a brown paper package secured with string lying close to the Down Fast main line. Turning it over with his foot he was shocked to see the hands and feet of a dead baby boy showing through a tear in the wrapping. He observed that the body had not been there long, as the paper was dry and the preceding night had been damp and foggy.

Ashton Signal box south of Victoria (Coronation) Bridge c1904
(Alvin Barby Collection)

CUTTING REMARKS

He proceeded to the Station at Roade to report the circumstance to Stationmaster Thomas Coxon and PC Avery. The subsequent investigations considered if the remains were thrown from a train or dropped from Victoria Bridge itself, which was a possible explanation. The Coroner asked when the last check of the line had been undertaken prior to the discovery and Thomas Coxon stated that it would have been around 5.30pm the previous evening and that 19 trains would have passed on the Up Fast line in the interim prior to the remains being discovered.

Having considered the evidence, it was concluded at the inquest that it was more likely that the bundle had either been placed by the line or rolled down the embankment. The previous considerations being thought not possible due to the small amount of damage sustained to the wrapping and the body within, in comparison to what such a method would likely cause. Dr Walter Ryan of Roade in his submission stated that it was in his opinion a case of misadventure in childbirth, the poor boy being asphyxiated due to the birth cord being around his neck during the birth. The jury's verdict was: 'Found dead, but not how it came by its death, the evidence does not allow the jury to say'. The mother of the unfortunate new-born was never identified.

Services were delayed through the Cutting on Saturday 3rd April 1898 when the wheels of two luggage wagons came off the rails. They remained upright for a considerable distance before the train was stopped, damaging the track bed such that platelayers were required to work till late in the day before normal services could be continued.

On 24th March 1899, Thomas Coxon retired following nine and a half years as Roade Stationmaster and an eventful length of service to the railways totalling 43 years. In the public waiting room, amongst family and colleagues, he was presented with a drawing room suite by the company in appreciation of his services. His successor as Stationmaster and Goods Agent was Alfred Reed.

CHAPTER 11

Into the 20th Century

On 27th February 1900, platelayers Thomas Malsher and Fredrick Clarke were engaged upon track work high on the Ashton Bank. They were, according to Clarke, working about 40 yards apart. A train approached on the Down Slow and both stepped back into the safety of the six-foot way just as another train, the Bletchley to Rugby service, passed on the Down Fast. Malsher was struck by the Down Fast service. At the inquest driver George Galvin stated that he did not feel the impact, but upon turning around saw the deceased falling down the embankment. He immediately applied the brakes in order to stop. Fredrick Clarke stated that after the trains had passed he could not see his colleague and upon looking found him down the banking, the back of his head had been crushed and he showed no signs of life. He was joined by the guard of the Up Fast train who had come to investigate. The fast train proceeded to Roade where assistance was requested from Stationmaster Reed. The inquest recorded a verdict of accidental death on the unfortunate Thomas Malsher, 58, who before his demise had performed 30 years of service on L&NWR. By an unbelievable coincidence, Thomas Malsher had seven years earlier witnessed the death of Alfred Clarke (a relative of Fredrick Clarke) of Ashton, on the same length of railway in almost identical circumstances.

In early March the *Northampton Mercury* was to report a humorous case headlined 'The Wandering Minstrels'. Frank Huber and Walter Winkle, both 13-year-old schoolboys from Kettering, were summoned for travelling on the L&NWR at Roade without a ticket on 27th February. One of the boys said they left home because they were told that they could earn more money by playing musical instruments than by work. One could play a mouth organ and the other was skilled at imitating birdsong. Detective John Mackay said he did not wish to press for a conviction and the Bench decided to dismiss the case on payment of three shillings and four pence costs each.

In July, Mackay apprehended Frank Bruce of Queens Park, Northampton, who had also travelled to Roade from Northampton on a single ticket which had been defaced. He was fined £1 and one shilling.

Throughout its existence, Roade Station was never blessed with the arrival of royalty. However, during January 1901 the village was decorated with flags, bunting and a resplendent triumphal arch of evergreens. These celebrations were to welcome home Lieutenant Hereward Wake (later to become the 13th Baronet) following his exploits during the Boer War. Lieutenant Wake, *Aide de camp* to Field Marshall Lord Roberts, had been involved in a number of celebrated engagements during his 14-month tour in South Africa. Travelling from Euston with his parents, he was welcomed upon his arrival at Roade by the distinguished ladies and gentlemen of the district who awaited him on the platform.

CUTTING REMARKS

Emerging from the booking office to the sound of 'Rule Britannia' played by the Militia Band, he was to see the Station approach full of carriages and a vast throng of people, some mounted on horseback. The school children of Stoke Bruerne, Roade and Courteenhall were all present, each clutching the national flag which they waved vigorously.

The returning hero with the welcoming local dignitaries 6th January 1901
(Johnny Wake)

The party proceeded to the green at the top of the high street where a raised dais had been erected. Lieutenant Wake was then formally welcomed home as a hero of Northamptonshire and a number of speeches were given. In his response, the Lieutenant was humble in relating his part in the actions in which he was involved, to which the crowd cheered and decried his modesty. The procession left for Courteenhall, following the marching band, past the decorated homes of the local residents. Upon reaching the gates to the estate, the horses were released from his carriage and ropes attached to the shafts, and over 100 men and boys then hauled their hero to his family home on the estate.

Abel Hurst, whose notebook recorded his daily life in the service of the railway at the turn of the century, tells of many of the incidents he witnessed whilst living at Bridge Cottages –

> *I was foreman platelayer over the Roade length (responsible for the safety*
> *& maintenance of the track over a set distance) through the girders, which*
> *was about 2¼ miles in length, and I used to walk it twice daily. That would*
> *be 9 miles a day. After I had done my weekly duty, and had a wash, off I*

118

would go along the banks with my dog and ferrets, sometimes I would have good luck and sometimes bad luck. Sometimes I would catch as many as 6 rabbits on a Saturday afternoon. So I don't think that was bad. I have caught brown ones, brown and white ones, and black ones. The number of rabbits I have caught I would not like to say, but I can truly say, it would be in four figures.

It would also seem that the railway continued to inconvenience the Grafton Hunt and the Wakes, as Abel recollected -

Another case when the fox hunters were round our place the fox came along the bank and round by the iron fencing by our door and then he jumped onto the stonework and run along the round nose stone to the centre of the arches and he curled himself up and laid there for the remainder of the day. In the evening I saw Sir Hereward Wake {the 13th Baronet} coming from hunting, so I stopped and told him he would see the fox. He could not believe me for some time, so he got off his horse and went and looked for himself, and found it was quite true. So Sir Hereward got on his horse and went to where the fox was and drove him off.

One day when the hunters were round our way some man came along and told me there was one of the red jackets fell at a fence and his horse was on top of him. So one of my men and I went to where he was, I found him in a ditch, the horse was lying on his back with legs up in the air, his master lay in the ditch with the horse lying on his legs and could not get out. A groom came up to us and got the horse out and up jumped his master none the worse for his fall. The gentleman thanked us all for what we had done and gave us a £1 to be divided between us.

London & North Western Railway Postcard of 1904
(Alvin Barby Collection)

119

CUTTING REMARKS

During June 1905 at the Northampton Assizes, Alfred James, alias Alfred Langton, a tramp, was charged with attempting to break into the booking office at Roade. The offence had taken place on 3rd April and the court heard that following Stationmaster Reed locking up the previous evening, the door lock had been tampered with and the wood around it gouged out. Signs of entry were discovered by Alfred Poole, a brass finisher employed at Wolverton Works.

The intruder, who was thought to have been in the building when the damage was discovered, escaped. He was found near Castlethorpe and arrested. At the trial he asked for legal aid under the 'Poor Prisoners Protection Act', but the request was rejected and he was dealt with accordingly.

Roade Station Postcard, c1906
(Alvin Barby Collection)

On Saturday 17th March 1907 a Mr Gray was busy in the sidings at Roade unloading a wagon containing the contents of his former residence. He was stacking his belongings onto a horse-drawn cart in readiness to transport to his new home in the village. To ensure that no damage was caused on that journey, all the goods were being packed tightly with straw. It was a very windy day and a spark from a passing train ignited the straw and within moments the flames had engulfed the wagon. The horses were quickly released and escaped injury. The furniture however was reduced to a charred mass, only a few items being saved. No doubt the railway company made good the loss suffered by the unfortunate Mr Gray.

During August, new signals were being erected over the loop line. Due to the difficulty in positioning the equipment, a wooden derrick was being used to lower equipment from the edge of the Cutting. The apparatus collapsed and trapped Welshman Robert Williams, 55, of Holywell, who had to be released by his fellow workmen. He was taken to Northampton by the engine of a train involved in the works and thereafter to the infirmary where it was discovered that he had sustained a smashed thigh and hip.

INTO THE 20TH CENTURY

A frightful accident was reported upon by the *Northampton Mercury* in its edition of Friday 20th September 1907, which had occurred at Roade on the previous Tuesday morning. John Smith and Fredrick Keech, two Cosgrove men, were walking along the line from the Station to their work on the new relief loop which was being constructed near Ashton. The purpose of this line was to move goods trains off of the Up Slow during busy passenger services; its long length being able to accommodate several trains simultaneously. Smith and Keech were run into by a goods train, running from Warrington to London, and instantly killed. There was no actual eye-witness of the fatality, but other persons were near at hand and the bodies were at once removed to The George Hotel, Roade, where, on Wednesday morning Mr C. H. Davis, the Divisional Coroner, held an inquest, at which all available particulars were laid before the jury. The L&NWR was represented by Mr H. T. Tait (solicitor to the company) and Mr Williams (Divisional Engineer). Superintendents Butlin and Norman were also present.

The following month, in its edition of 29th November, the *Northampton Mercury* reported upon the death of platelayer 31-year old Earnest Crane. He had been working upon the line in the vicinity of the crossovers opposite Roade Junction signal box and his death was witnessed by Arthur Howkins, a lamp man, and telegraph clerk Charles Sims. Howkins stated that at 7.40am that morning when the 5.30 Euston to Crewe service crossed from the Down Fast to the Down Slow at 15mph the buffer of the engine struck the deceased as he stepped forward. It was likely that the deceased was unaware that the train was in the process of crossing over. The body was identified by his brother Fredrick, a caravan traveller of Clifton near Rugby.

One measure which had been adopted by the Railway Companies to protect their employees and customers during the preceding years was the introduction of 'ambulance training'. This can be compared to modern day 'first aid', was not compulsory but volunteers could receive certain benefits if they became proficient. Competition was encouraged at local, district, and national levels with each company striving to have the best team.

One such event in the Rugby district was hosted during 1908 by the Roade team, and held in a local Co-operative hall. Among the 15 teams competing were Northampton, Rugby, Peterborough, Leamington, Castlethorpe, Warwick and Nuneaton. The winners were Rugby N°1 who attained 323 points; Roade finished last with 225 points!

During April, following prolonged wet weather, another serious landslip occurred in the Cutting. The *Chronicle & Echo* reported the slip to be over 100 yards in length, having fallen from the upper banking.

The same year the cross-country routes comprising the Stratford-upon-Avon, Towcester & Olney Junction Railway, the East & West Junction Railway and the Evesham Redditch & Stratford-upon-Avon Junction Railway were amalgamated. They jointly became the 'Stratford-upon-Avon & Midland Junction Railway,' (S&MJR). As a consequence the goods facilities at Salcey Forest Station were closed on 2nd July. 1908 was also notable for the establishment of Masters & Shuter Simplex Polish Works in Roade close to the sidings at the bottom of Station Road; these premises were destined to evolve into a major employer in the area.

On 3rd March 1909, the aforementioned George Tew was to make another gruesome discovery. Close to one of the bridges between Roade and Ashton he discovered a much damaged severed head which he removed from between the rails. Proceeding to the Station to report his find, he came upon the scattered remains of the rest of the body over the next 400 yards. He reported this to PC Day who returned to collect the remains.

The body was identified as that of Charles Bass, 26, of Shutlanger. PC Day and other officers in the area had been searching for Bass since the previous day following the brutal murder of 76-year-old William Robinson also of Shutlanger.

Circumstances of the murder were later told at the inquest. John Robinson, grandson and next door neighbour of the deceased, had been awoken by a disturbance. He went to the home of his Aunt, Mrs Margaret Inwood, to obtain a key to his grandfather's house, and upon entering with Mrs Inwood, found Bass within the premises, a hedge slasher in his hands.

Bass violently assaulted Mrs Inwood and fled. Then the younger Robinson discovered William dead with his throat slashed open. PC Balderstone, who investigated the scene, noted a window pane had been removed and a catch opened, which may have indicated robbery as Bass's intent, an act in which he was disturbed by the deceased. At the inquest into the death of Bass, a damaged notebook was found on his body, the writing was mostly illegible but the words 'times bad' and 'hope' were suggested by jury members. A verdict of suicide was returned upon Bass, *'Felo de Se'*. The verdict upon William Robinson was recorded as 'Wilful murder' by Charlie Bass.

On 27th June that year, William D. Sturgess & Son entered into an agreement with the S&MJR for a siding to be provided for their growing limestone quarrying activities at Roade, this siding Sturgess named 'The Jubilee Track'. A private siding was also opened at Easton Neston on 27th September of the same year to facilitate further mineral extraction at that place.

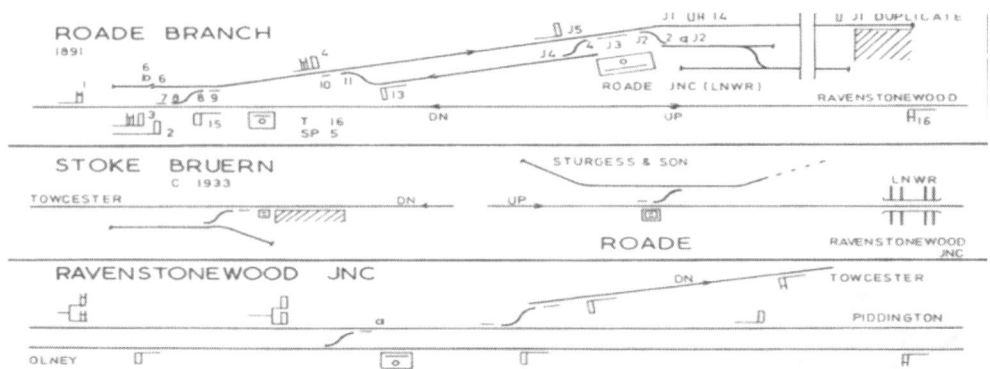

Local Sidings and Junctions on the cross-country route
(Chris Hillyard Collection)

In 1910, the bay platform, N°5, at Roade, originally built for the transfer of passengers and freight to the Towcester/Olney route, closed after 20 years. The S&MJR route and alignment still continued to frustrate the hunting fraternity, to such an extent that at the end of the fox hunting season the *Banbury Guardian* printed a rant from Captain Pernell-Elmhurst. He pontificated that the construction of the Olney to Towcester railway was: …

> *The most needless that had ever rendered broke the shareholders, and, that had ever interfered with fox hunting.*

The same year the Northampton & Banbury Junction Railway was absorbed into the S&MJR, with Towcester as the hub where all four lines converged. The combined lines were to become known thereafter by railwaymen and locals to the areas through which it passed as the 'Slow, Miserable and Jolty'!

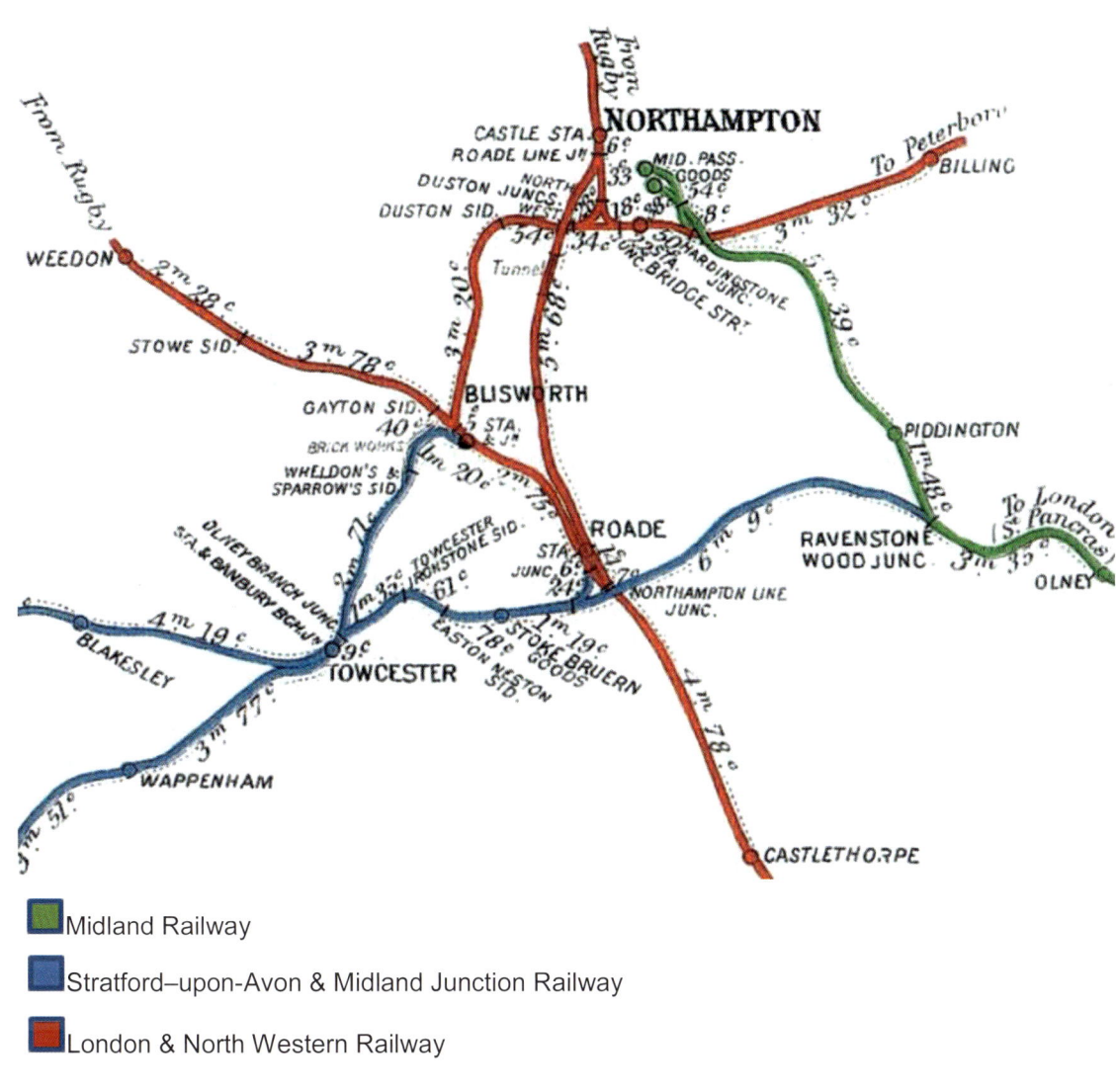

■ Midland Railway

■ Stratford–upon-Avon & Midland Junction Railway

■ London & North Western Railway

Railway Clearing House S&MJR Diagram 1914
(Wikipedia)

CHAPTER 12

A World First

1910 also saw an event that would see Roade prominent in national and international headlines and the location of a world-first in transportation history. This prestigious circumstance was the result of a challenge made four years earlier by the *Daily Mail* newspaper which offered a prize of £10,000 for the first aviator to fly from London to Manchester, 185 miles, within 24 hours and not more than two stops. When the challenge was set, it was believed to be an impossible target as powered flight of any notable distance had not been achieved.

The first pilot to attempt the feat was Englishman Claude Grahame-White. The 23rd April was the date scheduled for the well-publicised event. As navigational aids were at this time rudimentary, the plan was to follow the route of the railway. The L&NWR did its part by painting sleepers white at junctions as an indicator to the pilot of which route to follow. Unfortunately mechanical troubles and a high wind damaged the Farman aircraft at Lichfield which meant the flight ended in disappointment.

Upon returning to London to effect repairs, he was to learn that Frenchman Louis Paulhan, who was also keen to secure the prize, had arrived in England to make the attempt. Again the media trumpeted the contest as 'Not the greatest of the century, but of all centuries'.

On Wednesday 27th, Grahame-White was back in north London with his plane undergoing repairs. During the morning he went to Hendon to visit his competitor and discuss the flight. Paulhan's mechanics were busy assembling his aircraft at the time, also a Farman. Returning to Wormwood Scrubs in the afternoon, Grahame-White undertook a successful test flight in somewhat strong winds, but the 15,000 people who had arrived to see him take off were to be disappointed as he viewed the conditions unsafe and returned to his hotel for the night, his plane safely in its hanger.

According to Graham Wallace's biography *Claude Grahame-White* (written with the co-operation of Grahame-White himself) the two pilots had, "agreed that if, and when, the weather improved, neither would take-off without giving the other notice….By 4.30 p.m. weather conditions looked promising, so Paulhan sent his rival the agreed warning of his intention to take-off for Manchester. Inexplicably, this was never delivered and Grahame-White, who was in bed, slept on".

Among the crowd which cheered Paulhan's take-off at 5.30 were Claude's mother and sister. "They imagined that he intended to make a short test-flight; not until they saw him climb in ever-widening circles and fly in the direction of Hampstead did they realise that the race to Manchester had begun. It never occurred to them that Claude possibly did not know."

Grahame-White was to learn of his rival's departure when he was awoken in his hotel shortly before 6.00pm, and he immediately returned to Wormwood Scrubs and dressed for the flight whilst his plane was removed from its hanger. He would try and catch the Frenchman if he could. A few hundred lucky individuals from the crowd of thousands that had remained at the makeshift airstrip witnessed him take off in Paulhan's wake at 6:30pm.

The Daily Mail London to Manchester Air Race
(*ourwarwickshire.org.uk*)

Grahame-White pursued Paulhan until the receding daylight forced them both to land; the latter had made Lichfield by this time. Grahame-White successfully landed in a field south of Roade Station at around 7.55pm, from where he made his way to the signal box. The signalman, Frank White (a resident of Holly Tree Terrace), made him tea and telegraphed Rugby in order that the airman's mechanics could be notified of his location. Returning to his plane, he found the field full of well-wishers and was carried shoulder high and made to sign autographs by the light of a bicycle lamp. Retiring to the house of the local Doctor, Walter Ryan, he dined and discussed his strategy with his advisors, who had arrived in the interim.

Locals with the intrepid aviator (centre back to the camera) at Roade
(Unknown)

A World First

Village surgeon Doctor Walter Henry Ryan
(*RLHS Images*)

It was decided to take the bold step to attempt a take off by moonlight and, after a short nap, he returned to his aircraft hoping to depart at 2.00am. Initially clouds obscured the moon, but it cleared around 2.45 am. Surrounded on three sides by trees and hedges, and telegraph poles and bridge on the remaining side, he took off into the darkness with only a single car's headlights to guide him. The large crowd of well-wishers breathed a collective sigh of relief. Once airborne, he was reliant on limited night vision and the lights from signal boxes and stations guiding him on his route. A resident recollects being told that the excitement kept the pubs open nearly all night!

Mechanical trouble with the Farman biplane's Gnome engine forced Grahame-White to land at Polesworth at 3.50am, only 20 miles from Lichfield where Paulhan had landed the previous evening. Paulhan, on learning of the approach of his rival, took to the skies at 4.09am and was ultimately successful in reaching Manchester and claiming the £10,000 prize. Regrettably for Grahame-White, his mechanical troubles prevented him from taking to the air again. However his brave, somewhat foolhardy exploit had earned him a place in the history books for achieving the world's first night navigation flight. Following the event, Grahame-White's commentary regarding Roade appeared in the *New York Times* of 28th April, under the headline: 'Grahame-White's Description of His Perilous Adventure' –

> *After my journey from London to Roade where I alighted last night I had some rest but I was up at 2.30 am. At 2.54 am when I rose into the air it was completely dark. People were groping their way about the field with lanterns.*
>
> *As I stood by the side of my aeroplane, there was utter blackness facing me, faintly relieved in the distance by two or three twinkling lights which I knew to be those of Roade Station. I felt, well, I scarcely know how I felt. I did not know whether I should lose myself flying through the night.*

CUTTING REMARKS

My start was a confused jumble of scattered lights which swept away quickly below me, I could not judge my run along the ground but I rose as speedily as possible. Directly I was in the air the lights of the railway Station showed clearly below me and I headed toward them. I could see nothing of the ground below me; it was all a black smudge.

I went right over the railway Station lights and then, fortunately for only a second or so my engine missed fire and I began to sink towards the inky blackness below me. I could have picked no landing, and it would have been a swift steep glide to I know not what. And then, to my joy, my engine picked up again and I rose once more.

Great difficulty presented itself not knowing in the darkness if I was ascending or not, I had done no night flying before you see, but I soon became accustomed to watching closely the movements of my elevating plane which was silhouetted before me against the sky. I steered on for a spell with nothing at all to guide me. After leaving the lights of Roade behind the gleam from the occasional signal box far below helped me however, and so I picked my way through the night to Blisworth.

Claude Grahame-White, aviation pioneer and builder of aircraft 1879 – 1959
(*RAF Museum Hendon*)

A World First

There was one thing that Grahame-White omitted from his original commentary. The following was reported in the *Rushden Echo & Argus* on the 24th March 1935

> *My engine stopped over the railway Station just after I left Roade. There appeared nothing between me and destruction, but in a flash I diagnosed the cause of the stoppage he related. My coat sleeve had caught the engine switch. Instantly I switched on again and managed to clear the Station by inches.*

Night flight is commonplace now and in the intervening years man has flown to the moon. Roade's distinction as being the birthplace of night aviation has since been lost in the passage of time, less than a footnote in the history of flight, but nevertheless a world first that cannot be disputed. In October of the same year Claude Grahame-White restored national pride by winning the International Gordon Bennett Aviation Trophy at Belmont Park, New York.

CHAPTER 13

Prelude to Conflict & Supporting the Cause

In 1912 Masters & Shuter sold out to Thomas Henry Dey who incorporated the business as the Simplex Polish Co Ltd. Dey had made his fortune as a bookmaker and hoped to secure further rewards as an industrialist. He is reputed to have spent a considerable amount on advertising and is said to have erected a giant hoarding alongside the Station proclaiming: 'Watch us Grow'.

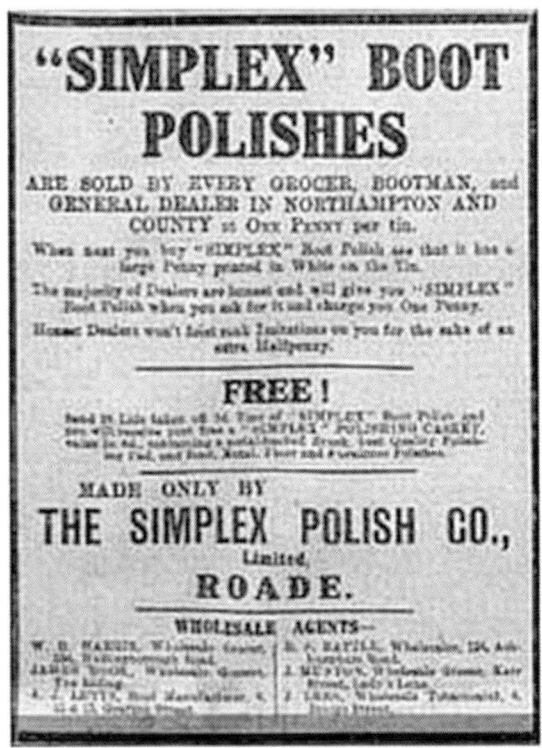

Simplex Polishes Advertisement
(*Northampton Mercury*)

On 23rd March of that year William Taylor, 54, of Ashton, a railway platelayer originally of Spratton, was killed by a passing train on the Ashton length. The inquest, which was attended by Roade Stationmaster Mr Reed, heard that Taylor's body was discovered by William Lawrence of Hartwell at 8.45am. It was a very foggy morning according to the driver of the train which struck the deceased, visibility being only 10-15 yards. Dr Ryan of Roade stated that the deceased had suffered a fractured skull, the extent of which had left his head 'quite out of shape', surmising that he had possibly been struck by the flange of a wheel whilst stooping down.

In October tragedy befell Herbert 'Bertie' Thomas Hillyard, 31, also known as 'Joe', a railway lamp-man at Roade. The inquest was conducted by the Divisional Coroner Mr C.H. Davis who heard from witnesses. The remains of Mr Hillyard were identified by his brother George of St James, Northampton. Dr Ryan had attended the scene and stated that the deceased had suffered a broken neck, back and ribs, in addition to fractures to his jaw and left thigh. The signalman at Roade Junction box, George

CUTTING REMARKS

Odell, stated that he had seen Hillyard going to the signal gantry carrying eight lamps just after 5.00pm. Shortly afterwards he was alerted by telegraph assistant George Crutchley Turner, who was with him in the box, that: 'Joe has fallen onto the train'. Turner told the inquest that he observed the deceased go to the home signal where he took four lamps to the lower landing and a further two to the top gantry. Whilst kneeling on the top gantry landing a train passed through the Station. Seeing the approaching train the deceased stood up, staggered, missed the handrail and was pitched from 50 feet onto a coach of the passing train. The weight of his falling body triggered the communication cord and stopped the train. Stationmaster Alfred Reed stated that the deceased was a sober man. A verdict of accidental death was recorded.

Abel Hurst also recalls this fatality in his notes, this is his account –

> *Joe Hillyard of Roade was a Lamp man at the Station, when he was putting his lamps in one Saturday afternoon in the Down home signals on the fast lines, he fell from the top of the signal onto an express train which was passing at the time, and was killed. They took his body to one of the waiting rooms on the Up (towards London) platform from Northampton. On the afternoon when I was walking my length an Inspector was on the platform and he asked me if I would come and help put him in his coffin, which I did. The undertaker was at the head and I at the feet. We put him in fully dressed with his boots and cap on as well. The undertaker told me to call at The George and there would be a pint of beer for me. I went up to The George, at the time Charlie Battams was there so he told me there was a pint of beer for me. I said, "No I could not have it" I said to him "I could not drink beer over poor old Joe's death". I said, "I would not mind having a cigar" which I did, so you see we put him away alright to his happy resting place I hope.*

Many years later the *Northampton Chronicle & Echo*, in its look-back to '90 years ago', printed a summary of the incident –

> *A railway lamp man Joseph Hillyard was lighting a lamp at the top of a tall signal post when he fell on to a passing express and received fatal injuries. It was surmised that the deceased, who was perfectly sober at the time, turned giddy as the train passed and lost his balance.*

On Thursday 28th May 1913 a cricket match was held at Roade between Mr Dey's Simplex Polish Works and local L&NWR railway employees. This was a return fixture of a match played a fortnight earlier in which the L&NWR had been the victors.

Team for Simplex Works, Walker, Tait, Alsopp, Passmore, Fowke, May, Cotching, Blackwell, Lucas, Parish and Warren.

Team for L&NWR, Smith, Boyle, Stamford, Hurst, Leech, Odell, Hobson, Clarke, Watkiss, Nightingale and Curtis.

CUTTING REMARKS

Roade Station c1920
(Alvin Barby Collection)

In November 1921 an alert unknown signalman raised the alarm after noticing a hayrick ablaze in a field close to the junction signal box, possibly the result of a stray spark from a passing locomotive. The hayrick was owned by George Skears, a farmer and the licensed victualler of The Swan public house. Unfortunately the rick was 400 yards from the nearest building and burnt to the ground before the fire could be put out.

An unusual accident occurred between Roade and Blisworth on Friday 3rd February 1922 as the Glasgow to Euston and the Euston to Wolverhampton express trains passed each other. An iron step fitted to one of the engine's tenders became detached and ricocheted from one train to the other as they passed, smashing windows down the length of each.

The two trains stopped at Blisworth and Roade respectively and doctors Jeffreyson [of Blisworth] and Ryan were summoned to attend the injured at each place. At Roade, Stationmaster George Bates found the tender step embedded in the partition of the last compartment of the first coach of the southbound train.

He also discovered the body of 25-year-old Ghanaian Caleb Jones Quaye, stage name Ernest 'Mope' Desmond, an actor/singer/pianist, who played in the Southern Syncopated Orchestra, that had previously taken London and the nation by storm. He was the only fatality in this unusual accident, his throat being cut by flying glass.

The Southern Syncopated Orchestra at Brighton in 1921
(brightondome.org)

Quaye was a particularly unlucky individual. Four months earlier he had survived another accident when the orchestra was sailing on the *SS Rowan* from Glasgow to Derry as part of the nationwide tour. On the west coast of Scotland, in dense fog, the ship was struck by an American vessel, the *West Camak*. Directly following this incident, it was struck again by the *Clan Malcolm*, and subsequently sank. Quaye escaped the tragedy but eight fellow members were drowned

Heavy lifting cranes were required at Roade Junction to re-rail the Bowen-Cooke designed Claughton Class locomotive N°2511 in early December 1922.

Recovery operations 4th December 1922
(Alvin Barby Collection)

CUTTING REMARKS

The engine, which had entered service two years earlier, had suffered a major axle failure and left the tracks at the crossovers opposite the signal box.

The war curtailed the opportunities for the potential rewards anticipated by Mr Dey and his Simplex Polish Company. Competition, coupled with wartime austerity, were the contributing factors which dictated that the business did not prosper and failed after about 10 years. The factory was left deserted and was nicknamed 'Masters Folly'.

Former Masters & Shuter Simplex Polish Works c.1920
(David Cochrane)

However, local economic and employment opportunities returned when Cyril Thomas Cripps, a former employee of the Simplex Polish Company, bought the now redundant works located at the end of The Leys in Roade.

It re-opened on New Year's Day 1923 to accommodate Pianoforte Supplies Ltd (PSL), a formerly London-based piano component business. Cripps's return to the village was due to him requiring larger premises, and soon 25 men were employed. The business expanded steadily, using road transport to take finished goods to London, although the works also retained access to the railway sidings. The business site would evolve in the following decades into the major employer in the village, along with the railway contributing extensively to the social and economic development of the area.

CHAPTER 15

London Midland & Scottish Railway - All Change

LM&SR Armorial device
(*Chris Hillyard Collection*)

Also in 1923 many railway companies, including the L&NWR and the S&MJR, were amalgamated to form the London, Midland & Scottish Railway (LM&SR). This in itself was a drive to standardise and integrate the business to increase productivity and compete with the threat from the expanding road transport network. Roade was one of many Stations renovated and improved by this newly formed company and its design lasted until closure, albeit with a number of enforced alterations. The layout was similar to the original L&NWR Station. The waiting room on the centre platform was upgraded with doors on each side, allowing it to serve trains on both sides. Toilet and parcels facilities remained much as before.

In March, Henry Harrison, on leave from his position as a ship's steward on the White Star steamer *Philadelphia*, boarded the 11.50 pm Euston to Liverpool service. Two other passengers travelled with him in the compartment and soon after leaving all were asleep. Passing through Roade at an estimated 50mph, the train was stopped after the communication cord was pulled.

Upon investigation by the train guard, it was learned that Harrison had risen from his seat, in the process disturbing a fellow passenger who witnessed him enter the carriage corridor open the exterior coach door and step out. Alerted by the train staff, a signalman based in the Cutting arranged for the line to be searched. Harrison was found alive but in an unconscious state, a condition from which he was not to recover. At the inquest it was determined that, in a sleepy state, he had confused the exterior door with that of the coach lavatory, with fatal consequences.

The late Sir Hereward Wake of Courteenhall, in his talk to Blisworth Heritage Society recalled some of his boyhood memories of travelling by train and the local Stations –

Remarkable to think of it today but I remember when as a boy travelling home with my father on an express train from Euston. He arranged for the guard to make an unscheduled stop at Roade Station and he quickly let us out. Blisworth Station excited us as children. There was a Nestle's chocolate machine there and for one penny in the slot behold a small slab of milk chocolate appeared wrapped in red and silver paper. From the ticket office near the entrance, we descended into what seemed a long tunnel, to climb up to the platform and see and hear the mighty steam engines roaring through with their long, dark red London Midland & Scottish coaches.

He also recalled –

My Nanny in the 1920's driving me and my brothers and sisters fearlessly in the pony and trap along the road to Blisworth. Of course the express trains in the Railway cutting were our chief excitement and standing up in the pony trap we could see over the high sides of the bridge down to the cutting below.

The Wake family were to be involved in another incident connected with the railway on 17th December 1923. Lady Wake, accompanied by two of her sons, was out driving during the afternoon and had a collision with a van on one of the Cutting's over-bridges as smoke and steam from a passing train had obscured the van driver's vision. None of the occupants were hurt, it was reported in the *Northampton Mercury*, although both vehicles sustained such damage that they were not driveable as a result.

The late
Sir Hereward Wake 14th Baronet

At Courteenhall in 2010
(*Courteenhall Estate*)

London Midland & Scottish Railway - All Change

On 12th December, the *Northampton Mercury* published the names of individuals who had been appointed as magistrates to serve the County. One of these was the aforementioned William Thomas Elliott, of Helen Cottage, The Leys, Roade. He was in the employ of the railway company in the village as a signalman, a position he had held at various other locations for the previous 16 years. His railway career had begun as a junior porter at Althorp Station. He was, the newspaper noted, the only working man to be appointed to the position.

William Thomas Elliott County Magistrate & Roade signalman
(Northampton Mercury)

In 1924 the most comprehensive geological account of the Cutting was published by a geologist named Beeby Thompson, who thirty-two years earlier had walked through it making many notes. This was during its closure for the remedial work following the major landslip in 1892.

In its edition of Thursday 10th September 1925, the *Northampton Mercury* reported upon the inquest into the death of James Tite, a 52-year-old described as a signalman's labourer and resident of Park Wood Street in the St James area of Northampton. Tite had been working in the Cutting with three colleagues when he was struck by a London to Northampton train and killed instantly. Police Sergeant Shead from Collingtree gave evidence and the inquest heard that at the time of the incident none of the deceased's colleagues had heard the train approaching. The verdict recorded was: 'Accidental death from injuries received while in the execution of his duties'.

In the early post-war years, the resourcefulness of railwaymen continued just as in Abel Hurst's day, using the opportunities which presented themselves in their daily endeavours to improve their somewhat subsistence living.

On the Blisworth to Towcester route, one of the best 'un-kept secrets' was the regular additional man on the footplate of the engine. On his day off, he would be dropped in a Cutting between the two places for the purpose of hunting game for the cooking pot. Evidently it was not unknown for a gun to be part of the engine crew's

CUTTING REMARKS

'unofficial equipment' with pot-shots being taken from the engine whilst in motion and sudden unexplained stoppages being to enable a successful kill to be retrieved.

To add credence to this tale, a correspondent to the Blisworth Heritage Society shared the following –

> Listen! Those 'sayings' were supposed to have been secret - and they were very, very true. As a lad, waiting for my call-up to go into the army, I was often threatened with a thick ear if ever I 'opened my gob and spilled the beans'. And yes, if we had to work a Saturday shift my old driver Bert always took along his 410 shotgun which he secreted under his coat. On one occasion this practice impaired his getting up onto the footplate and he fell backwards onto the ground. The loaded shotgun discharged itself, tearing a chunk out of his boot. Luckily, he survived without actual injury to himself. Old Bert was made of sterner stuff - you couldn't imagine him being killed off like that!

Claude Molcher of Roade recalled his boyhood memories of Roade Station's goods yard activities during this time –

> There was a big yard at the bottom of Station Road past the bridge where two lines came in from Northampton, and wagons were reversed into sidings carrying a variety of cargo such as coal, bricks and livestock. There was a special loading bay for the livestock. The coal would be placed in separate heaps for various people; as children my friends and I would 'help' weigh the coal and bag it up. We also helped with the bricks which came for the building of new houses in The Leys.

In *Kelly's* 1928 edition, Alfred Clarke was joined in the goods yard by Wiggins & Co Ltd, a coal merchant, who would supply all the local dealers.

Wiggins' coal delivery receipt
(Alvin Barby Collection)

London Midland & Scottish Railway - All Change

Passenger trains on the former S&MJR route were a rarity. One exception was for the Grafton Hunt steeplechases which were held at Towcester racecourse. Race day specials ran at Easter and Whitsun from 1927 to 1939. An estimated 5,000 race-goers regularly travelled by special trains from Leicester, Bedford, Luton and Stratford-upon-Avon, as well as additional services from Northampton via Blisworth.

A race day Special from London St Pancras to Towcester, c1929
at the Ashton Road Bridge.
(Alvin Barby Collection)

George Fredrick Bates retired as Stationmaster at Roade 1929 and was succeeded by Mr Hubert (Bert) White. During his short time in the village he became well known in the community. At a meeting of the Women's Institute, established the previous year, he gave a lantern lecture to the members on 'a tour of North Wales' which included 60 slides loaned by the LM&SR.

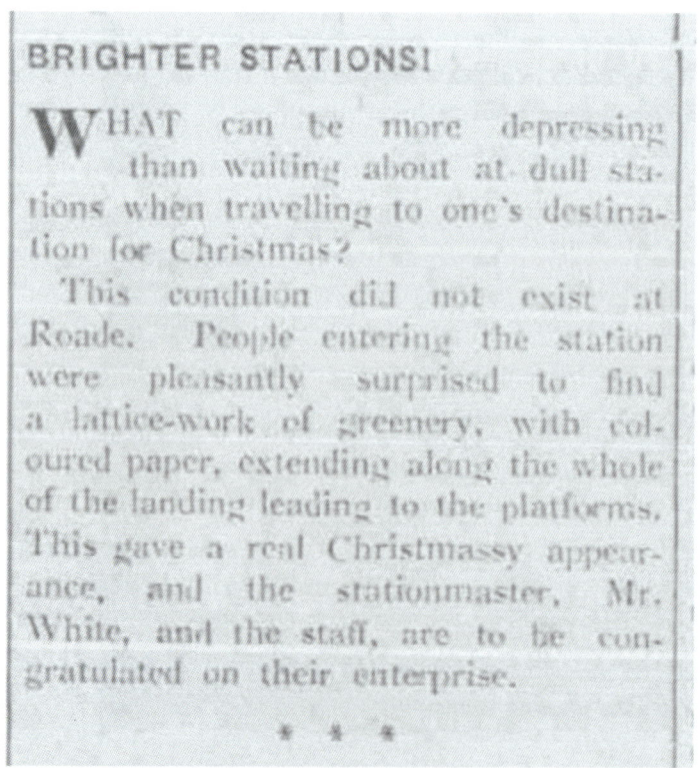

BRIGHTER STATIONS!

WHAT can be more depressing than waiting about at dull stations when travelling to one's destination for Christmas?

This condition did not exist at Roade. People entering the station were pleasantly surprised to find a lattice-work of greenery, with coloured paper, extending along the whole of the landing leading to the platforms. This gave a real Christmassy appearance, and the stationmaster, Mr. White, and the staff, are to be congratulated on their enterprise.

* * *

Accolade for the Station Staff 1932
(Northampton Mercury)

He also arranged with Mr Janes, the headmaster of Roade School, an outing for the children to Bristol. They were joined by children from Ashton and Hartwell and many parents and friends were in attendance. The *Mercury and Herald* reported that the special train departed at 10.30am and returned at midnight.

The Sunny South Express Roade Station, 12th March1932
(Alvin Barby Collection)

Towcester-based men would maintain the former S&MJR line. Fred White, who lived in Stoke Bruerne, would patrol the line from there into Towcester, where he caught services to Northampton Castle Station via Blisworth. Upon reaching the town, he walked the short distance to St John's Station where he caught a Bedford bound service which dropped him off at Ravenstone Wood Junction, and from there he patrolled the line back home to Stoke Bruerne.

1933 saw the retirement of Stationmaster Bert White, who was succeeded by Mr Harry Lane, arriving from Welford. The same year the *LMSR Magazine* reported the death in Northampton Hospital of Roade signalman W. Taylor, at the age of 50, after a short illness. His career had begun in the Locomotive Department at Northampton. Thereafter he had worked at Willesden, Kilburn and Hanslope. His fellow workers acted as bearers at his funeral.

Roade Station c.1932
(Alvin Barby Collection)

London Midland & Scottish Railway - All Change

In March 1935 the *Northampton Mercury* featured an interview with retired 80-year old Thomas Gardener of Ashton who had worked on the 'Roade-length' for 40 years as a platelayer. In his estimation, he had worked upon and examined over 61,620 miles of track during his career. His greatest stimulus, he said, was sitting in his garden watching the trains travelling to Roade.

Roade Junction 22nd July 1933
(Alvin Barby Collection)

Roade Cutting was to feature in a report in the *Northampton Independent* in July of 1936. In an article headed 'The Romance of Roade Cutting' the author enthused upon the great diversity of mature trees and shrubs which bedecked its banks and ridges. The numerous species listed included: Ash, Acacia, Holly, Larch, Sycamore, Lilac, Maple, Oak, Holm Oak, Common White and Black Poplar, Pine, Rowan, Willow, Whitebeam, Laburnum, Elder, Privet, etc. Quite how such a great diversity coexisted was put down to the mixture of soils and minerals which had been thrown up and blended from the excavations. This is testimony to the foresight of the then Duke of Grafton and his fellow horticulturists during the previous century, whose legacy must have exceeded all expectations.

The local railwaymen who maintained the Cutting, its banks and track were permitted by the company to cultivate areas of allotments on the rim. In addition, the banks teemed with rabbits and pheasants. The ever resourceful railwaymen never missed an opportunity to reap nature's bounty, as diarist Abel Hurst wrote –

One Sunday when I was walking my length, there was a cat crossing the line near the ram [water pump]. It had been caught in a trap, and it had got one leg broken. I caught hold of the trap; the cat turned round and bit me through the thumb. Another Sunday when I was walking my length I heard a squealing noise, I went up the bank and on the other side I found my dog Billy struggling with a great big hare in a snare. So I went to his help and we landed it back home. Another Sunday I found a fox in a snare but he was dead, I took him home and skinned him, and had it dressed and my daughter wore it for a fur for many years.

The allotments were still in evidence in the mid-1980s, as were the game trapping activities and collection of nature's other bounties by the locals.

Arthur Curtis on his Hyde Road bridge
Embankment Allotment, c1970s
(Freda Bennett)

A collision occurred on 19th November 1936 between an express sleeper train and another engine at Roade Junction. This involved the 12.50am sleeping car service from Manchester to London (hauled by Patriot Class locomotive N°5541 DUKE OF SUTHERLAND*), which was routed to run via Northampton, and a parcels train which was also bound for the capital.

It became clear at the subsequent inquest that a train that preceded the sleeper from Northampton had encountered a mechanical failure in Roade Cutting. This service, the parcels train, had originated from Holyhead and, whilst passing through the Cutting, a drawbar coupling had failed and the train had divided. A locomotive had been sent to the 15 stranded wagons and the brake van, to which it was coupled, and thereafter proceeded to propel the stranded vehicles forward to Roade.

At the junction the signalman, James Grimes, stopped the rescued train at the south end of the crossover and set the points and signals for the express sleeper service, which had departed Northampton at 3.50am. It was to cross from the Down Slow to the Down Fast and approached at a speed of 20mph. However, the engine of the parcels train, N°2821, had been stopped in such a position that it left insufficient room for the locomotive and a collision occurred. The force of the impact derailed the locomotive and its coaches were telescoped, blocking all four lines.

Collision site
(Alvin Barby Collection)

Crash Damage
(Alvin Barby Collection)

The driver of the engine at the rear of the parcels train, James Lowton, was severely injured and the rude awakening saw seven of the sleeper passengers sustain minor injury and shock. Two breakdown crews from Rugby and Watford respectively were required to remove the debris which blocked all the lines completely for several hours. At the subsequent inquest, signalman Grimes told the jury that he was sure that he had stopped the engine at the rear of the parcels train, leaving sufficient room for the express to pass as it crossed to the Up Fast. In his defence, he stated that Stationmaster Harry Lane, who was in attendance, should have advised him that the positioning of the parcels train was causing an obstruction. Lane responded by stating that the actions that should have been taken were not in his realm of responsibility or competence. The Coroner did not accept Grimes's position, stating that it was his responsibility to ensure the safety of the line before allowing the express sleeper to proceed.

Also in 1936 Frank White, the signalman at Roade who had witnessed Claude Grahame-White's heroics in 1910 (see Chapter 12) retired from the post of Chief Controller at Rugby Signal & Telegraph Department on Christmas Day. His prize memento from his 26-year career was a leaf from the signal box log-book signed by the intrepid aviator.

Additionally in 1936 the embankment excavation for accessing Roade Station Platform N°5, built for the S&MJR in 1890 and unused since 1910 was filled in.

Another local railwayman, Walter Richardson, was employed at the Wolverton Carriage Works and was a member of its Ambulance Team, which in the 1937 Coronation year won the Dewar Shield, the most prestigious award in the National Finals, for the second time. They were on duty for the procession along Oxford Street. Subsequently, all the English-speaking countries that had sent a contingent to attend the Coronation competed for the 'Empire Medal', which the Wolverton Team won for England.

Frank Edward White (left) and Walter Richardson
(Northampton Mercury/RLHS)

In July of that year, Newport Pagnell resident Laurence Froggart Henry Warner Soames, 27, was charged with improperly pulling the passenger communication cord at Roade. When the train guard advised him beforehand that the train would not be stopping at Wolverton and that he would have to alight at Northampton, Soames had replied: "It will stop". Realising that the train had passed Wolverton, he pulled the communication cord and attempted to climb down from the train when it stopped and the guard was forced to restrain him for his own safety. He was fined the maximum £5, with 10 shillings costs.

London Midland & Scottish Railway - All Change

1937 saw the publication of *Northampton Vindicated (Or, Why the Main Line Missed the Town),* by Miss Joan Wake. Included within it was a footnote to the main text regarding the landowner's initial opposition to the railway –

> *In justice to the landowners, there was a good deal to be said for their point of view. It did not improve an estate to have a portion cut off and rendered difficult to access from the rest by a railway line. A considerable acreage of good land, part of the Wake and Grafton estates at Ashton, Roade, Courteenhall and Blisworth, has been completely obliterated by the immense railway cutting. By the deepening of the same cutting towards the end of the last century the water supply at Courteenhall was seriously endangered, but that's another story. With regard to the hunting, a fair estimate of the landowners attitude can probably be arrived at by trying to imagine the outcry that would be raised if anything were done to interfere with the amusement of the classes now in power, for instance, if an attempt were made to seize football grounds in various parts of the country for the use as landing places for public aeroplanes.*

The mid 1930s saw a village water tower constructed. This followed serious concerns expressed by the Parish Council during the previous decade about the inadequacy and poor quality of the village's supply. This shortage was directly attributed to the negative impact of Roade Cutting's excavation 100 years previously, when, as a consequence, most of the natural watercourses had been severed.

The Revd William Henry Sharland, vicar of Roade since 1908, retired in 1936. He was known as an enthusiastic and accomplished croquet player. On one occasion, returning by train from the sport's headquarters at the exclusive Hurlingham Club in London, he found himself in some discomfort. During the day he had been sitting on the grass and he became aware on the journey home that his trousers were full of ants. As he was in a compartment on his own, he whipped off his trousers and dangled them out of the window to rid them of the invaders, when along came a passing locomotive which snatched the trousers out of his hand, so he arrived at Roade Station trouser less. His dignity was in part restored by the Stationmaster who provided him with a blanket and sat him in the waiting room whilst a boy was sent to the vicarage to fetch another pair.

Webb tank engine 6686
passing Roade signal box 1938
(Alvin Barby Collection)

CUTTING REMARKS

In September 1938 the *Northampton Mercury* reported the Golden Wedding anniversary of diarist and railwayman Abel Hurst who had moved from Courteenhall Bridge Cottages to 'Woodlands', a cottage within the village, following his retirement.

Although dark times were on the horizon, the centenary of the opening of the world's first long-distance intercity railway was not to be overlooked. In mid-September, an exhibition was staged at Euston Station to celebrate this milestone and featured two famous locomotives of the period, 'COPPERKNOB' and 'LION', the latter still in full working order. These were complemented by period vehicles including a First Class coach of the Liverpool & Manchester Railway, the Dowager Queen Adelaide's saloon and an L&B brake van.

On 9th October the exhibition moved to Birmingham, the ancient engines and rolling stock loaded on 'well trucks' for the journey by means of a special freight train which left Willesden at 7.15am. It made a brief stop at Roade at 11.00am on the way north.

(RLHS Image)

153

CHAPTER 16

Once more into the Breech

1939 saw hundreds of London children evacuated by rail to the area due to the threat of air raids on the capital. The *Northampton Mercury* detailed the numbers to be sent to each location. Locally Ashton would receive 50, Roade 301, Blisworth 175, Stoke Bruerne 31 and Shutlanger 32. One of these who arrived in Roade on 2nd September via Northampton was the children's teacher who stayed after the war and became Mrs E. Malin. Another evacuee that arrived was Mike Connelly who later worked at the Station as a porter upon leaving school.

In 1939 Roade welcomed 301 wartime evacuees
(Express.co.uk)

Stationmaster Harry Lane retired at the end of 1939 and his replacement was Percival Stephens who took up residence in the Station house with his wife Una.

Percival & Una Stephens
(Alvin Barby Collection)

CUTTING REMARKS

As a consequence of the outbreak of the Second World War, Pianoforte Supplies' factory greatly expanded; the company produced parts for both aircraft and road vehicles in addition to a variety of munitions. By 1940, almost all production was for war and munitions requirements. The sidings for the receipt and despatch of goods were certainly busy during this period, and Wiggins & Co Ltd's wharf was still supplying dealer Alfred Clarke and the local area.

Pianoforte Supplies Ltd & goods loading platform
(David Cochrane)

The elevated signal box in Roade Cutting was removed in 1939/40, officially for reasons of economy, but it is assumed that the installation of coloured light signals had rendered the semaphore signals redundant as they were often obscured by smoke from the engines' chimneys.

The elevated signal box within the Cutting c1937
(Alvin Barby Collection)

155

Once more into the Breech

Late in the evening of Wednesday 8th March 1940, a cattle train arrived at the sidings with 39 beasts for Mr Rossiter, a farmer from Heathencote. Due to delays in transit, the animals had been confined in their wagons for in excess of 35 hours without food or water and it was determined to be absolutely necessary for their welfare to remove them to a field close to the Station. In complete darkness due to the blackout enforcement, the farmer, assisted by the Station porters and others unloaded the animals and proceeded to herd them to the pasture. At the top of the Station Road, the beasts became excited and charged onto the highway where they collided with a confectionery van travelling without headlights from Stony Stratford to Northampton, causing considerable damage.

Harrison Whitlock & John Pell Station porters
(Martin Whitlock)

The confectionery company, Crystal Sweets, sued farmer Rossiter for damages and in the subsequent court case, although all precautions were noted to have been taken, the farmer was found liable and fined £11 and 4 shillings.

The late Eric Pickles of Roade commenced his railway career in August 1941 at Towcester as a junior porter. In his recollections of the time, he remembered limestone from Sturgess's Roade quarry being taken to the brickworks at Towcester, along with wagons of coal and coke, and deliveries of sugar beet to Stoke Bruerne. He regularly worked trains to Stratford-upon-Avon and back and recalled working wartime race specials to Towcester from London and Leicester, as well as trains with wagon-loads of maps for the military.

CUTTING REMARKS

Eric Pickles, (left), at Towcester Station
(Eric Pickles)

The war was again to reduce the available manpower as industry once more released staff to join the services. As a consequence, wives and daughters became essential in supporting the war effort. Relief Inspector James Campion's daughter Dorothy worked in the booking offices at both Towcester and Roade. When required at Roade she would cycle from her home in Towcester or her father would take her with her bicycle on the pedal-powered velocipede which was used to inspect the track, dropping her in the vicinity of Sturgess's siding from where she was able to walk the track bed of the former S&MJR junction to reach the Station.

During 1942, a Royal Air Force maintenance unit (72 MU RAF Roade) opened in Salcey Forest. Provisioning of the 38 storage buildings scattered throughout the forest was mainly from Roade Station's goods sidings, where a secure holding shed was positioned on the cattle wharf. The locality, which had largely escaped the terrors of war, was to witness a stick of bombs dropped near Ashton, one of which hit the railway embankment damaging a number of sleepers and lifting a section of the track. Some residents allegedly sheltered, unwisely, under the railway bridge.

72 Maintenance Unit RAF Building and the General Goods Office in Roade goods yard c1955
(David Cochrane)

Once more into the Breech

Although Roade was fortunate to escape many of the harsh realities of the conflict, the strategic importance of its railway Cutting was known to German Military Intelligence. In preparation for Operation Sealion, the Nazi invasion plans for the occupation of the British Isles, a 'Top Secret Guide Book' was produced. The Cutting's location is identified within its pages as one of the 'important and vulnerable points in Great Britain'. The description was supported by an annotated image of John Cooke Bourne's 1839 lithograph!

Translation-

> GB8, BB23, N°55. 'The Railway Cutting near Blisworth (Northamptonshire) The 2.5km long Cutting with several lines of the London Midland & Scottish Railway, between Blisworth and Roade, South from Northampton is 19.8 metres deep. In the background is an old flat, arched road bridge.

(RLHS Images)

As a consequence of the war the village had its own Home Guard Unit & Auxiliary Fire Service, the former's task being to defend the locality against enemy invasion. Two young recruits, Ray Battams and Vic Johnson, joined the latter unit and were sent to London to be trained in how to deal with incendiary devices. Approaching Roade on their return journey, the lads noticed sparks and smuts passing the carriage windows, far too many to be emitted from the engine. On reaching the Station they found the booking office destroyed by fire, completely burnt out…! The only fire on their entire wartime watch and they were away on training!

CUTTING REMARKS

Auxiliary Fire Service Volunteers Ray Battams (left) & Vic Johnson
(Johnson Family Archive)

This was not a consequence of enemy air raids however, for reports state that the fire was started by detonators stored in the building's brick under-croft, ignited by a discarded cigarette (these explosive devices were used to alert drivers to danger when the locomotive ran over them).

Booking Office fire damage still visible in1955 (The Austin 7 still exists)
(Alvin Barby/Fred Blincow Collections)

Booking Office fire damage 1955
(Alvin Barby/Fred Blincow Collections)

Once more into the Breech

Alternative rudimentary arrangements were hastily provided, many of which lasted for a number of years. **'We are Carrying On'** was chalked on the side of the footbridge.

Station Staff at the time of the fire.
(Martin Whitlock)

From the time of the fire the original booking office remained derelict for over a decade. During the interim tickets were issued from a wooden hut erected on the adjacent embankment accessed via a small wicket gate to the left of the old structure. Thereafter the route to the platforms and waiting rooms required a perilous walk, highlighted on the image below, over boards to the footbridge.

Aerial view of the damage, note the temporary ticket hut centre left c.1950
(John Armitage)

CUTTING REMARKS

On 7th July1944, the wife of Roade signalman Cyril Parry gave birth to a daughter, Glenys Elizabeth, in one of the railway cottages situated at the bottom of the Station Road. In later years, the daughter remembered that these dwellings had no gas, running water or electricity. The family moved to Wales soon afterwards and Glenys trained as a teacher. She was to become Baroness Kinnock of Holyhead, FRSA, wife of the former Labour Party leader Neil Kinnock (later Baron Kinnock of Bedwelty).

Baroness Kinnock of Holyhead who grew up in the Station Road Railway Cottages
(en.wickipedia.com/Northampton Library)

Memories of this era were recorded by Vincent Miller, who, as a child from Kilburn, North London, was evacuated to Roade for the duration of the conflict.

> *I spent many hours train spotting on the railway embankment, the main L.M.S. London to Scotland railway ran through the village. The fast steam engine on its journey to Scotland was a wonderful sight; I collected all the train numbers of the different class of steam engines. I was very friendly with a young lad his name Peter Wilding, he would be about 14 years old from the village. I am not sure if he actually worked on the railway, sometimes we would take tea and food to Mr Parry's signal box, he lived at number 2, Railway Cottages, it was great fun, walking over the railway crossing, looking out for the fast trains, down line to London and up line to Scotland. Once over the wooden crossing, turn left then under the footbridge and the signal box in sight up those steep wooden steps and we were in the signal box. I remember those big levers all shiny and the thrill to see a fast train on its way to Scotland, that line was nearest to the box.*

The same year saw the retirement of Richard Widdows, foreman platelayer on the Roade length. His railway career began as a young boy engaged upon the remedial work following the landslip in 1892.

Post-war, the coal merchants operating from the Station yard were Messrs Wiggins & Co Ltd and Mr Percy Chaplin, whose business later became the general haulage company P. Chaplin & Sons.

Once more into the Breech

Following the end of the conflict, eight families who had been evacuated to Roade decided to remain in the locality.

The heavy snowfall in the winter of 1947 was to make local roads impassable. At Gordons Lodge, near Ashton, Alan Malcher's sister Brenda was stricken with a serious case of tonsillitis. With no chance of the doctor from Roade attending by established means, the Glasgow to London Sleeper train was stopped at Roade Station to convey the doctor to a spot as close to the farmhouse as possible. Treatment was administered and the doctor returned to Roade in the same fashion while Brenda recovered.

Inspector Albert Chambers overseeing the Roade Gang
Lifting & Packing on the Up Slow, 1940s
(Alvin Barby Collection)

CHAPTER 17

Nationalisation – British Railways - All Change

BR Armorial device
(Chris Hillyard Collection)

The effect of the war on the railways was that its control had virtually passed to the Government and the industry was in a desperate financial position, as only essential maintenance had been undertaken during the conflict. The whole system was in a 'tied state' with no finance available for investment or improvements. In an effort to stabilise the industry, the Government nationalised the entire system on1st January 1948, it collectively becoming British Railways (BR).

National Service was introduced in 1948 and the former S&MJR route was used to transport those called-up and assembled at RAF Cardington in Bedfordshire to travel from Bedford via Towcester to Bridgenorth, a journey described by one serviceman as '*an interesting journey, which ended in hell'*.

In 1949 extensive remedial and repair works were undertaken on the Cutting's retaining walls to overcome erosion of the exposed soft rock formations on both the east and west embankments.

In June 1950 the Railway Executive announced its intention to close the goods facility at Stoke Bruerne Station, due to the very small volumes of traffic handled over the previous post-war years. The Rural District Council complained of the considerable hardship that would result for local farmers and K.G. Smith, coal merchant of Hartwell, complained that he would be seriously affected by the closure as he received part of his supplies (one wagon a month) at the Station. Widow Mrs E.R. Woodward was the Goods Agent, earning 15 shillings and 6 pence a week. She paid the railway 5 shillings and 4 pence per week to live in the three-bedroomed Station house which was shared with her daughter, plus an additional 7 shillings and 6 pence annual sum for the gardens. Traffic at this time was four trains daily. The goods facilities were terminated on 1st May 1951.

CUTTING REMARKS

Northbound express 29th July 1950; the recent repairs to the Cutting walls are evident
(Alvin Barby Collection)

On Friday 28th September 1951 the *Northampton Mercury* reported upon the Fire Brigade's attendance at Roade sidings to extinguish a burning wagon, the contents of which were considered dangerous –

> *Northampton Fire Brigade saved Roade Railway Station from a 'big bang' in the early hours of Tuesday. At 12.45 am they received the first call. Arriving at the Station a water tender team under Deputy Chief Officer Weir found a goods wagon was alight and a large wooden container was becoming involved. As the wagon was some distance up the line, an engine was hitched to it – and the fire brought to the fire engine which stood on the platform. A first-aid hose and a jet from the water tender were brought to bear and the flames were soon extinguished. A water tender from Towcester was also in attendance. When the container was opened and the contents salvaged undamaged, it was found to contain thousands of – Christmas Crackers!*

On 25th May 1953, history was to tragically repeat itself when the remains of a baby girl were found on the trackside at Roade, 545 yards from the Station. George Tew had made a similar discovery 55 years earlier at Ashton.

On this occasion, the new-born was wrapped in old newspaper. Medical opinion was that the infant had died from a want of skilled attention at birth and that the marks of violence upon the body happened after death. The mother was never found and the child's mortal remains were buried in the village cemetery, where fresh flowers were placed upon the grave for many years thereafter.

Following post war housing developments on the western side of the Cutting pedestrian traffic within the village to the Primary School, local shops and PSL engineering facilities significantly increased. This caused serious public safety concerns on the A508 Northampton – Stony Stratford road bridge, N°207, where no footpath existed. Following a long campaign by Alderman William Sturgess and the Parish Council, a bolt-on footway was opened in July 1953. The following image shows Primary School Headmaster Mr Harper (on the road!) escorting a group of schoolchildren across at the official opening.

Mr R N Saunders, Arnold Bailey, Alderman W.D Sturgess & Alderman J D Brown
(Fred Blincow Collection)

Also that year, the Coronation of Queen Elizabeth II was attended by Roade resident Walter Richardson as a member of the Wolverton Works Ambulance Team. They were again the National Champions, winning the Dewar Shield for the fifth time. As a reward, the team were on duty inside Westminster Abbey, with Walter receiving the Queen's Coronation Medal for his selfless endeavours.

During 1955 Roade's Station was refurbished. The improvement work included the removal of the canopies on the waiting rooms and the stripping down to the iron stanchions and rebuilding of the footbridge. The storage areas under the previous ticket office were bricked up and the complete Station was repainted.

No. 92028 Franco-Crosti 9F through the rebuilt Roade station c1955
(Northampton Library)

CUTTING REMARKS

Roade Station looking south1956
(Alvin Barby Collection)

Finally in 1956 a new brick-built, flat-roofed ticket office was opened, sited a short distance south of the previous building, with the entrance from Station Road leading straight through to the footbridge which allowed access to the platforms.

On the right-hand side was the ticket office counter and on the left a parcels office/cycle storeroom. George Parish was the porter during the 1950s and would call out "Roadee-oh-doh" as the trains halted and passengers alighted.

1956 New Booking Office on Station Road
Graham Onley)

George Lucas Parish, Porter
(Mark Webb)

On 26th May 1956 tragedy would strike deep within the Cutting at the entrance of the girders, or the 'Birdcage' as it is known to railwaymen. Reginald Yates, a railway ganger, was struck by a train and killed. His body was covered in sacking until the undertaker could be brought to the scene.

Relaying the crossover Mid 1950s
(Alvin Barby Collection)

William John 'Jack' Hillyard retired on 11th October 1957. He was presented with his retirement gift, a mantle clock, outside the platelayers hut sited close to the bridge parapet on the western side of The Gravel Bridge N°206. The hut contained a heater and in snowy conditions local lads would toss snowballs from the bridge down the chimney and scarper before those inside could vent their anger!

Retirement of William John Hillyard
. *(Alvin Barby Collection)*

CUTTING REMARKS

Charlie Beechey, Signalman 1950s
(Terry Beechey)

Walter Judkins & Nell, Signalman,1950s
(Ron Johnson)

On the S&MJR 44587 hauls an Olney – Gloucester freight over the WCML, December 1955.
Pianoforte Supplies Limited Offices under construction in the centre background
(Alvin Barby Collection)

The line from Ravenstone Wood Junction to Towcester was closed during May 1958 due to the construction of a bridge over which the new M1 motorway would pass. This bridge, Nº169A, is recorded in the LM&SR bridge register as: 'London and Yorkshire Motorway Structure Nº66'. After a very brief reopening the line closed to regular traffic at 8.30am on 28th June of that year.

Loco passes under the M1 Motorway on 20th August 1964 prior to track removal
(Ian Lyman/RLHS)

By October of the same year, the *Railway Observer* reported that over 1,000 redundant wagons were stored on the old line. The late David Blagrove, at that time a teacher at Roade School, recalled that students spent lunchtimes 'faggin it' in the old wagons. This practice stopped after someone released the brakes, sending the wagons hurtling towards the West Coast Main Line before crashing with considerable force into another set of stationary trucks, 'scaring the lads out of their wits'.

Mr Percival Stephens retired as Roade's Stationmaster in 1959, being replaced by Mr Jack Jennison from Leeds, who was to be the final person to hold the position before its closure five years later. His wife Sheila was the porter.

CHAPTER 18

Steam Decline – Diesel Dawn – Spotting Heaven

Throughout the 1950s the gradual modernisation of the railways saw the introduction of diesel locomotives and the inevitable decline of steam. Numerous prototype diesel engines were tested on the West Coast Main Line through the village. One notable example was the very first diesel hauled Royal Train, conveying HRH the Duke of Edinburgh to Mossley Hill, Liverpool, passing through Roade on 28th October 1959.

Above 'The Birdcage' Spotters observing at the Courteenhall Bridge
(*Graham Onley*)

Roade was a long established location for railway enthusiasts and attracted train 'spotters' from far afield along the entire Cutting length. Furthermore, as the electrification of the main lines was completed it was common to simultaneously witness steam, diesel and electric locomotives all hauling freight and passenger services, as well as new diesel and electric Multiple-units.

Prototype English Electric diesel 10201, introduced in 1950,
leaving Roade Cutting on the Down Slow towards Northampton.
(*Robin Patrick*)

CUTTING REMARKS

Memoirs of these times and the Cutting remain fresh and clear for many Railway enthusiasts evidenced by the following recollections many years later.

The following is recalled by John Evans in his publication *Last Rites –From the Track to the Scrapyard*, Google Books.

> *When I stood on a bridge at Roade Station on the West Coast Main Line in the summer of 1960 and watched N° 46200 'THE PRINCESS ROYAL' roar underneath, gleaming in crimson paint, it hardly seemed possible that just over four years later, not a single Stanier Pacific would be at work. Bob Mullins, a friend from school, had got me train spotting again after a couple of years on the side-lines. We usually caught the 08.46 for London out of Northampton on a Saturday and visited a field at Roade next to the main line. That first summer in 1960, back with my old Ian Allan spotting books, I was surprised to see Peak N° D3 'SKIDDAW' on a northbound express, later N° D1 'SKAFELL PIKE' was seen heading an Up passenger train.*

Diesel prototype DP2, built by English Electric,
northbound through the Cutting, 22nd June 1962
(*Graham Onley*)

An extract from *Northampton Memories* by Christine Jones, Google Books, includes the following recollection of.

> *We often got up to mischief of some sort or other. The first hobby was to put our pennies on the line and then try to find them after an express had run over them. Also in Roade Cutting, under the black bridge, there was an access hatch between the two fast lines that you could climb down and watch the trains thunder past your head. At Roade Station you could see how long it would be before the Stationmaster chased you off the platforms.*

Steam Decline – Diesel Dawn – Spotting Heaven

Train spotters John Butt & David Winter on platform No 3.
Note the Ian Allan Combined Volume on the bench
(*David Winter*)

Roade Junction, 29th September 1962
(*Northampton Library*)

The 108th edition of *Roade News* (Winter 2003), contained an article entitled 'A Child of Roade'. It was written by David Chambers, who had moved away from the village 30 years previously, recalling his boyhood recollections of train-spotting. -

> *As a lad I lived only one hundred yards from what is now the West Coast Main Line, at Roade where my father was a permanent way (track) ganger. Roade Junction in those days was where the former London & Birmingham Railway and the Bletchley and Rugby Railway diverged, it was known locally as the Northampton Loop. Railwaymen still use the term 'down the bank', to describe trains heading via that route.*

> *The main lines direct to Rugby via Blisworth ran parallel with the Northampton lines, which were at a lower level through the vast earthworks that is Roade*

CUTTING REMARKS

Cutting. The mountainous blue brick walls are supported at this lower level with steel reinforcing, known as 'the girders'.

Roade Station had four through platforms and before the diversionary route via Blisworth to Northampton was closed, trains occasionally used different platforms from those scheduled. The platforms were in the Cutting, with the booking hall some distance away high above on the embankment, and the signalman would ring a gong corresponding with the platform number, at which a train would be stopping. The number one hobby for many lads in those days was of course train spotting, and our favourite place was on the embankment of the Cutting, by the large signal gantry. This gantry spanned four tracks and carried the outer-home and junction signals. The semaphore signal arms were nicknamed 'pegs'. The term 'peg on the main, or slow' would mean that a signal had been cleared for a train to pass. Trains, mostly freight, would be brought to a stand here when other trains were crossing the junction into their path. Semaphore signals could be read from both the front and rear, and served as a wonderful early warning system for the spotter, lest his, or her, attention be distracted by a ripe bush of blackberries or whatever!

An unusual train working or a locomotive uncommon to the area would always give delight, especially if the engine was seen by someone for the first time. They would call it a 'cop', and it could then be underlined in their Ian Allan record book. There is one memory though that surpasses all of the modern-day laser and light shows – the passage on a dark night of a Northbound express with the firebox door open, illuminating and dancing on the undulating contours of the Cutting walls and embankment. Now that's what I call Northern Lights!

A footnote suggested that a subsequent edition would include the following poem composed by David reflecting upon his school summer holiday activities in the early 1960s, it was finally published in the 173rd edition of Roade News, (Spring 2020).

PEG ON THE MAIN

Close your eyes and squander, a few moments of your time,
And let your memory wander, until your heart doth pine,
Back to journeys that we made, when you were just a lad,
Many friends, whom with you strayed, such happy time you had.

The travels start at break of school, six whole weeks of freedom,
Same routine as a rule, with warnings, but do you heed them?
No, for the embankment beckons, it's off with pad you go,
Be a good day I should reckon, pegs off on main and slow.

So get over the fence and settle, put your sarnies in the shade,
See the cowslip, mind the nettle and guard the pie that Lyon's made,
Now await the action, which should not be too long,
Up-Slow is cleared for traction, as we hear the Station gong.

Steam Decline – Diesel Dawn – Spotting Heaven

A stopping train to Euston, through the girder does appear,
Black-Five for us to feast on, but sadly no 'cop' here,
Lakes Express with Jubilee, the next train down the bank,
A loco rare for us to see, with Holbeck shed to thank.

The temperature is rising, Grasshoppers start to sing,
Is it so surprising, that to these memories we cling?
While Super D is vented, by the gantry where she waits,
Further passage being prevented by crossing fitted freights.

Onward runs our journey, with the sun now on our backs,
The Callie's running early, well, a Duchess never slacks,
Wire starts to rustle, signals again are cleared,
Spotters start to bustle, a double-header does appear.

Into the twilight kingdom, as the last commuters pass,
Fading hours of freedom, spent seated on the grass,
Occasionally a cheer is heard, and pads are thrown aloft,
'Oh' so quickly spread the word, loco from Patricroft.

Still on our journey goes, into darkness as it falls,
An open firebox glows to dance, upon the Cutting walls,
The Postal has been signalled, although we dare not wait,
For supper and our beds have called, so run, don't hesitate.

Dream away contented, of the treasures that you saw,
Sights and scenes lamented, all have gone before,
Yet even in your slumber, you still wait for the train,
With that one elusive number, Pegged along the Main

Steam and Diesel train await signals. The electrical supply structures are being erected.
(*Graham Olney*)

Roade Junction Autumn 1963
(Bernard Webster)

In its 110th edition *Roade News* featured another poem by David who wrote -

Thanks to my father's employment on the railway the family was entitled to discounted and free travel, to which every advantage was taken. Roade Station was conveniently placed and blessed with at least one special train to Margate and Ramsgate, also one to Blackpool for the illuminations annually. We were fortunate in having relatives in each of those resorts. As children in the 1950's these day trips were something to look forward to. The poem "Excursion Train" hopes to impart the mounting excitement prior to and during such an event. The destination will become fairly obvious by the final verse, but this wonderful station and host to millions of holidaymakers since the 19th century was lost, as was Roade, thanks to Dr Beeching.

British Railways Holiday Posters

EXCURSION TRAIN

Early to bed for tomorrow we ride,
To the sun and the sand of a northern seaside.
Up with the larks, show no hesitation,
Dress for the day and the walk to the Station.

Set off with father, my brothers and I,
With a spring in our step and blue in the sky.
But, alas on the platform we are short of one other,
There's sight of the train, but where is our mother?

She'll not be in time, said father, I bet,
Well it's awfully tight, but she's not missed one yet!
Just a minute to spare, as mother appears,
And with her the picnic, so everyone cheers.

A compartment is free, once aboard we find,
Black Five at the front, with fourteen behind.
Is it back to the engine, or facing for you?
Were there really a choice, I would ride with the crew!

Still, at last we are settled and well on our way,
With our privileged tickets there's no price to pay.
A seat at the window is like the first prize,
As the vistas unfurl, to light up our eyes.

Last pick up has passed and the road ahead clears,
Sit back and relax, until our goal nears.
Father is thirsty so a beverage quaffs,
Likewise our loco, as we're splashed from the troughs.

On northwards we travel till Preston we reach,
To be switched from the mainline and steam toward beach.
At Lytham we catch first sight of the tower,
There'll be ice creams to taste within the hour.

So wipe smuts from your eyes and stack the hamper,
Up front on the engine, they'll close the damper,
As we're slowed to a crawl, to roll the last mile.
Each train in its turn, into platform will file.

At last we arrive, there's no motion, its still,
Doors they fly open, and out we all spill,
To be swept with the tide, in anticipation,
For what treasures await us, outside Central Station?

CUTTING REMARKS

Built by English Electric in 1947, LMS N°10001 at Roade Junction
with a southbound mixed-freight service in 1964
(Robin Patrick)

Andrew Newbery, an enthusiast from the Blisworth end of the excavation shared the following memories of his train-spotting days 1962-66, on the Blisworth Heritage Society website.

Waking to the sun shafting through wrinkled curtains, and sparrows chirping around my window, I would eagerly leap from my bed, full of anticipation of another day at the Cutting in the sun and the possibility of plenty of "cops".

Summer holidays were times to savour, normal breakfast of cornflakes gobbled down or a hastily prepared slice of burnt toast, but we were off school for seven weeks! And it was like another world.

I will never forget the sense of excitement at breakfast times during those seemingly endless summer weekdays. Breakfast gave way to "kitting up" for the day - notepad, shed-book, pencil and well-worn blazer covered in dry grass.

At last Wilf would arrive on his bike. 'Hello Mrs. Newbury' - he would politely say at the door – 'Is Whiff there please?'   It was like an angel's voice to my ears. 'Okay Wilf, come on then!' Onto my rusting Hercules bike with Wilf following on his gold Triumph with clanking chain-guard, we would head off along the Courteenhall Road in the direction of our days pilgrimage - "Black Bridge".

Steam Decline – Diesel Dawn – Spotting Heaven

Black Bridge - a sight that needs no further description except in the way we would experience it at first sight. An eternity of ten minutes from home would find us dropping bikes at the far end of the parapet, leaping the fence and then down onto the steep grassy bank of the Cutting.

I shall always remember how, with the early morning sun in our faces, the bridge seemed peculiarly massive, dwarfing everything around it, giving the whole place a feeling of exhilaration and excitement. The evocative aroma of sulphur and steam smoke would hang heavily on the dewy dawn air; evidence of trains which had already broke through the day's first light. I will never know what kept the two of us so spellbound, sitting on that verdant bank, but there we would sit for the whole day - time would stand still for us!

Local train to Northampton
(Alvin Barby Collection)

Wheezing goods engines laboured their way beneath us up the bank from Northampton with trains of coal, ore and chalk filling the still air with swirling smoke, the blast echoing back from blackened arches of the bridge. The main line had its own mystique - along its metals ran the fast and famous expresses, "The Royal Scot", "The Midday Scot", "The Caledonian" and "The Lakes Express", all graceful, swift and powerful. Headboard up front on a gleaming "Duchess" bursting with power. Then a tailboard behind the last coach took the magic into the fading distance.

Wilf would by now be catching grasshoppers in the long grass or blackberry gathering from the bushes on the slope if it were autumn. Hard work this but we were totally engrossed. Quick, there is one coming!, a distant whistle and the roar of a rapidly approaching engine would bring us scampering down the bank, pencils out, books open ... A grimy Scot. Can't see the nameplate! Under the bridge at 80 with a trail of white smoke drifting down the Cutting with a wake of maroon coaches ... Copped it! Must be a special! ... back to the grasshoppers.

CUTTING REMARKS

So it went on, hour by hour brought moment upon moment of thundering, rumbling, speeding, grinding procession of men and machine passing on their way before us, leaving their presence in our hearts and above all, like a silent sentinel, the bridge. The day would draw to its inevitable close, the trains hissing, snarling and barking onwards, their work never done. We, our cups full, our hearts content, would pedal our weary way back in the dying light of evening, our books full of the day's tally.

So would pass each summer day in those long lost days of youth.

The bridge watched over it all, and still watches as we journey on, out of the halcyon days of boyhood into the harsher reality. But the bridge knows the blissful hours that Wilf and Whiff shared under its solemn arches. What we shared was no less a reality - perhaps the purest kind - that of sheer joy and beauty of existence in two innocent hearts.

Paul Mason spotting at Roade in the late 1950s
(Paul Mason)

CHAPTER 19

Upgrade – The High Wire Act

In the 1960s the overhead electrification of the route brought the return of gangs of railway engineers to the locality. Temporary accommodation was provided with obsolete carriages positioned in the Station Road sidings. Thankfully, they shared none of the characteristics of their forebears.

Roade Station 1962. Wireless
(Bernard Webster)

F. W. Chambers, (platelayer). Overhead gantry footings being excavated.
(David Chambers)

CUTTING REMARKS

The first stage locally began in late 1961 and involved the demolition of part of the bridge carrying the Ashton road over the railway on the southern edge of Roade parish. The existing roadway and base were removed and the two supports each side were increased in height. Reinforced concrete beams were positioned to form a new base and a new road surface was applied.

Ashton Road Bridge, being demolished 1961
(David Farrand)

Ashton Road Bridge being reconstructed, 1961
(Fred Blincow Collection)

Upgrade – The High Wire Act

Shortly afterwards, following removal of the S&MJR track east of Roade, work commenced on the demolition of the Tin Bridge which spanned the main line.

The Tin Bridge embankment following demolition
(Unknown)

In addition, the bridge carrying The Gravel footpath over the lines at the south end of the Station was raised by giant cranes in two sections. This was to allow two of the three brick supporting piers to be increased in height, the western pier with more brickwork, the centre pier with a huge reinforced concrete slab. The two footpath sections were thereafter lowered back in position

A Mineral Train passes under The Gravel Bridge after it had been lifted.
Note the concrete insert on the pillar
(Robin Patrick)

CUTTING REMARKS

At the Courteenhall end of the Cutting, an even bigger civil engineering task was the systematic removal of each of the 99 individual horizontal cross beams bracing and supporting the deeper Cutting sides for the Northampton loop lines, the 'Birdcage'. The vertical supports were then increased by the required amount and the cross beams replaced. These works had to be completed before the wiring trains could commence the electrification of the loop.

N° 42106 with an Overhead Gantry crane, 22nd June 1962
(Grahame Onley)

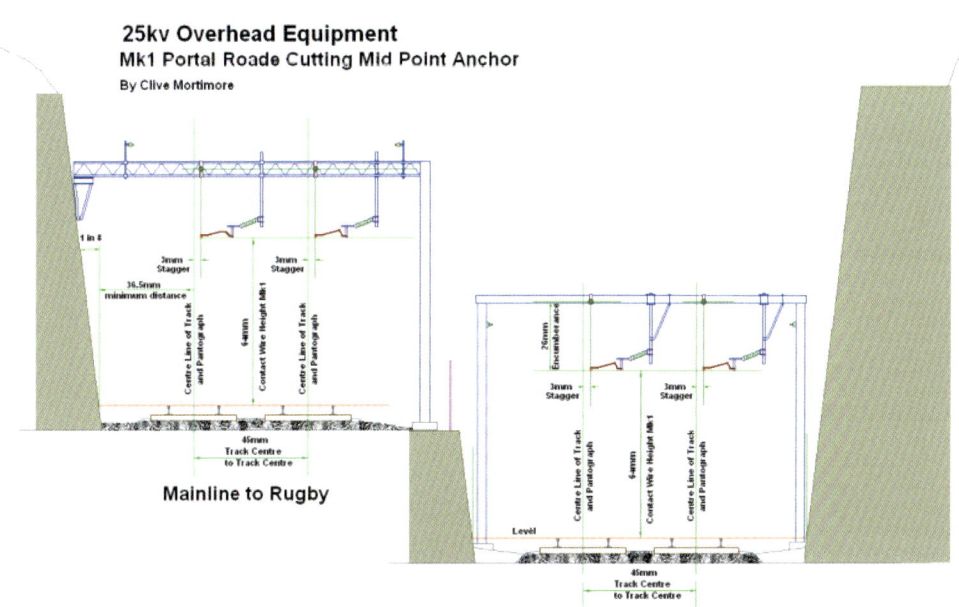

Overhead gantry section illustration
(rmweb.co.uk)

Upgrade – The High Wire Act

Image showing the main line to Birmingham electrified.
The Northampton loop would follow
(Neil Hodson)

On 25th October 1963 at 12.07am, a rear-end collision occurred close to Ashton. The accident was caused by the driver of a southbound train on the slow line missing the danger signals at Roade Station, and so colliding with a slower train which was preceding his. Half a mile of track was damaged.

The collision at Ashton 1963
(Unknown)

CUTTING REMARKS

During the electrification of the line deep in the Cutting on the Northampton Loop in 1966, an accident occurred resulting in a railway worker suffering fatal injuries. At the subsequent inquest held in a room at The George, Stephen Clements, the local doctor who had attended the accident, made a dramatic entrance tripping over a step and falling headlong onto the floor. A former signalman recollected that the good doctor was a frequent visitor to the signal box whilst 'on his rounds'. He would, he said, cross the tracks near the sidings and sit with the signalman for hours, fascinated by the operation of the railways.

Dr Stephen Clements addressing RLHS, November 2007
(Bill Hudson)

All lines electrified mid 1960s
(Alvin Barby)

185

CHAPTER 20

Severed from the Network

Whilst the upgrading of the West Coast Main Line progressed, the government became increasingly concerned at the railway industry's significant on-going financial losses. In March 1961 the then Minister of Transport, Ernest Marples, appointed Dr Richard Beeching as chairman of British Railways, his remit being to produce a report on how the industry could be restructured and become more sustainable.

The report's publication two years later under the title *The Reshaping of British Railways* would lead to a reduction of over 4000 route miles, hundreds of thousands of goods wagons scrapped, significant job losses and the closure of one third of the network's 7000 Stations. Like hundreds of other rural locations, Roade Station was one of those designated for closure, resulting in a vociferous campaign by the Parish Council and local residents to have the decision reversed; regrettably it was to no avail.

THE CLOSURE OF ROADE RAILWAY STATION

When Dr. Beeching produced his plan titled "The reshaping of British Railways" it was argued against it that the **social and economic consequences** to the nation had not been within its terms of reference.

If Roade Railway Station is closed to passenger traffic in November many parishioners are firmly of the opinion that this will be of great dis-service to the community. Some use the station frequently, others use it daily, and there are those who may use it less frequently but **ALL** use it as an essential social and economic necessity. Our protest against the withdrawal of passenger services is: **(a)** the substitute service is inadequate and it takes longer to do the journey added to which is the considerable inconvenience for long distance travel. **(b)** Invariably the arrival and departure of main line trains at Castle Station **FAIL** to synchronize with the Derngate bus service and is frustrating and time-wasting. **(c)** For those (especially) with fixed incomes the cost of travel is increased. **(d)** The inconvenience and awkwardness of travel to be offered reduces the opportunity of pleasurable outings, to, say, a London theatre for a matinee, or a day in London shop gazing. **(e)** The suggested substitute mode of transport offers **NO** convenience to mothers with perambulators and is quite inadequate (and wholly unwilling) to accommodate the holiday luggage for a family and other bulky shopping parcels either. **(f)** There are some older parishioners finding pleasure at travelling with convenience from Roade who would think twice otherwise not to mention the added expense.

So there are, consequently, a number of parishioners who should be concerned at the possible closure of the Station and who have a justifiable reason to protest against it.

NO ONE SHOULD ALLOW the passenger service **TO BE WITHDRAWN** without a protest. Our position is a little different from those on a branch line: ours is a main line and the trains will still continue to pass through Roade Station. We have a strong case for **INSISTING THAT TRAINS WILL CONTINUE TO STOP** for passengers.

YOUR PROTEST should be made by **19th OCTOBER AT THE LATEST** by **WRITING A LETTER** addressed to:-

The Secretary,
Transport Uses Consultative Committee,
44 Friar Street,
DERBY.

Or by **SIGNING A PROTEST** which Mr. J. Howard is holding and it will be forwarded to the proper authority in due course.

Transcription of the Parish Council letter to residents
(RLHS Images)

CUTTING REMARKS

A further outcome of the Beeching report was the closure of the Olney – Towcester cross country line.

In its edition of 25th January 1964 the *Crewe Chronicle* reported a bomb scare had caused the 10.10 Liverpool Lime Street – London Euston service to be stopped at Roade Station on Sunday 18th. Four hundred passengers had to be evacuated to the platform and waiting rooms whilst the train and luggage were searched by the police. Thereafter the train was removed to sidings for further inspection. These proceedings delayed services for two hours. The unfortunate passengers were picked up by following train; it was perhaps the busiest day in the Station's history.

The following month George Lucas Parish, the Station porter, retired after 50 years' service to the railways. At the Booking Office he was presented with a certificate and gifts from colleagues. Recalling a memory of the 1930s, he told the *Northampton Chronicle & Echo* of an amusing incident involving a pack of disoriented foxhounds. They were howling around the platforms after arriving unattended from the depths of the Cutting.

George Lucas Parish centre with Mr Jack & Mrs
Sheila Jennison, Stationmaster & Porter
(*Alvin Barby Collection*)

On Sunday September 6th 1964, the last train stopped at Roade. The following day the booking office doors were closed, Stationmaster Jennison locking them for the final time. The impact on the community and local commuters, shoppers and workmen alike was inconvenience and hardship. Each was required to find alternative ways of getting to their employment.

The United Counties Bus Company added additional services to its timetable to help alleviate the problem. Roade's principal employer, Pianoforte Supplies Ltd, found it necessary to hire private buses to bring its employees from Northampton.

Severed from the Network

Shortly afterwards the footbridge, platform building and the platforms themselves were completely demolished to track level. The booking office on Station Road was boarded up by BR, thus severing the village's link to the system after 126 years. These final acts marked the end of an era.

Roade Station demolition
(Peter Alliot)

CUTTING REMARKS

Throughout its existence Roade's signal box had been the boundary point between the London and Rugby operational districts. This made it an important train reporting location, and it was staffed accordingly.

Ray Williams, Signalman1960s
(*Robin Patrick*)

However, new electro-mechanical equipment dispensed with the manpower requirement, and its importance declined. In addition, a new high-speed crossover was installed near Hanslope, between Castlethorpe and Ashton, as part of the line's electrification and signalling upgrade which effectively moved the district boundary. The box was closed on September 27th 1964, and was demolished the following year. The signal box at Ashton, sited high on the embankment close to the Hartwell Road, was also closed in 1965, and the long relief siding removed.

Demolition of Ashton Signal box
(*David Farrand collection*)

Severed from the Network

Following the closure of the booking office, it began a new lease of life, being used by a number of businesses for workshop and storage purposes for many years. Coal wagons continued with deliveries to the goods yard for distribution by Wiggins & Co Ltd, but this was short-lived. The sidings became redundant as Pianoforte Supplies Ltd had long before begun removing its waste and products by road haulier.

Former Booking office after closure
(Unknown)

The Royal Train conveying HM The Queen & HRH The Duke of Edinburgh
to London Euston following an extensive tour of Scotland,
passing Roade on 1st July 1964
(Robin Patrick)

CHAPTER 21

Scratter Lament - the end of the S&MJR

In July and August 1964 the *Railway Observer* reported that the removal of the track on the profusely overgrown former S&MJR between Roade and Towcester had commenced. The rails were also removed eastward between Roade and Ravenstone Wood Junction.

Over-bridge N°167 for farm track east of the village, 2020
(Chris Hillyard Collection)

Images looking west from the Hartwell Road
Bridge N°166 and east towards it
(Alvin Barby Collection)

CUTTING REMARKS

The remains of Hartwell Road Bridge N°166, prior to demolition
(RLHS Images)

The image above shows the Hartwell Road bridge N°166 which stood at the eastern end of 'Roade's other Cutting', immediately prior to its demolition. Earth mounds either side of the arches consist of the material which formed an embankment 500 yards to the west of the bridge, this being the original excavated spoil removed in the late 1880s to form the embankments for the Bridleway bridge N°165.

The remains of bridge N°165, prior to demolition following
the removal of the embankments c.1970
(Brian Battams)

View from the Ashton Road Bridge N°164 towards Towcester
(RLHS)

Bridge N°162 over the A508 looking east
(Chris Hillyard Collection)

Many local people witnessed the track's removal, most being children at the time. Their recollections include riding on the engine, cooking breakfast on the fireman's shovel and wandering around with their parents.

CUTTING REMARKS

Roade's 'Railway Children' during track removal 1964
(Fred Blincow Collection)

Recalling this old line in his autobiography, Mr Joseph Smith, who was born in Hartwell in 1911 and was a former employee of the S&MJR & LM&SR, included a chapter on railways, which his son shared with members of the S&MJR Society. These memoirs were to reveal the origin of the local nicknames of the cross-country route, 'The Scratter'.

Mr Smith recorded his recollections under two headings. The first heading was: 'The Bread and Herring Line', which derives from the habit of the Irish navvies who built the line eating bread and herring sandwiches for their lunch. In his recollections he states –

> *To the north of Hartwell at 1.5 miles was the Stratford-upon-Avon and Olney Railway. It was, in reality, a link line travelling East to West; linking two main lines. All along this single track were hazel, by the pools, willow and watercress; primrose and cowslips. Rabbits sat on sleepers, cock pheasants honked and curtsied, moorhens scuttled between water. I spent hours just wandering on this line looking for anything of interest, particularly mushrooms in adjacent fields, blackberries and nuts. We loved this old line.*

In another of his recollections he refers to fox hunting: 'once a fox escaped the Grafton Hunt by jumping off a bridge into a coal truck on a passing train'.

Mr Smith's second heading for his memoirs was; 'The Scratter'. The origin of this local nickname has long been questioned and thought lost over the passage of time. He writes –

> *In my day, it had only four trains a day, usually two each way carrying freight pulled by 0-6-0 tanks. There was a steep 1 in 96 rise near Courteenhall, so we had these coughing and spluttering engines opened fully scratching their way up the 1 in 96 like old hens scratching for daylight from the sound of the engines. We would listen eagerly for an engine to fail, which they sometimes did: but usually they made it, and with a sigh, free wheeled down the other side.*

The term 'hens scratching for daylight' is a reference to the birds being less productive during winter months when daylight hours are shortest and their natural instinct being to seek it out if confined in a coop at sunrise. Mr Smith used these nicknames as the basis for a talk he did for the BBC programme 'Home in the afternoon' in about 1963.

The only significant physical evidence that remains is Bridge N°164, adjacent to the new housing developments on the former Pianoforte Supplies Ltd site, on the Ashton Road adjacent to the water tower.

Engine N°47873 Olney-bound crossing the
West Coast Main Line, 27th June 1957
(Alvin Barby Collection)

CHAPTER 22

Off the Rails – Double Trouble

On 11th April 1967, as a goods train of 69 empty 16-ton mineral wagons passed over the junction at Roade, the suspension on the 18th wagon collapsed causing it to derail and turn on its side. The train continued through the length of the Cutting for over one and a half miles, causing damage to the track and sleepers in its wake. Eventually further wagons became derailed which in turn fouled the adjacent line directly in the path of an approaching multiple-unit. Close to Milton Malsor village, with its brakes fully applied, the unit struck the wagons at speed, resulting in the first two coaches being deflected down the embankment, demolishing the overhead gantries.

The crash scene.
(Jim Patrick Collection)

CUTTING REMARKS

There were 45 passengers on board, of whom 22 were injured, though only two were detained in Northampton General Hospital. The driver of the passenger train was seriously injured but had made a good recovery by the time of the official report. The lines were re-opened to traffic on 20th April.

Recovery operations
(Jim Patrick Collection)

On New Year's Eve 1969 an almost identical accident occurred, this time deep in the Cutting itself. A wagon of a goods train, consisting of 49 wagons and two brake vans hauled by an electric locomotive, derailed south of the Cutting. The cause of the derailment was the failure of a main bearing spring on an empty 16-ton mineral wagon. The wagon ran for about two miles before becoming derailed. It then ran for a further two and a half miles with one pair of wheels derailed until passing over the connections at Roade Junction, where it turned on its side, though remaining coupled at each end. The guard observed this and attracted the attention of the driver by applying his van brake, but before the train was brought to a standstill, a derailment had occurred blocking all four lines.

Surveying the damage
(Chronicle & Echo)

Off the Rails – Double Trouble

At this moment a four-coach passenger train was passing on the Up Northampton line at approximately 70 – 75 mph and it collided with the derailed wagons, also coming off the line. The wheels and wheel frames (bogies) were completely removed from the first coach by the force of the collision and the second coach vehicle rode up over the displaced bogies, coming to rest with the leading end up in the air, but still coupled to the leading vehicle and leaning towards the Cutting side.

All lines blocked
(Chronicle & Echo)

The emergency services were alerted by seventeen year-old Stella Weston who, when interviewed by the *Birmingham Post* stated:

> '*I heard a noise like a clap of thunder and ran out of the house, I saw the crash and ran across the bridge to call the ambulance and fire brigade, there was not a lot I could do to help*'.

The location, deep in the Cutting, caused a major headache for the fire and rescue services.

Emergency Medical Services reached the scene using a platelayers' trolley
(Images: Pauline Lever)

CUTTING REMARKS

Local medical professionals, Dr Sutton, Sister Bonham and Nurse Margaret Hart from Pianoforte Supplies Limited, rushed to the scene. Nurse Hart, pictured front right on the trolley on the previous page, recalled that the majority of the 38 injured were attended to at the scene. The closest point that ambulances could get was at the bottom of Station Road. Dr Stephen Clements went down a long ladder and managed to reach the driver, Gilbert Wharton, but regrettably could not save him. Nine passengers suffered minor injuries, though none were detained in hospital.

The train with the derailed wagon had been observed and photographed by 15 year-old local lad and 'train spotter', Leslie Ashby, who was interviewed by a national television crew reporting on the accident. His witness testimony was included in the Department of the Environment's official report, as were the thanks expressed to him by the investigating officials.

Northampton Chronicle & Echo headline and image.
(Alvin Barby Collection)

199

Off the Rails – Double Trouble

20. *Master Leslie Ashby*, a schoolboy aged 15 years, was train watching in the neighbourhood of the footbridge at Roade (Overbridge No. 205). He saw the goods train approaching and took a photograph of it. He then heard a scraping noise and saw a wagon in the centre section of the train skidding along on its side with its wheels away from him. He thought that when he first saw them, the wagons in front and behind the one on its side were on the rails but as he watched the train going away from him towards Underbridge No. 207 it seemed to him that the trailing wheels of the wagon in front were derailed to the right. From where he was standing the train passed out of his sight before he heard the sound of the collision.

Extract from official accident enquiry report
(Alvin Barby Collection)

The repair work to the overhead electric lines and gantries was hampered by difficulties of access to the site and extremely cold weather. However, the Down Fast line was reopened on 1st January and the Up Fast the following day. The slow lines were brought back into full use on the 5th. The intense brightness of the lights illuminating the recovery site was visible for several evenings as work continued to remove the wreckage and repair the damage.

Recovery operations
(David Winter)

CUTTING REMARKS

Recovery operations
(Michael Hager)

During the early 1970s, a major restructuring of the labour force resulted in a number of permanent way workers moving to other areas. The Roade Gang was disbanded, with staff moving either to Blisworth or a newly formed group called the Wolverton Gang. Three of the former Roade Gang, Frank Reid, Jonnie White from Ashton, and Roade resident Bert Bream moved to the Wolverton group.

Whilst undertaking maintenance at Wolverton in about 1974, Bert Bream was working within the confines of the Station area and, when alerted by a look-out to an approaching train, attempted to climb onto the platform. Unable to do this, he was forced to crouch down between the running line and the platform face, where there was limited clearance. He suffered serious injuries from which he would not recover. He was a well-respected individual, well-known in the area as a local cricket umpire.

CHAPTER 23

This is the - Age of the Train?

In the late 1970s BR adopted a fresh marketing strategy to revive its fortunes with the catchphrase 'This is the Age of the Train', using high profile media personalities to promote the speed, comfort and reliability of its 125 mph High Speed Train services. Whilst it did see an improvement in Inter-City passenger numbers, little was to change for rural communities seeking to have former Stations reopened.

A goods train ran into the rear of another train of liquid nitrogen tanks in August 1980, in the area of the former Roade Station. Firemen had to release the driver who was trapped.

A further collision at the site of the former Station on 31st January 1982 resulted in the death of railwayman Mohammed Rashid, 45, of Luton. Seven others were hurt, sustaining chest, shoulder and head injuries. It happened when two track engineers' trains collided. The dead man and the injured workers were all in a brake van whose train reversed into the engine of the second train. They had been working through the night engaged upon routine maintenance and track renewal and were at the end of their shift.

Collision Damage
(Alvin Barby Collection)

In the spring of 1984, the 34th edition of *Roade News* reported that the re-opening of Roade Station was proposed. The Parish Council was actively pursuing this possibility and called a public meeting on 30th April to explain their hopes and expectations; 200 residents attended. It was further reported that a questionnaire was to be produced, to gauge the feelings and opinions of local residents and those within a three-mile radius of the village.

The *Northampton Chronicle & Echo* reported in its edition of 1st May that over 120 residents had attended the meeting and were wholeheartedly in favour of the reopening. However, representatives from the County Council and BR made it clear that there was a long way to go before trains stopped at Roade again. Parish Council chairman Alan Maskell explained; "The reaction of BR was that if the capital could be found elsewhere, they would be prepared to open the Station". Costs varied from £100,000 to £300,000. BR's passenger officer Jeremy Cobb said: "There is certainly no question of BR financing this project or developing it".

The paper reported in its 17th May edition that plans were to be unveiled by the County Council the following month. On the same day the *Northants Post* featured an interview with Mrs Marjorie Hemming who had been living in the former Station master's house for the past 14 years. Mrs Hemming stated that; "The bus services have been run down because they are not used enough, I cannot see that a railway Station would be economical now". She added that it would bring down the value of her three bedroomed property, for which she had paid just £2000 originally.

Mrs Hemming and children
(Northampton Chronicle & Echo)

In the following winter edition of *Roade News* the result of the questionnaire was published, 63% having been returned. The responses indicated that should the Station be reopened, 4,902 journeys per month would be undertaken, generating an annual income for BR of £72,000. The County Council estimated that the cost of the Station would be £200,000 and were keen to know if BR would contribute to the costs. The Parish Council, which had researched other reopening schemes, proposed that it would contribute a sum to the project, equivalent to the product of a 1p rate on the annual precept over the following three years. The forecast being that the Parish contribution to the project would be approximately £12,600.

This is the - Age of the Train

A further public meeting was called for 10th December. The outcome of the meeting was reported in the *Northampton Chronicle & Echo* on December 11th. Residents voted almost unanimously in favour of supporting the 1p rate towards the reopening costs.

The *Northants Post* reported in its edition of 11th April 1985 that BR backed the plan to reopen the Station and were preparing an independent survey to investigate the cost and viability. This was also reported in the spring edition of *Roade News*. In addition, BR had reiterated that they would stop trains again at Roade if they were given substantial help with the rebuilding costs. In edition N°38 *Roade News* reported that BR's estimate for the building work was 'somewhat higher' than expected. However, the scheme had the support and backing of MP Michael Morris and County Councillor Bill Morris.

In May Glenys Kinnock, wife of the Labour Party leader Neil, returned to the village where she had spent her early years. In a letter to a parishioner afterwards she wrote; 'I thoroughly enjoyed my visit to Roade, and was very interested to learn of your efforts to re-open the railway Station'.

In the spring of 1986 it was reported that negotiations continued with the full and active support of the MP and interest from 'elsewhere'. However, a major setback was news that the BR Property Board was planning to auction off the former sidings.

For Sale boards on the Station Road
(Alvin Barby Collection)

CUTTING REMARKS

Following representations from Michael Morris MP and the Parish Council, the Property Board withdrew the land from auction as this action would potentially remove the car parking space from the site. It further stated that negotiations continued with Northamptonshire County Council and the Network South-East sector of BR.

Roade News Edition N°43 brought the news that another questionnaire was to be undertaken, the following issue stating that the Parish Council had been 'swamped' with responses and the results were being analysed; the return had exceeded expectations.

On the 21st July the Northampton *Chronicle & Echo* reported that Roade Parish Council were taking the case for reopening to Northampton Borough Council. RPC Clerk Mrs Susan Smith stated "We believe the Borough Council should give serious consideration to this project". The outcome of that meeting was that the Borough Council's Policy Committee decided to back the campaign. Councillors in Northampton voted overwhelmingly to back the Roade Station campaign. However, Labour councillor Geoffrey Howes warned: "If there was an Inter-City Station at Roade, BR could close Castle Station in Northampton down".

In its edition of 15th August 1986 the *Northampton Chronicle & Echo* reported that plans to reopen the Station were set to fail. Five days later it further advised readers that County surveyor Michael Sharpe had stated that the scheme was ranked only third in the County Council's rail improvement strategy. Roade Parish Council's Clerk Susan Smith lamented that the County's view could prejudice the Parish Council's efforts, stating; "The last thing we need after all the hard work is a resolution from the County Council giving the scheme low priority and saying no finance is available". The paper reported in November that the County Council had agreed to undertake a wider survey into the possibility of the Station's reopening.

One highlight of the year was Roade Cutting being awarded the prestigious status of a Site of Special Scientific Interest (SSSI), under section 28 of the Wildlife and Countryside Act 1981. The citation stated that; 'This is a new site identified as of national importance in the Geological Conservation Review', together with the following –

> *Roade Cutting exhibits one of the most complete Bathonian (Middle Jurassic) sections in central Northamptonshire, potentially exhibiting complete Rutland Formation and White Limestone sections together with the basal Forest Marble (Blisworth Clay). The Cutting is particularly important because it shows the typical rhythmic rock units developed within the Rutland Formation in this area.*

> *The White Limestone section, which shows features comparable to White Limestone sections in both Oxfordshire and the East Midlands, is of the utmost value for establishing detailed correlations between those two*

areas. The section is a particularly important one for reconstructing the environment of deposition at various times during the Bathonian period.

The conclusions are that Roade railway Cutting displays sections in the Rutland, Blisworth Limestone, Blisworth Clay and Cornbrash formations. The Blisworth limestone formation in the Cutting is representative of the East Midlands generally.

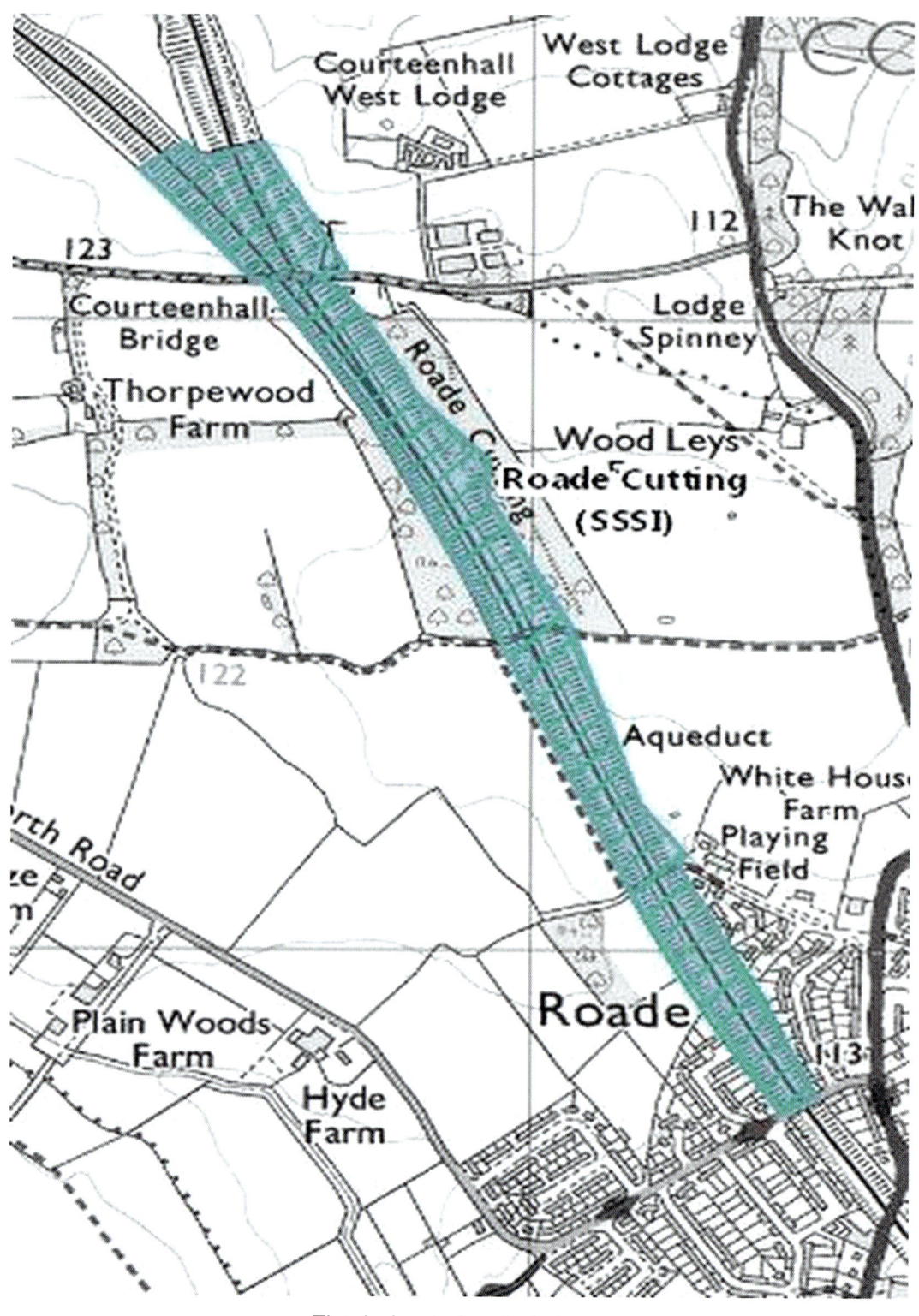

The designated protected area
(naturalengland.org.uk)

CUTTING REMARKS

On 27th February 1987 the *Northampton Chronicle & Echo* reported upon a further development. Commenting upon proposed expansion south of the town, Roade Parish Council Chairman Alan Maskell commented "There is a vast expansion in the Southern District, and this will give added impetus to the reopening of the railway at Roade".

No further news on the possible reopening was forthcoming until the winter of 1988, when *Roade News* N°48 advised residents that the survey had indicated an even larger revenue income for BR if the Station reopened.

However, the total estimated cost had risen to £1,000,000!

And that was the end of that decade of indecision!

CHAPTER 24

Railway Privatisation – All Change

RAILTRACK

In 1994 the railways were returned to private ownership. This split the train operating companies away from the track and infrastructure maintenance both of which came under the stewardship of Railtrack. One of the changes made was the erection of the high palisade fencing throughout the Cutting's length as part of the West Coast Main Line improvements. This put an end to the allotments, the trapping of game and unofficial public access.

In July 1994, Transport Consultants Steer Davies Gleaves prepared a report on behalf of 'West Coast 250' entitled 'Development of the West Coast Main Line Preliminary Assessment'. It stated; 'A further element of joint guideline puts emphasis on providing for new development locations of high accessibility by public transport'.

What the document considered were the benefits of building further Stations and infrastructure giving direct access to the Channel Tunnel and mainland Europe. Northampton County Council, in reviewing the report, considered the likely impacts on the existing County Structure Plan, which had already forecast that a population increase of 50,000 people would be likely from the known 1991 figure and that predicted for 2006.

One consideration was the building of a new Station near to the Cutting's northern end on available land close to the former Blisworth Station site. This would give direct access to Intercity and International rail services locally, without the need to travel to Milton Keynes or Rugby, whose facilities the context document considered inadequate. The new Station was to be called 'Northampton International Parkway' and its inclusion in the 1996–2016 County Structure Plan – declared 'transportation led' – was being considered.

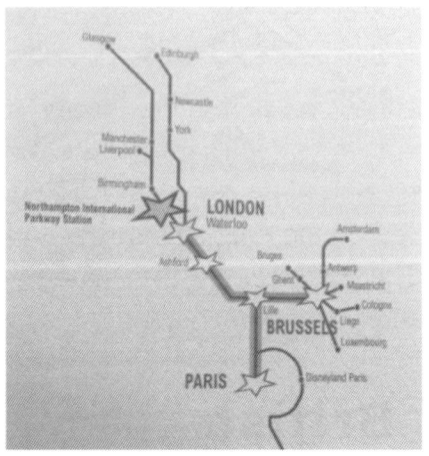

Northampton International Parkway
(Northampton Borough Council)

Artist's impression of Northampton
International Parkway at Blisworth
(Northampton Borough Council)

Nothing was to come of the proposal, which would have had multiple impacts on the adjoining parishes and railway infrastructure. However, later in the decade Northampton Borough Council produced a document which reviewed the town's existing rail services and the potential benefits of the West Coast Main Line Upgrade. It described the town as being buoyant within an area of significant economic growth and, whilst recognising that services had been improved in recent years, pointed out that it was still without an Inter-City type service.

Northampton Central Library
(Northampton Borough Council)

The document stated that the Council strongly supported the further upgrade as a project of national significance – so long as its benefits were shared with communities such as Northampton. However, unless a new junction with the main line and additional platforms were provided on the line, all services to Northampton would still have to use the slower lines. The document further stated that Silverlink had promised to fund this new junction and provide new trains if they were to obtain a new franchise. They were successful in winning the franchise, though the additional infrastructure and Station facilities south of the town never materialised.

The Advanced Passenger Train in Roade Cutting. London – Glasgow service
(flickr.com)

CHAPTER 25

A 21st Century Railway

NetworkRail

In 2002 track and infrastructure maintenance became the responsibility of Network Rail.

The former booking office was last actively used as a private workshop in 2006, before becoming unoccupied.

In the autumn of 2006 a group of volunteers under the auspices of Roade Parish Council began a process to devise a Parish Plan for the village; it was intended to guide planning and development policies that affected the Parish. A questionnaire was produced covering a multitude of topics, seeking the views and opinions of residents in devising a forward-looking strategy up to the year 2020. One question asked residents if they supported the Station's reopening and 60% of the respondents who answered that question were shown to be in favour when the Plan was published in 2008.

A further outcome from the Parish Plan results was the need for social facilities for teenagers and young adults. A number of potential sites were considered and an enquiry was made to Network Rail in 2009 regarding potential use of the empty booking office as a youth café for the village. This request was declined on the basis that it had become structurally unsafe. It was demolished in 2013.

Demolition of the Booking Office
(Alvin Barby Collection)

End of an era!
(Roade Remembered Helena Musselwhite)

The George public house, originally The Stephenson Inn, closed its doors for the final time in the spring of 2008; demolition began in February 2009, 170 years after its initial opening. Perhaps only the Revd Maze W Gregory, Vicar of Roade in 1862, who lamented that the village contained six pubs to a population of 669, applauded its demise from his celestial pulpit. At present (2021) the village population is estimated to be in excess of 3000; only one pub remains!

CUTTING REMARKS

The George built 1839 demolished in 2009
(urbexforums.com)

Today few railway-related buildings remain from the time of the Station's closure in 1964. Two are former Stationmasters' houses. The original 1830s building, much altered since and relocated to London Road, remains a private dwelling.

The original Stationmaster's residence of 1838 in 2020. See page 86
(Peter Mawby Collection)

The1880s Stationmaster's residence on the Station Road is also a private dwelling, having been considerably altered and extended from its former railway design.

Former Stationmaster's house
(John Farebrother)

In addition two rows of cottages survive, which were built by the railway stone masons. One is sited at the eastern end of Hyde Road, and is built of stone excavated from the Cutting. The other stone-built cottages form Yew Tree Terrace in the High Street, built by the Railway Contractor Richard Dunkley. Both were to accommodate railway employees

Hyde Road railway cottages
(Northampton Library)

Yew Tree Terrace railway cottages
(David Hornsey)

Of the S&MJR line very little visible evidence remains. There is still a platelayers' hut hidden in deep undergrowth between the A508 and Stoke Bruerne, which can be accessed from the footpath to Stoke Bruerne from Roade. In addition, the only remnant which is still used for its original purpose is the overbridge on the Ashton Road.

SMJ platelayers' hut
(Peter Mawby Collection)

Ashton Road Bridge N°164 looking west.
(Alvin Barby Collection)

Since the overhead electrification of the line was completed in the 1960s, no significant major engineering work has been undertaken. The on-going maintenance of the Cutting itself is a never-ending task, its tall banks and retaining walls requiring regular inspection and examination. Pumps and rams installed many decades ago are still required to remove the tremendous volume of water that flood the drains. Over the last 50 years the track has been renewed and realigned. The signalling has been upgraded as new faster trains speed through the historic excavation.

CUTTING REMARKS

Pianoforte Supplies Ltd, which for many years was connected to the railway system and was the major employer in the area, finally closed its doors in 2010. Its empty workshops deteriorated to a state of semi-dereliction thereafter, until demolition commenced five years later. This was followed by land decontamination and the construction of a major housing development covering the entire site.

During 2015 a Strategic Rail Freight Interchange (SRFI) was being planned by Ashfield Land Management Limited. This proposed development, called 'Rail Central', would be sited at the northern end of the Cutting, on the western side of the Northampton Loop line and linked to M1 Junction 15A and the A43 dual carriageway. An application was submitted to the Planning Inspectorate in September 2018 but was not accepted. A further application was submitted in October 2018 but after various difficulties and delays it was withdrawn in October 2019.

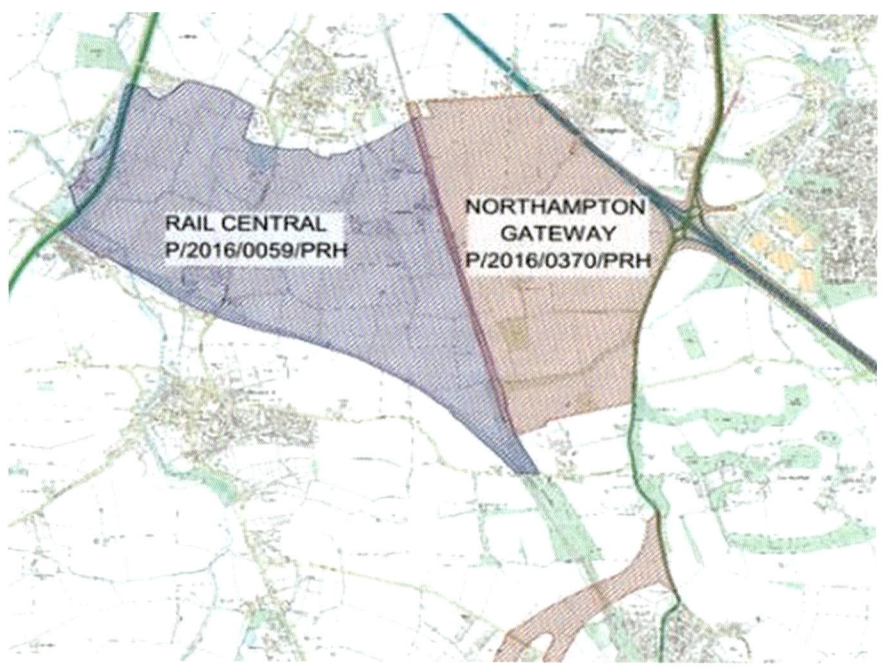

Proposed Rail Central & Northampton Gateway developments
(northamptonchron.co.uk)

In May 2018 Roxhill Developments Limited submitted an application to the Planning Inspectorate for another SRFI at the eastern side of the Northampton Loop line at the northern end of the Cutting. This development would be linked to M1 Junction 15 and the A508 and be called 'Northampton Gateway'. The forecast completion of all phases was predicted to be 2025. The application contained within its environmental impacts assessment a commitment to provide a bypass for Roade village. On the 10th of October 2019 the Northampton Gateway SRFI was given the go-ahead by Secretary of State for Transport, Grant Shapps. The new road will pass over the 19th Century excavations of the Cutting.

The proposed Roade bypass would
cross the Cutting between
Dirty (Muddy) Lane Bridge, N°209 &
the Aqueduct, N°209A
(planninginspectorate.co.uk)

Area of the proposed bypass bridge
(Peter Mawby Collection)

In the autumn of 2019 drainage problems at the Cutting's southern end were investigated by Network Rail. The causes were determined to be a combination of blocked drainage pipes and insufficient soak-aways. During renewal and remedial work in the area of The Gravel footbridge N°206, evidence was uncovered of the original London & Birmingham Station building footings, and the associated underground service ducts. Efforts were made to drain the blocked pipework that resulted in considerable quantities of water cascading from the long redundant 19th century subterranean works.

Foundations of the 1838 L&BR station
(Mark Jasper)

CUTTING REMARKS

Following stability concerns in early 2020, bolstering work commenced on the embankments south of the village, either side of the Ashton Road over bridge, N°204.

The geological stratifications which were revealed in these excavations show the same blue limestone layer that is found in the designated Site of Special Scientific Interest surrounding Roade Cutting. It suggests that the striations which disappear at the Cutting's southern end rise once again at this point; and serve to illustrate how these latest works mirror the contemporary descriptions of the initial excavations published in the1830s.

(Images Peter Mawby)

Tragically, whilst this work was being undertaken by Network Rail contractor Amco Griffin, on Wednesday the 8th of April, despite safety procedures being in place, track worker Aden Ashurst from Wigan was struck by a train and killed. Unconfirmed reports suggested the train was running out of sequence with the scheduled planned movements. The Rail Accident Investigation Board and British Transport Police commenced a full inquiry; the RAIB's findings were published in June 2021.

CHAPTER 26

STEPHENSON'S LEGACY RECOGNISED

In 2016 Roade Local History Society began a process to have Roade Cutting recognised as a National Transport Heritage Site. This was instigated by Alastair Inglis, a Society founder and Committee member since its establishment in 2005

This prestigious accreditation is awarded by the Transport Trust, now the National Transport Trust, to significant buildings, structures and transport heritage sites, and promotes and encourages the restoration and preservation of transport projects. Its award recognises historical uniqueness, innovative design and ground-breaking contributions to our nation's transportation evolution. Physical recognition is in the form of a distinctive 'Red Wheel' plaque.

In August 2018 the Society received a Red Wheel, the 102nd to be awarded. This was in respect of the enormous physical and engineering challenges overcome during the construction of Roade Cutting, an enduring legacy which Robert Stephenson and his engineers have left to Roade, the county of Northamptonshire and the nation.

The commemorative plaque was unveiled by Mr Stuart Wilkinson, Transport Trust Chairman, on 8th September at the Society's Grand Exhibition, nine days short of the 180th anniversary of the Cutting's official opening in 1838.

Stuart Wilkinson Transport Trust Chairman, The Rt. Hon Andrea Leadsom MP,
John Martin and Chris Hillyard, RLHS.
(Anthony Hall)

CUTTING REMARKS

Red Wheel sited on Overbridge N°208.
(Peter Mawby)

The plaque is sited on bridge N°208, the Hyde Road bridge, a busy thoroughfare for residents, school students and passing vehicle traffic. It is a visible and lasting reminder of the Roade's railway heritage.

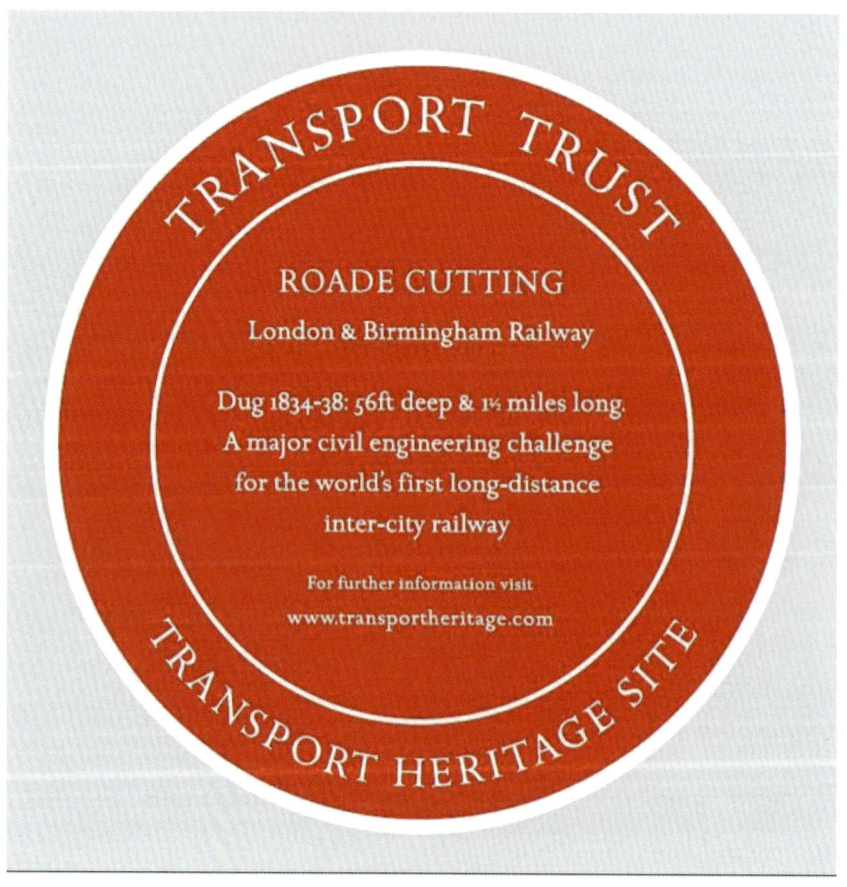

(RLHS Images)

CHAPTER 27

Roade Cutting's 180th Anniversary Grand Exhibition

The decision by Roade Local History Society to stage an exhibition to recognise the Cutting's 180th anniversary was made in late 2017, planning for it to coincide with the National Heritage Open Days to be held the following September. The exhibition was supported by Northamptonshire Community Foundation and Milton Keynes Heritage Association. It was also sponsored by many local businesses.

The two day exhibition, September 8th & 9th was officially opened by the Rt. Hon. Andrea Leadsom, Member of Parliament for South Northamptonshire, Lord President of the Council and Leader of the House of Commons.

RLHS welcomed exhibitors from a variety of national and local railway societies. Strong additional support came from local history, industrial archaeology and transport heritage organisations and many local community groups and individuals. For a small Society, this was a mammoth task involving the organisation of over a hundred willing volunteers that helped. Foremost among these were The Ramblers Association who, with local resident Christopher Clayson, organised guided tours of the Cutting itself, and Roade Women's Institute, who organised the refreshments and whose branch banner depicts the Cutting as one of its features.

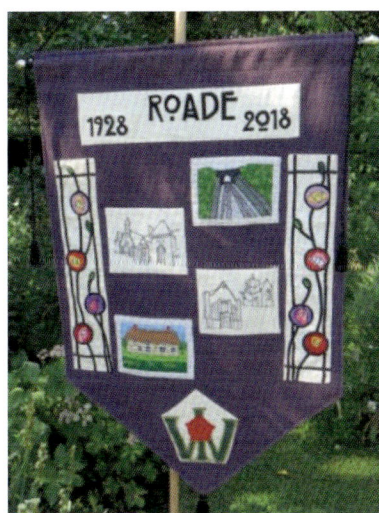 

Roade WI Banner
(Lesley Armstrong)

Exhibition Cutting Walk at Accommodation Bridge
(Anthony Hall)

The principal RLHS exhibit was a model of the Cutting, former Station and diverse railway infrastructure. The model is indicative of the village's social and economic development since the railway came to the locality in the 1830s.

One of the Society's prime objectives in building the model was to give future generations an insight into the village's rich railway heritage, especially as the number of residents who can remember catching a train from the Station, and have first-hand knowledge of the village's railway history is, regrettably, diminishing.

CUTTING REMARKS

Overall, the project was a community-inspired initiative undertaken by Society members, local artisans, artists, technical specialists and Elizabeth Woodville School staff and students.

History Recreated
(Anthony Hall)

The two day exhibition attracted local and national media attention and in excess of eight hundred visitors, Northampton Transport Heritage's vintage buses bringing many from the county town.

(Images, Aldo Brustenghi)

On 4th July 2019 RLHS was delighted to receive the Best Event Award for 2018/19 from Northamptonshire Heritage Forum. This was a considerable achievement against competition from long-established county museums and country houses and a welcome reward for the community effort and support. The model is now on public display at Rushden Historical Transport Society Museum.

(RLHS Images)

CHAPTER 28

Recreating our History

The concept of building a model of Roade Cutting was discussed and agreed upon in January 2018, with little forethought of the enormity of the task, initially fuelled by overactive imaginations and an over-indulgence in 'best bitter'.

The challenge was to produce the finished item within eight months. In the Society's favour was the reassurance that the project was supported by a reasonable degree of local knowledge of the subject matter, and a wealth of research material gathered by individuals over many years.

The first stumbling block was the realisation that a scale model, using one of the smallest proprietary model railway gauges, would require its length to be in excess of 43 feet (over 13 metres!). Obviously this was impractical and much thought went into how a reasonably representative outcome could be achieved which was both manageable and transportable. This resulted in 'back of a fag packet' solutions using 'modellers' licence', wallpaper and inspired compromise; the outcome being a two sectioned design overall measuring 14' x 3' when combined to enable easier transportation.

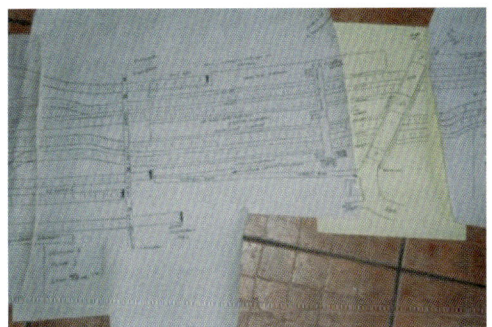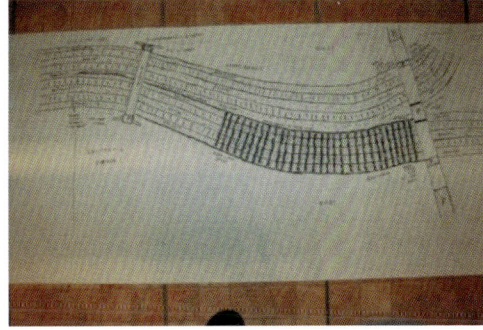

Patchwork drawing and wallpaper sketch
(*Peter Mawby Collection*)

Initially the production was undertaken by John Martin, Chris Hillyard and Peter Mawby, who were equipped with fairly competent organisational and practical skills. However, to enable the finished item to satisfactorily reflect the ambition of the team it was realised that specialist help would be essential.

EWS 2D Laser Cut Bridges – work in progress
(*RLHS Images*)

CUTTING REMARKS

The active involvement of Elizabeth Woodville School teacher Michael Pearce and student Jarred Chapman at the Deanshanger Campus, supporting the project with innovative construction solutions for bridges, buildings and feature structures, coupled with hands-on practical application, proved inspirational in driving the project forward. The Caretaking Staff at the Roade Campus provided ongoing logistical support.

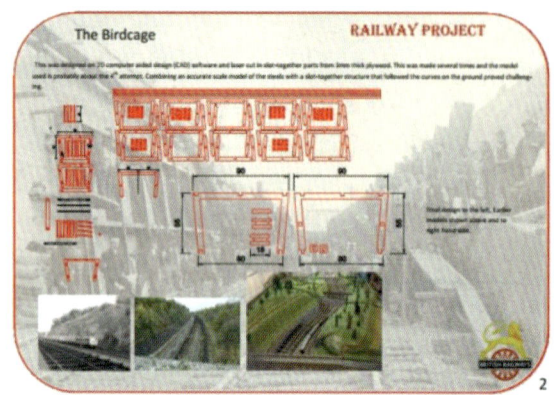

EWS Project Write-up
by student Jarred Chapman
(*EWS Images*)

EWS Teacher Michael Pearce
guiding student Jarred Chapman
(*Peter Mawby*)

It was determined at the outset that the model would include as many distinctive features of the railway as possible, and a selection of line side structures illustrating the railway's impact on the village. This was to prove challenging as no off-the-shelf representations were available. The solution was at hand via a Roade Local History Society member, John Armitage, equipped with a 3D printer. His accurate and detailed replications were to add significant realism to the finished items.

The sectional construction process
(*RLHS Images*)

222

Recreating our History

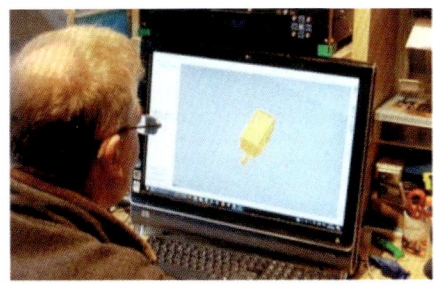

John Armitage's 3D representation of period rolling stock
(*RLHS Images*)

A further required element was applying the scenic details. Once again the Society was fortunate to be given assistance by a local artist Alan Atkinson, who produced masterful end panel depictions of a realistic quality.

(All the following images - RLHS Images)

One of the most innovative features of the model was the concept of physically recreating specific events described by local diarists, and instances from the RLHS photographic record. This was achieved by creating a number of cameos of social and economic significance in the growth of Roade during the Cutting's 180-plus year history. The scenes that follow can be linked to references in the preceding historical record in this publication.

Recreating our History

Following the Exhibition the Roade Cutting model was entered into a national competition, jointly organised by *British Railway Modelling* magazine, The London & North Western Society and Bachman Europe PLC. The Society was up against strong opposition from both professional and established amateur modellers. Despite this, it was awarded 'Highly Commended' by the judges at the Stafford Model Railway Exhibition on 2nd February 2019. This was a tremendous accolade for a team with no previous experience of modelling.

THE LONDON & NORTH WESTERN RAILWAY SOCIETY

The 2019 Model and Engineering Railway Competition

CERTIFICATE OF ATTAINMENT

This is to certify that

Roade Local History Society has been awarded

HIGHLY COMMENDED

In the Infrastructure Category

Ken Woods
President

Dave Bond
Chairman

(RLHS Images)

225

CUTTING REMARKS

The Modelling Team:
Jarred Chapman, Peter Mawby, Michael Pearce, Chris Hillyard,
John Martin, John Armitage & Alan Atkinson.
(All images in this chapter - RLHS Images)

A final accolade was awarded to Roade Local History Society member John Martin, whose selfless efforts in supporting the Society in the model's construction were recognised by the Northamptonshire Community Foundation (NCF) in November 2019, being 'Highly Commended' in the 'NCF Volunteer of the Year' category for 2018/2019.

John Martin
(Peter Mawby)

TAIL LAMP

Francis Roscoe wrote:

> *When railways were first established, every living being gazed with astonishment and fear: ploughmen held their breath; the loose horse galloped from it, and then, suddenly stopping, turned round, stared at it, and at last snorted aloud. But the 'nine days wonder' soon came to an end.*

Mogg's prophecy in his 1839 '*Handbook for Travellers*' contains the following:

> *The little village of Roade, which lies close to the railway, has suddenly become invested with all the bustle and activity of a town; and will, no doubt, enjoy increasing consequence and prosperity from its locality to this great line of communication.*

It is perhaps somewhat difficult to imagine the impact of the changes we would have witnessed, were we fortunate enough to have lived throughout the entire period of the railway's influence upon Roade.

Villagers ceased to be ruled by the 'Tyranny of Place' and were given the opportunity to travel and wider choices of employment. Many left the land to become servants of the railway, some families for three or more generations.

Northampton's initial exclusion from the 'railway family' saw the village slowly expand as further opportunities arose. In the first decade of the twentieth century the establishment of Masters polish factory, with the convenience of its closeness to the railway, brought new employment opportunities which increased considerably after its acquisition by Mr Cripps, (later Sir Cyril), founder of Pianoforte Supplies Limited.

PSL's continued expansion, railway connection and ability to transport and house additional workers boosted Roade's economy to the extent that between 1931 and 1971 the population increased from 701 to 2,529. Sadly, by this time the Station had closed, the sidings were redundant, and the community's direct link to the railway network had been severed. By 1991 the population had fallen to 2,239, partly because of the decline of PSL but also because families had become smaller.

A time traveller who had first marvelled at the enormity and splendour of the Cutting and later witnessed the equally dramatic spectacle of its widening, would have become used to the passage of the train through the Cutting's length and no longer been daunted by the massive enveloping walls towering above.

However, he would have observed with interest over the years what little of the village was visible as he passed. The expansion of the line-side factory would have been noted over the decades, and he would thereafter have observed its decline, dereliction and demolition, and then witnessed a new housing development rise like a Phoenix from the ashes. This and other large developments on the opposite side of the railway have helped the village population increase to over 3000.

CUTTING REMARKS

Roade Station closed in 1964 but nearly 60 years later the village will benefit from a bypass and enhanced employment and commercial opportunities as a result of the Strategic Rail Freight Interchange, at SEGRO Logistics Park Northampton Gateway.

Fear not; be rest assured, above the high Cutting walls all is well. The London to Birmingham Railway was the making of our village community, and we are proud of the legacy and National Transport Heritage Site that Robert Stephenson and his engineers left us all to enjoy.

As for the troublesome navvies; perhaps the final words should be those of Elizabeth Garrett, Secretary of The Navvy Mission Society, who devoted her life to the welfare of these workers. In 1879 she wrote-

> *"Certainly no men in all the world so improve their country as Navvies do England. Their work will last for ages, and if the world remains, people will come hundreds of years hence to look and wonder at what they have done".*

Cutting Remarks cover picture
The scene from Hyde Road bridge N°208, site of the Red Wheel plaque
(David Chambers)

ACKNOWLEDGEMENTS

Roade Local History Society expresses its sincere gratitude to Alvin Barby for sharing his research, which allowed us to begin this challenge with almost a 'full tender'. Especial thanks and gratitude to India Abbott, Elizabeth Woodville School student, for the initial proof reading of the text, and Roger Colbourne for his invaluable and meticulous proof reading and guidance in bringing the manuscript up to an acceptable publishing standard. The Society is sincerely grateful to Peter Mawby for his positive suggestions, ideas and constructive criticism when aspects of the project were in danger of 'passing signals at danger'. Especial thanks to fellow local railway enthusiasts Christopher Clayson, Johnny Martin and David Chambers, for reading the proof in order to weed out any potential 'derailments', errors or misconceptions. That said, the author accepts full responsibility for any errors or inaccuracies contained herein.

Every effort has been made to trace copyright owners of all the images used. If you own the copyright of any of the few that are not – or inadvertently inaccurately – accredited, please contact the Secretary of Roade Local History Society via the website www.roaderemembered.org.uk, in order that retrospective acknowledgement can be made in any future display or publication.

We are indebted to the following for the loan of documents, technical assistance and the provision of incidental anecdotal information; India Abbott, John Armitage, Lesley Armstrong, Leslie Ashby, Alan Atkinson, Alvin Barby, Brian Battams, Terry Beechey, Peter F Blincow, Vivian & Stephen Blyth, Graham Brant, Susan Campbell, David Chambers, Thomas Chaplin, Christopher Clayson, David Cochrane, Roger Colbourne, Lydia & Mick Collins, Christopher Denton, Nigel Elliott, David Farrand, Jackie Gilson, Michael Hager, Sue Hagon, Anthony Hall, Joan Hedger (nee Hurst), Richard Hennessy, Neil Hodson, the late Rodney Howkins, the late Bill Hudson, Alastair Inglis, Mark Jasper, Ron Johnson, Pauline Lever, Gail Ling, Philip Marsh, John Martin, Paul Mason, Peter Mawby, Mike Musson, Andy Newbury, Graham Onley, Les Pace, Emma Parker, Robin Patrick, Adrian Perkins, Christopher Perry, the late Eric Pickles, David Saunders, Barry Taylor, Andrew Thompson, Lionel Tibble, Susan Travell, Johnny Wake, Mark Webb, Maureen Williams and David Winter.

LITERARY SOURCES

A Force on the Move - The Story of the British Transport Police 1825-1995. Pauline Appleby. Published: 1995. ISBN: 1897817673.

50 Years of Foxhunting with the Grafton and Other Packs of Hounds. Frank Beers. Published: 1901.

A History of the London & Birmingham Railway Volume 2 Bletchley – Rugby. Peter Richards & Bill Simpson. Published; 2009. ISBN: 1899246223.

A Scrapbook of Ashton 1953. Ashton Women's Institute

Bourne's London and Birmingham Railway Guide. Bourne. Published: 1839.

Branch Lines Around Towcester. Vic Mitchell & Keith Smith. Published: 2008. ISBN: 9781906008390.

Claude Grahame-White A biography. Graham Wallace. Published: 1960.

Kelly's Directory of Northamptonshire. Various.

Fifty years of the London & North Western Railway. David Stevenson. Published: 1891.

Grafton Regis The History of a Northamptonshire Village. Charles FitzRoy and Keith Harry. Published: 2000. ISBN: 1898937419.

History of the English Railways. John Francis. Published: 1851.

Life and Work among the Navvies. The Rev. D W Barrett. Published: 1883.

Lives of the Engineers George & Robert Stephenson. Samuel Smiles. Published: 1857.

Locomotives of the LNWR Southern Division. Harry Jack. Published: 2001. ISBN: 0901115894.

London and Birmingham Railway Guide. Osbourne. Published: 1839.

Lost Railways of Northamptonshire. Geoffrey Kingscott. Published: 2008. ISBN: 9781846741081.

Photographic Memories of Hackleton, Horton, Piddington and Preston Deanery. Maureen Williams. Published: 2017.

Practical Treatise on Railways. Peter Lecount RN. Published: 1839.

Railway Images around Northamptonshire. Richard Coleman & Joe Rajczonek. Published: 1992. ISBN: 0951855719.

Railway Practice - A collection of works and plans. Samuel C Brees. Published: 1859.

Railway Reminiscences. George P Neale. Published: 1904.

Road Book of the London & Birmingham Railway Drake. Published: 1839.

Roade Review a Parish Appraisal. Produced by the Roade Appraisal group. Published: 1995.

Roade Through the Camera. Roade Local History Society. Published: 2009. ISBN: 9780956349606.

Roade Village Scrapbook 1953. The Women's Institute and Parish Council. Published by Roade Local History Society. 2012. ISBN: 9780956349613.
Steam Nostalgia around Northampton. Richard Coleman & Joe Rajczonek. Published: 1987. ISBN: 090539111X.

Steaming into Northamptonshire. Richard Coleman & Joe Rajczonek. Published: 1988. ISBN: 0905391128.

The History of the Railway Connecting London & Birmingham. Peter Lecount RN. Published: 1839.

The History of the Railways of Northamptonshire. Peter Butler. Published: 2006.

The Iron Road Book. Coghlan. Published: 1970. ISBN: 0851040128.

The Iron Roads of Northamptonshire. C A Markham. Published: 1904.

The London & Birmingham - A Railway of Consequence. David Jenkinson. Published: 1988. ISBN: 1854141023.

The London & Birmingham Railway 50 Years on. David Gould. Published: 1887.

The London and Birmingham Railway Guide. Joseph W Wyld. Published: 1839.

The Railway Navvies - A History of the men who made the Railways. Terry Coleman. Published: 1968.

The Railways of Northamptonshire. David Blagrove. Published: 2005. ISBN: 1871918200.

The Stratford-upon-Avon & Midland Junction Railway Volume 1. Barry Taylor. Published: 2017. ISBN: 9781911038252.

The Stratford-upon-Avon & Midland Junction Railway Volume 2. Barry Taylor. Published: 2018. ISBN: 9781911038467.

The Stratford-upon-Avon & Midland Junction Railway. J M Dunn. Published: 1952.

The Stratford-upon-Avon and Midland Junction Railway. Arthur Jordan. Published: 1982. ISBN: 0860931315.

Victorian Northamptonshire - The Early Years. Eric Jenkins. Published: 1995. ISBN: 0952248107.

The Wakes of Northamptonshire. Peter Gordon. Published: 1992. ISBN: 0905391152.

JOURNALS, MAGAZINES, BOOKLETS
& OTHER DOCUMENTS

A Century of Progress - London & Birmingham 1838-1938
LMSR Publications. Published: 1939.

A Northamptonshire Village Childhood.
Freda Bennett (nee Curtis). Published: 2015.

Appendix to the Working Time Tables & Book of Rules and Regulations. SMJ Railway 1916.

Backtrack Magazine, Pendragon Publishing. July 2017.

British Railway Journal Number 76, Paul Karau.
Wild Swan Publications.
Published: 2017. ISBN: 9781905184866

British Railway Journal, Special L&B Edition.
Wild Swan Publications. Published: 1985?
ISBN: 9770265410982.

British Railways Illustrated Annual No 10.
Irwell Press. Published: 2001. ISBN: 9781903266229.

Census Records. 1861, 1871,1881,1891,1901 & 1911.

Diary Extracts (Unpublished), Abel Hurst.

Encyclopaedia Britannica 9th Edition 1902.

History of Wesleyan Methodism in Roade (Unpublished).
Mrs S G Caswell. 1924.

Illustrated London News. Various.

London & Birmingham Railway Directors Reports,
Robert Stephenson. Various.

London and North Western Railway Society Journal. Various.

London and North Western Railway Staff Gazette. Various.

New York Times. 28 April 1910.

Northampton Independent. July 1936.

Northamptonshire Past and Present. Various.

Police Gazette, Various.

Railways around Roade. Alvin Barby. Published: 2010.

Roade Master Plan. South Northamptonshire Council 2011.

Roade News. Various.

Roade Parish Council Minutes. Various.

Roade Parish Plan. Northamptonshire ACRE Published:
2006.

The English Illustrated Magazine July 1897.

The Geology of Roade Cutting. Beeby Thompson 1924.

The Geology of Roade Cutting. Bradshaw. Published: 1978.

The Geology of Roade Cutting. Torrens. 1967.

The History of the Parish of Roade. The Rev. Maze W Gregory. Northampton Mercury 8th February 1862.

The Penny Magazine. 1838.

The Practical Mechanics Journal. Various.

The Railway Magazine. Mortons Media Group Ltd. Various.

The Railway Observer. The Railway Correspondence & Travel Society. Various.

The Wolverton Express. Various.

Towcester Memories of the "Slow Miserable & Jolty".
Robert Stevens, Published: 1994. ISBN: 0952461900.

ONLINE & WEBSITE RESOURCES

agefotostock.com

alamy.com

ancestry.com

antiques-atlas.com

blackcablondon.net

Blisworth Heritage Society - *blisworthheritage.org.uk*

brightondome.org

british-history.ac.uk

burtonlatimer.info

Castlethorpe Local History Society -
castlethorpevillage.org.uk

devianart.com

express.co.uk

northamptonchron.co.uk

nsimblog.wordpress.com

Olney & District Historical Society - *olneyonline.com*

ourwarwickshire.org.uk

pinterest.com

planninginspectorate.co.uk

Railway Correspondence & Travel Society - *rcts.org.uk*

reframingthevictorians.com

rmweb.co.uk

Roade Local History Society - *roaderemembered.org.uk*

steamscenes.co.uk

The LMS Society - *lmssociety.org.uk*

fighthistoryextra.com

Findmypast.com

fineartamerica.com

flickr.com

Gayton Local History Society - gayton-northants.co.uk

Hanslope Historical Society - hanslope.org.uk

havershamvillage.co.uk

leominster1941.tumblr.com

lookandlearn.com

naturalengland.org.uk

The London & North Western Society - lnwrs.org.uk

The National Newspaper Archive - britishnewspaperarchive.co.uk

The SMJ Society – thesmjr.ning.com

The Transport Trust - nationaltransporttrust.com

Towcester & District Local History Society mkheritage.co.uk/tdlhs

tringlocalhistorymuseum.org.uk

urbexforums.com

victorianweb.com

World History Archive

wikimedia.org

OTHER SOURCES

Courteenhall Estate

Johnson Family Archive

New York Public Library

Northampton Borough Council

Northampton Central Library

Northamptonshire Record Office

RAF Museum Hendon

Official Roade Trade Union Branch Stamp
(RLHS Images)

232

INDEX

INDEX

INDEX

INDEX

INDEX

Please advise any errors or omissions to us at:
info@roadehistorysociety.org.uk
Any updates will be made available on our website:
www.roaderemembered.org.uk
www.roadehistorysociety.org.uk